THE SEARCH FOR HIDDEN, SACRED KNOWLEDGE

DOLORES CANNON

OZARK
MOUNTAIN
PUBLISHING

Library of Congress Cataloging-in-Publication Data

Cannon, Dolores, 1931 - 2014

The Search for Hidden Sacred Knowledge by Dolores Cannon

Many of us lived previous lives as keepers of sacred knowledge that was taught in the ancient mystery schools. Much of this knowledge was lost through time due to disasters and destruction or death. The knowledge was reserved for a select few who devoted their lives to understanding and teaching it.

1. Hypnosis 2. Reincarnation 3. Ancient Knowledge4. Metaphysics

1. Cannon, Dolores, 1931 – 2014 II. Metaphysics   III. Reincarnation IV. Title

Library of Congress Catalog Card Number: 2014957838

ISBN: 9781940265230

Cover Design: Victoria Cooper Art

Book set in: Felix Tilting & Times New Roman

Book Design: Tab Pillar

Published by:

OZARK
MOUNTAIN
PUBLISHING

PO Box 754

Huntsville, AR 72740

800-935-0045 or 479-738-2348 fax: 479-738-2448

WWW.OZARKMT.COM

Printed in the United States of America

Dear readers,

Shortly after Mom finished this book, she passed from this world and into the next. These past few years not only was she diligently working on this book, and several others, but also spending a lot of time developing training programs and personally honing the skills of her global QHHT practitioners to ensure that her lifelong work and legacy will continue through them and future practitioners. To her last days here she insisted 'the work and quest for knowledge' must continue and promised that she would assist from the other side, a promise I'm happy to report she is keeping.

Love,

Julia Cannon

Books by Dolores Cannon

Conversations with Nostradamus, Volume I
Conversations with Nostradamus, Volume II
Conversations with Nostradamus, Volume III
Jesus and the Essenes
They Walked with Jesus
Keepers of the Garden
Between Death and Life
The Legend of Starcrash
A Soul Remembers Hiroshima
Legacy from the Stars
The Custodians
The Convoluted Universe - Book One
The Convoluted Universe - Book Two
The Convoluted Universe - Book Three
The Convoluted Universe - Book Four
The Convoluted Universe, Book Five
Five Lives Remembered
The Three Waves of Volunteers & the New Earth
The Search for Hidden Sacred Knowledge
Horns of the Goddess
A Very Special Friend

For more information
about any of the above titles, or other
titles in our catalog, write to:

Ozark Mountain Publishing, Inc.
PO Box 754
Huntsville, AR 72740

info@ozarkmt.com
479-738-2348 or 800-935-0045
www.ozarkmt.com

DEDICATION

This book is dedicated to all who work in the "light" to bring forth knowledge and particularly to the worldwide practitioners of my QHHT method who lovingly work to raise the vibration for us all.

*I write for the same reason I breathe –
because if I didn't, I would die.*

Isaac Asimov

TABLE OF CONTENTS

TABLE OF CONTENTS

INTRODUCTION

For those of you who are familiar with my work in hypnosis, I say, "Welcome back!" For those who have not read any of my other books, I say, "Welcome aboard!" All you need for the journey is an open mind, and the ability to suspend disbelief for the little while that it takes to read this book. I have been working in the field of the strange and the unknown for so long that it becomes normal. I no longer question the information that I receive through my thousands and thousands of clients who come to me for therapy. I know beyond the shadow of a doubt that nothing is impossible in my work. I do not intend to try to convince anyone of the things I have discovered. I think my work speaks for itself.

A strange phenomenon has been occurring in my work in the last few years. I can definitely see a big change happening. Now when I lecture before large audiences all over the world, there will be many who say they have never heard of me. They say they only discovered my work as recently as a month or a week before the lecture. They are discovering me on the Internet. So I call this the Internet generation. I have definitely not been hiding. I have been doing my work in hypnosis, writing many books and lecturing at conferences all over the world continually for over 45 years. The majority of people who are just now discovering me seem to be young, so it would make sense that the Internet is now reaching many more than my books and lectures could ever touch. We are truly living in the computer age of electronic information. I have been privileged to watch this phenomenon develop.

I am a hypnotherapist that deals with past life regression and therapy. Over the many years I developed a new method of hypnosis that uses the power of the client's own mind to instantly heal them of any disease, illness or malady. This is my main focus now, teaching this amazing method all over the world. I began teaching the method in 2002 and have now trained over 4000 people who are discovering the same miracles that I have found. But it wasn't always this way. It may be hard to believe, but when I discovered reincarnation and past lives in

1968 it was unheard of to use hypnosis in this way. At that time hypnosis was only used to take away habits (stop smoking, lose weight, etc.) and to help the client relax. In our western world the words "reincarnation and past-life regression" were unknown for the most part. The story of my introduction into this fascinating world of time travel is told in my first book *Five Lives Remembered*. Instead of being frightened, my curiosity took over and I was compelled to investigate this further. Today I am considered a pioneer in the field of past-life regression because I have found a way to take it further and use it to help the client with therapy and healing. Because there was no one teaching this type of therapy in the 1960s, I was free to develop my own technique.

In this technique I found a way to speak directly to the greatest power in the universe. It happened gradually, but I found a way to call it in to help the client. It has the answers to any questions, has total knowledge of anything known and unknown, and can perform instant healing. When I discovered this power I did not have a name for it. Others have referred to it as the Oversoul, the Higher Self, the Higher Consciousness or the Universal Consciousness. At the time I was not familiar with those terms so I called it the Subconscious. It must be stressed that this is not the same as what the psychiatrists refer to the subconscious. I have found that is a childish part of the mind and it does not have the power of the part that I work with. I call it the Subconscious because I didn't know what else to call it. "They" have since said that they do not care what I call it. "They" said they don't have a name anyway, so they will respond to that and work with me. For the purposes of this book I will refer to it as the SC. My students are also feeling more at ease to call it that.

I work in the deepest possible level of trance, called the "somnambulistic" level. At this level I can get the conscious mind out of the way, and converse directly with this great power, the SC. I am not a psychic, I do not channel. All of the information that I write about comes from my thousands of clients that I have worked with over 45 years. I consider myself a reporter, an investigator and a researcher of lost knowledge. I take all the information that comes from my clients and put it together like pieces of a puzzle. I am always amazed at what is discovered, and the information has been becoming increasingly more complicated with unknown metaphysical concepts and theories. These have been the foundation of my *Convoluted Universe* books. The information I am receiving now I could never have understood twenty or thirty years ago. It had to be given to me gradually, or it would have been overwhelming. They have said, "Give you a spoonful of information, digest that, and then give you another spoonful." I am glad they did it in that way, or I would never have understood it.

From my research in hypnosis, I have discovered that secret mystery schools have been around forever. There was always a fear that sacred and hidden knowledge would be lost, and much was. In the beginning it was preserved orally, not through writing. The oral traditions and histories were passed down through generations. There was usually one person entrusted with the keeping of the knowledge and it was passed down through stories told on special occasions (as in my book *The Legend of Starcrash*) or preserved as legends. Much knowledge was lost through time, either through disaster and destruction of the tribe, or death of the Keeper of the knowledge before he could transfer the information to another student. Normally the keeper would begin teaching special students long before his demise. If there was much knowledge to transfer and preserve, it could take years of dedicated study. This was the beginning of the secret mystery schools. The knowledge was not for everyone because the average person could not understand it. It was only for the select few who devoted their lives to understanding it and teaching it. They usually had to live in isolated and secluded areas because the possession of such knowledge put their lives in danger. Down through time there have always been people (usually those in power) who felt threatened by anything they couldn't understand. This was the real reason for the witch trials and persecution in the early days of the Catholic Church. They felt threatened by the Gnostics and their secret knowledge. They wanted it for themselves, but the Gnostics would rather die than divulge it. They were sworn to secrecy. (These stories are told in my book *Jesus and the Essenes*.) So the Church decided that was the only answer; these people would have to die. So it had nothing to do with witches or devils, it had to do with the desire for more knowledge and power. The Inquisition is a perfect example of that terrible time period. The Essenes were also a perfect example of the extent people went to preserve and protect the ancient knowledge. They lived in complete isolation and secrecy.

I had a recent session where a woman went back to a lifetime where she was a monk (apparently in the mountains of Tibet) who had spent his entire lifetime with a group in isolation studying the mysteries. Because of their separation from the distractions of the world around them, it was very easy to concentrate and learn the mysteries. He learned how to easily go out of his body and would journey and help create universes and galaxies. As he grew older in that lifetime, he taught the young students how to do the same thing, so the knowledge would not be lost. I would like to believe that these talents are still being taught in the isolated monasteries of Tibet and Nepal.

One of my students had a case where the client went back to a lifetime where he was a guardian of secret knowledge (very similar to the stories in this book). Of course, when we got to the SC, one of his requests was that he wanted to know more about the type of secret knowledge that he was protecting. The SC laughed loudly (*they* do have a sense of humor) and said, "All he has to do nowadays is google *Sacred Geometry*. It is all there, it is no longer such a secret." So the knowledge that people died for in other time periods is now readily available as we move into the new dimension of the New Earth. All knowledge and psychic abilities are being brought back at an astounding rate.

I work a lot with ashrams and Swamis and give lectures at their teaching retreats. I talk about the information I have written about in the *Convoluted Universe* series. After one lecture in the Bahamas, everyone was leaving the temple to go to bed, and I looked back and saw a group of students crowded around the Swami. I was later told about the conversation. They were asking if my information was correct because it is certainly radical. The Swami told them, "She speaks with truth. Truth is not new information. It is new *old* information." It was always kept for those who spent their lives studying and learning and going to caves in Nepal to meditate and become enlightened. It was always kept for a select few who wanted to dedicate their lives to study. The difference is that now it is being brought back for the ordinary person. Many will not understand and that is all right because it is not their path. Yet many will, and it is important for our time to regain this knowledge because in the times we live now, we will not be hung or burned at the stake out of fear of being different.

In my work I often receive information that is similar, applying to the same subject. When that happens I accumulate the cases and put them in a separate book. This is what happened in this book. It is not another in the *Convoluted Universe* series. This book stands alone (the same way my earlier books did), and it deals with information that has been lost or hidden away. For hundreds of years the information was only taught in secret mystery schools and only passed along to disciples or initiates who were capable of understanding it and using it. These were cases that came from many isolated sessions. I saved them and have put them together in this book. Enjoy the journey!

Chapter 1

ISIS AND THE MACHINE PEOPLE

I n my books *Keepers of the Garden* and *The Custodians* the story was told of how the extraterrestrials developed life on Earth. It all took an inconceivable amount of time as life was established and began to flourish. After the animals developed, humans were created by manipulating the genes and DNA of the apes. As the species grew and began to develop intelligence then the ETs came and lived among the savages to educate them and give them basic skills so they would be able to survive and eventually develop a civilization. The ETs lived among them for many, many years because they didn't die until they wanted to. Thus these beings were treated as gods and goddesses and these legends were born. Because they knew they would eventually leave and return to their homes they tried to pass the knowledge on to specific beings that they thought were capable of carrying it on. They also interbred with the natives to produce those who would have some of their abilities and be able to help the people after the originals left.

The knowledge and abilities continued to be passed down over centuries through several generations of selected people. These were initiates. This was the beginning of the Secret Mystery Schools where some were chosen to learn and practice the various techniques. As time went on they secluded themselves in temples and centers where they were isolated from the general populace. Because of their special talents they were treated differently and set apart and above the others. They became priests and priestesses specializing in various abilities. They were expected to also select others they could pass the knowledge on to, those whom they recognized as being able to understand it.

Down through countless centuries this knowledge was protected and shared only with the chosen few. Wars have been fought and terrible injustices have been committed (for example: the Inquisition) in attempts to gain access to this knowledge. Those with the knowledge often died rather than let it fall into the wrong hands. The knowledge had to be safeguarded and protected. They knew that it must not die.

Now it is no longer reserved strictly for oracles in temples, hermits in caves or wise men cloistered in hidden schools. It is returning to our time and is now available for all to learn. This is because the veil is thinning; we are experiencing an awakening as we move into the New Earth. Our vibrations and frequencies are being raised so we will be able to understand these ancient mysteries. They are being returned to our time and are available for anyone to use.

However, the regressions reported in this book take us back to when much of this was unknown to the average person and available only to a select few.

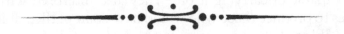

O riginally temples dating back to Babylon were designed with pillars evenly spaced all around the outside. Some had the roof open to the sky. (As long ago as 3000 B.C., Babylon had a well-developed complex culture.) These temples were intended as observatories. The priest would sit at a designated spot in the center of the building and observe and record the movement of the stars and planets as they passed between the open spaces of the pillars. These records would have been kept and observed for hundreds of years. Thus a record of the movements could be accurately measured. These records would become part of the sacred knowledge, and only those of the secret mystery schools would have access and be able to interpret the meanings. This would have been the birth or the beginning of astrology and astronomy. Of course, the original teachings (and what stars to observe) would have come from the ETs. Much of the knowledge originally given would have meant observing planetary bodies that were invisible to the naked eye. Thus they used highly advanced instruments such as telescopes. (Probably similar to the "far-seeing devices" used at Qumran. See my book *Jesus and the Essenes*.) Much of this information was essential to the ETs, because it related to their home planet or constellation. They wanted to keep track of the movements so they would know the best times to journey there or communicate. So some of the astrological information would have been important for Earthlings to plot the passing of time and the seasons, and some was important for the ETs themselves.

This pattern also continued with the building of stone circles and monoliths such as Stonehenge, New Grange and many others throughout the world. They were a marker for the passing of the seasons and the positions of certain important stars and planets. Their courses were plotted in relation to the lintels and stones.

This was a highly advanced science by the time of Atlantis. The knowledge was carried by the survivors to Egypt and other parts of the world. This is explored in my *Convoluted Universe* books.

Why was the building of the temples and stone circles, and the marking of the passing of the seasons so important? The monuments and the knowledge date back so far in time that primitive man was just beginning to master agriculture, planting, harvesting and the caring of livestock. The traditional explanation is that these basic humans built these masterpieces. How is that possible when they were just beginning to move from savagery to the rudiments of civilization? We know that during these early times ETs lived among the developing people and gave them information and gifts to help in their steps of evolution.

Every civilization in the world has their legends of the culture-bringers. These were stories of beings who came and lived among them and taught them the basic skills they would need to survive and progress. For instance the American

Indians had their corn woman who taught them how and when to plant. Also other beings came who taught them how to hunt and use fire. In every one of these worldwide legends the culture-bringer came from the sky or from across the sea. In *Convoluted Universe, Book One* there is the story of ETs who built machines that were able to harness the energy of the Sun, moon and stars.

Because these beings could live as long as they wanted they were treated as gods by the people.

It was very important to be able to calculate time, especially the passing of the seasons, so the developing species would know when to plant and when to harvest. Thus the importance of erecting the structures. To keep track of the seasons and to train certain people to be able to interpret the information and give it to the people. Through the sessions I have conducted over so many years I have found that the original structures were built by the ETs, not the primitive humans who were living there at the time.

The knowledge of the use of the mind to create and levitate stone etc. was perfected in some highly advanced civilizations. And was carried to Egypt and other places by survivors after the destruction of Atlantis. The ETs were still living among men and sharing advanced knowledge during the time of Atlantis.

It began with the basic tracking of the seasons, then later developed into the more sophisticated system of astronomy. This was done so the ETs could keep track of their own home planet and its position. The structures could also be seen from space and served as markers for spaceships orbiting the planet, so they could know where their brothers were located and working.

Terry was a single woman who lived on her ranch in Texas and spent her time breeding and selling horses. She came to me to find the answers to personal problems. We never know what type of past life the SC will choose to show the client. The SC has its own special and unique logic, and I never know what it will choose or the connection it will have for the client's present life.

When Terry came off the cloud she was standing in a big temple with tall columns. She was watching a boat with a dragon's head on the front coming towards her. The boat with about twenty people was coming into a dock on a large river. She was observing a woman with long dark hair and a gold bracelet around her arm. "She's very pretty. She has bangs. She has something on her head, too ... something gold." As she talked she merged with the woman. "I'm an acolyte. I study there. I hear the word Isis."

The dictionary defines an acolyte as someone who is an attendant [presumably in some type of religious capacity].

D: What are you studying?

T: The stars. And the planets.

D: You said you think it has something to do with Isis? (Yes) Who is Isis?

T: She's the queen. That's who lives in this temple.

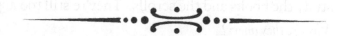

Isis was a very popular goddess figure in ancient Egypt. According to the myth that surrounds her, she was the first daughter of Geb, god of the Earth, and Nut, goddess of the Sky. She married her brother, Osiris, and had the son, Horus, who became Pharaoh. This was probably the beginning of intermarriage to keep the line pure. In the myth she had many magical powers and unusual abilities. The star Sirius is associated with Isis. The appearance of the star signified the advent of a new year, and Isis was considered the goddess of rebirth and reincarnation, and as a protector of the dead. She was the only goddess worshiped by all Egyptians. The ancient historian Plutarch described Isis as "a goddess exceptionally wise and a

lover of wisdom, to whom knowledge and understanding are in the highest degree appropriate."

She was served by both priests and priestesses throughout the history of her cult. And many of these had a reputation for wisdom and healing, and were said to have other special powers, including dream interpretation and the ability to control the weather. The cult of Isis and Osiris continued up until the 6th century CE when Justinian enforced the Theodosian degree that ordered all pagan temples to be destroyed. Many beliefs and rituals in the Isis cult were incorporated into the emerging Christian religion.

This story seems to have taken place during the time that Isis was alive, before it became a cult. I wanted to be sure we were talking about a real person and not a statue in a temple.

D: Is she a real person? (Yes) I was thinking of gods and goddesses with statues.

T: No, she's real. Many people study with her.

D: Are they all studying the same thing?

T: No, we each have different jobs. Some people don't get to study the books and the scrolls. They're still too angry.

D: Why are they angry?

T: They don't want to be there. They want to go home.

D: Isn't this home?

T: No, we come from all over to be with her.

D: From all over the Earth, you mean?

T: No, they come from the skies. They're from neighboring galaxies, or neighboring stars. And women aren't anything where they come from. They don't like being here because of that. They don't want to study with her.

Apparently they didn't like studying under a woman, if women were not respected where they came from.

D: *Can't they go home if they're not happy there?*

T: No, they have to stay a certain length of time. It's so different on their world. Where they come from it is very dark and has a lot of machinery. This place is very green, very fertile, very pretty, very warm. – They've been ordered to stay here to bring back information.

D: *Do these people look like the rest of you?*

T: No, they wear some type of spiky coverings on their hands, and they wear masks. You can't see their face.

D: *Oh? I wonder why they wear masks?*

T: To hide the machinery. They are not very pretty people. They're dark. They're black, like metal.

D: *What do the masks look like?*

T: We would call it a bird. It's a pointed beak. A large opening for the eyes, but the eyes are sunk in. And their eyes look dead. They're quick, bird-like. Their voices sound like a machine, not soft, and there's no melody when they speak.

D: *But you've never seen them without the masks?*

T: I can see beyond the masks.

D: *You have the ability to do that?*

T: Yes. Their flesh looks like leather.

D: *You said it was like machines too.*

T: No, that's underneath this covering.

D: *But it's alive?*

T: Yes, but they don't have organs like we have. They don't need them. I'm afraid of them. I don't like them.

I thought it sounded like some type of mechanical person, or something computerized. Maybe a robot?

T: It has intelligence. It has the ability to think and react to things, but it's fake. Something tells them how to answer and what to say.

D: *Then it's rather like a robot or a machine, isn't it?*

T: Yes, but more advanced.

D: *If they are angry that means they can feel some type of emotion.* (Yes) *And they don't want to be there. Well, how does Isis feel about having them there?*

T: She says they're necessary. That we have to befriend them. There has to be peace.

D: *There wouldn't be peace if she didn't let them come?*

T: Yes, that's right.

D: *Maybe there's something they can learn.*

T: Kindness. Some of them get over that anger and they stay. They're learning to have feelings. They already know about the stars. They say they're from the Milky Way. We study their culture.

D: *Are there other people in this temple that are different?*

T: Yes, there are very large people. They wear white robes. They are bald and very tall. Seven feet tall. They don't speak very much. They don't have to. They can just tell you mentally what they want. They are studying the power points of this planet. They use them to generate energy. That's how they travel.

D: *Do they need a craft to do this?*

T: Sometimes, but then sometimes not.

D: *What about the dark ones, do they use a craft?*

T: Yes, they have to have something. They don't know anything but machinery. Their craft is long and narrow, like a tube. Certain ways it turns, you can't even see it. It looks just like a flash of light. But the tall ones just appear. They don't like the machines.

D: *It sounds like this place has many unusual students, doesn't it?*

T: Yes, there are many different people. Some come from the Earth. They are humans that are native to the Earth, as I am.

D: *Are there more of the other ones than the natives of Earth?*

T: No, she doesn't let those people come very much.

D: *Do you like being there?*

T: Oh, yes, it's very peaceful. So many books.

D: *With all those different type of beings there, you could also learn about planets and stars by traveling, couldn't you?*

T: We're not allowed to leave.

D: *I was thinking that way you could get firsthand knowledge.*

T: Oh, no. The dark ones want to take us, but they won't bring us back.

D: *They probably want the knowledge for their place. (Yes) So you'd rather learn from the books.*

T: Yes. I study by myself a lot.

D: *That boat that you saw, do you know who those people are that are coming?*

T: They're pilgrims. They're from a long way away, from a very cold climate. They know of Isis. They want to see her for themselves. They have never come before.

Sounded maybe like Vikings.

D: *Does that happen very often?*

T: No, there's a veil. You can't find the temple unless it's right.

D: *So the average traveler couldn't find this place?*

T: No, they would never see it.

D: *This is done for protection then. (Yes) Do you think they want to study, or just to see Isis?*

T: They want the knowledge. They want to take it away with them.

D: *Everybody wants to take it away, don't they?*

T: Yes, but they can't. She knows who to tell it to and who not to.

I condensed time and moved it ahead to see if the visitors were able to meet Isis.

T: They don't talk to her. She doesn't talk to them. Some people think there's nothing there. Some people see a statue, but I know that she's real.

D: *I'm surprised they can even find the temple if they weren't the right kind of people.*

T: They stumble on it sometimes.

D: *Could they see you and the rest of the people?*

T: No, it looks like a ruin to them. It is a form of protection. It will appear different to different people. They would want the power. They would misuse it.

D: *So they could walk through this temple where all of you are, and not see any of you.*

T: Yes. Sometimes they walk right over the knowledge that's been hidden there. It looks like broken columns and a dirt floor. So they'll go back and say there wasn't anything there.

D: *That is a good way to protect.* (Yes) *What are you going to do with the knowledge you're learning?*

T: Teach children. They do not come here. I'll be sent out to teach. There are groups of people that I will be told to see.

I then moved her out of that scene and instructed her to go forward to an important day. She surprised me when she "leap-frogged." This is what I call it when the subject suddenly jumps into another unrelated lifetime. She came in on the day of her death. She found herself in the middle of a war as a male soldier in what appeared to be Greece or Rome. There was a lot of noise and yelling and metal banging. She couldn't see, because her head had just been hit from behind by some type of club. "I was a warrior. I had a shield. Someone hit me from behind. I can't see. Everything's dark. I'm lying on the ground. And I hear noises around me." He didn't know what the war was about. "It's probably about money and gold. They don't tell us. We're just told to fight." It was in a foreign land, so his group was the invaders. "Now I just see myself lying there, and I'm just walking away. My body's still there. I don't think it's alive anymore. It was horrible. I'm just walking away. I don't want to be a warrior anymore."

D: *What are you going to do now?*

T: I haven't decided for me yet.

D: *Did you have to go somewhere to find out?*

T: Yes. It looks like a library, many books. I'd rather stay there. My teachers are here. They wait for us in there.

This was obviously the spirit side where we go after death, which was described in my book *Between Death and Life*.

D: *Do they tell you what you'll have to do?*

T: Oh, they say I have to go back. I'm not done yet.

D: *Why do you have to go back?*

T: I'm still teaching.

D: *Have they decided where you're going to go?*

T: I just hear them say, "Far into the future." The End Times. "We need you in the End Times."

D: *Why do they want you to go that far into the future?*

T: Because of Isis.

D: *Of Isis? What's the connection between her and the End Times?*

T: She's coming back to bring gold light.

D: *Had she come back since the time you knew her?* (No) *And she's going to return at the End Times?* (Yes) *And they want you to be there at the same time?* (Yes)

There was a chapter in *Convoluted Universe, Book Two* about Isis. In that story Isis had returned to Earth to complete this mission. She was very upset with the way humans were treating Earth.

D: *Where did Isis come from originally? Was she a native of Earth?*

T: No, she's from ... she was with God.

D: *Did she ever tell you how she got here?*

T: I don't know. I just see this really shiny crystal bridge. And she can come and go.

D: *But then she stayed on Earth for a while to teach?*

T: Yes, but it didn't work out. Those machines. Too many of them came, and so she just had to leave. You couldn't trust them. You can't teach them.

D: *When she left did they go back too?*

T: No, they just kept coming. They wanted this place, Earth.

D: *The person you were at that time, did you stay to see all these things happen?*

T: Those machines, they took me because they thought I knew what Isis knew, but I didn't.

D: *Where did they take you?*

T: I don't know this place. It's on another group of stars.

D: *Is it their home?*

T: Yes. It's a dark place, no sunshine.

D: *Could you exist there?*

T: It was hard. I couldn't breathe. They didn't keep me long. I never got back home. I transitioned. There was nothing there for me.

D: *Were you able to teach them anything, or give them what they wanted?*

T: No, I didn't want to.

D: *It sounds like they didn't understand that you couldn't live there.* (No) *They didn't try to take Isis though.*

T: She's too powerful.

D: *But then the other beings stayed on Earth after Isis left?*

T: I don't know what happened. I wasn't there. All I know is that more of them came and they stayed for awhile on Earth.

D: *But now you said they want you to come back in the End Times when Isis would also return. Why do they call it the "End Times"?*

T: It's just the end of the way of thinking. She brings harmony. She brings peace. She brings understanding. She will reveal, show people the light. They can't survive if they don't accept the teachings. It's the last of those machines. They're leaving.

D: *Those machines stayed that long?* (Yes) *Wouldn't people have noticed them?*

T: No, because they change their covering. They look like other people.

D: *Were they trying to learn things?*

T: Yes. They're failing, though.

D: *Were they trying to change things?*

T: Yes, they wanted the sunshine. They wanted this beauty, but they can't survive here. Their thinking is wrong.

D: *Couldn't they have gone home?*

T: Not anymore. Their planet doesn't exist now. It just blew up. They're stranded here now. They wanted things from this Earth. The flowers and the trees, and the beauty.

D: *Wouldn't that have changed their negativity?*

T: Sometimes it did.

D: *I was thinking if they were machines they couldn't really die, could they?*

T: No. They inhabit, they use a body, and then they leave it. They go get another one, and when the body can't function anymore they get another one.

D: *Are they allowed to do that?*

T: They have to, or they can't survive.

D: *I was thinking that the body would have a soul inside it, wouldn't it?*

T: Yes, but that's different.

D: *How is it different? I'm trying to understand.*

T: They don't take a body if the soul is still there.

D: *You mean it's a body that doesn't already have a soul in it?*

T: Yes. They – I can't describe. The soul is separate from the body.

A body that has recently died? This sounds similar to a case I wrote of in *The Convoluted Universe – Book Three*. The chapter is entitled "A Totally New Alternative to a Walk-In." Normally, a walk-in occurs when the person decides they do not want to be in the life anymore, for whatever reason. They want to leave, but suicide is not an option. Why destroy a perfectly good vehicle when another soul would be more than happy to use it. So they make an agreement with another soul (usually one that they know and have association with) that they will leave, and the incoming soul will take over the body at that exact moment. None of this is done with the conscious involvement or motivation. The consciousness of the person usually has no inkling that anything has occurred, except that things seem to change in their life. The incoming soul makes an agreement that it will take on and complete any agreements the person has made with others as well as any karma that must be repaid and any contracts made before coming into this life. The walk-in must honor these commitments and complete them before it can go on with its own reasons for coming in. This is a normal walk-in.

What makes this alternative walk-in case different is that the incoming soul does not know them from any prior incarnations. It is sent from a higher power. It is still with agreement with the original soul. It must always be understood that these cases are definitely not possession, invasion or taking over the body. It is always done with permission.

D: *They create a body?*

T: They can do that. They can create a thing that looks like a body.

D: *That's what you mean. But then it gets to a point where it doesn't function anymore.*

T: Yes, it wears out.

D: *They do this so people won't see what they really look like. (Yes) But you said at the End Times the last one would be leaving?*

T: Yes. When she comes back they can't stay. Everything will be different. It will be beautiful again.

D: *So then they will have to go someplace, won't they?*

T: She says they'll just disintegrate.

D: *While they were on Earth were they able to get the things they wanted?*

T: No. They couldn't, they didn't have a soul. They did mean things. They had power, they have power. They hide in this cover that looks like a body.

D: *Can the average person recognize them if they saw them?*

T: Their eyes look dead.

D: *But if you saw them you'd know there was something different about them. (Yes) But you said after being killed in the life as a soldier, you're going to go far in the future? And come back at the same time as Isis? (Yes) Can you see what kind of body you'll have in the future time?*

I was expecting her to describe the body of Terry, but she surprised me. "She's very tiny. She's five feet tall. Blonde hair, blue eyes." That certainly wasn't Terry. She is dark haired and average height. I questioned to be sure she was talking about her own future body, or perhaps the body of Isis. But she insisted she was the blonde. "Very well known."

D: *What do you do that causes you to be well known?*

T: I don't know. I don't see that. – The people, we all come back together. We bring our scrolls with us. The knowledge.

D: *Were those scrolls left on Earth?*

T: Yes. They're kept somewhere in a gold box.

D: *Did you hide them long ago or what?*

T: No, they were taken. They didn't know what they had. They're in a big gold box. They can't read them, but they're afraid of these scrolls. Because it would destroy what they have made people think. They've lied about everything, and so when our scrolls are brought back the truth will be told.

D: *They lied about history or what?* (Yes) *Does your group find these scrolls, the box?*

T: They're just saying we're instrumental in bringing them to light.

D: *And this will be what this one* (this body) *I'm talking to, will be doing in the far future in the End Times.*

T: Yes, in 2050. Those machines have left by then.

D: *That's what you meant by an end of a way of thinking.* (Yes) *Is the world different?*

T: Yes, it's more peaceful. No more fighting, no more war. People are here to learn now. And our group will help teach them.

D: *But that is a long time in the future.*

I moved her from the scene where she was talking about these things with the advisor, and called forth Terry's SC. "Why did you pick that life to show her today?

16

T: To surprise her, to help her realize that she's a teacher of great ability. She has been a teacher many, many times.

D: *What does that have to do with her life now?*

T: The way she lives her life by teaching other people about spirituality, about the light, about goodness, about harmony. You have to understand that a life well lived is a lesson for people. She didn't realize she was living her life well, doing what we asked her to do.

D: *Why did you take her into the future to see the future life?*

T: Because she thought this was her last lifetime. She wanted it to be her last, and it's not. It's been hard, very hard for her.

D: *So she's not going to get out that quickly. She's got work to do.*

T: Yes, lots of work. (Laugh)

They then explained that she was shown the death of the soldier to explain Terry's present back problems. "She always feared being incapacitated, and we wanted her to know that we protect her. That was another lifetime, not this one. We are trying to tell her 'Let us help you. Don't fight us. Let us help you.'"

ANOTHER CLIENT

B: Her job is to work with the feminine energy. *The* feminine energy. It's awakened and needing human expression. And it's not easy to create the link. She's linking it to women who can carry it forward. It's like the mouse in the maze; it's not always a straight path. And it takes many people to light the way. She is the midwife for the birthing of what's to be. It has to be done through her consciousness. And others can see it through her eyes. She will be working with only eight aspects of the personification of the feminine energy. There are more, but there are eight to give direction. She will work with this energy. It's who she is, but she doesn't know it. She's supposed to implant it into the human consciousness. She's been absorbing knowledge of this planet for centuries. Alignments have to be made. Every alignment has to be anchored. It's about change. The Earth splits in half and opens itself up. She cries over it sometimes. She thought maybe she was responsible for destruction.

D: *What, in another life?*

B: In the coming life. This life now.

D: *She thinks she's going to be responsible for destruction?*

B: She's afraid of it. She's afraid that she might trigger it in something else.

D: *That won't happen, will it?*

B: If it's meant to be, it will.

D: *I mean, she won't be the one responsible, will she?*

B: Not alone, no.

D: *She's mostly just to pass on information?*

B: And sometimes to implant it. – It's like an arrow of light that needs to have a target. She creates the target so the arrow can hit its mark. It takes time and alignments to create the mark, the bull's-eye of concentric circles. The divine feminine is her main focus. The divine feminine is what's needed to tweak the consciousness of humankind to bring it into balance. To be creative enough to make changes on a grand scale. And the grand scale changes are fluctuating. And there is a division that is occurring, a splitting of the consciousness. It is that splitting that she is concerned will manifest into a physical form of the Earth splitting. She's confused as to whether it's going to be physical, or spiritual. And she does have enough power to manifest the physical. That's what she's afraid of. She has that much power. She knows how to channel it. She's done it before in another life.

B: She's trying to be very careful, and it's slowing things down. She needs to not slow things down.

D: *Did it happen on Earth or somewhere else?*

B: It was stopped on Earth, out of her control. Someone else triggered it. She saw it happen. She couldn't stop it.

D: *So that's why she's afraid she might do it again.*

B: Because she knows how. She doesn't want the outcome. But that's not her purpose this time.

This sounded similar to George (*Convoluted Universe, Book Three.* Chapter 38, The Final Solution) when he said he had the power to destroy the Earth, and had been on Earth when it happened before. We were told he is not the only one on Earth now with this latent power. I am discovering more of this type in my work. Of course, they do not know this consciously, and they are not supposed to know it. They are here to live as normal a life as possible on this hectic planet we call "Earth."

Chapter 2

THEY THINK WE ARE GODS

In the beginning, the ETs came and lived among the developing people. They brought much knowledge to help the people advance. This is where the legends of gods and goddesses originated because the ETs lived as long as they wanted and only died (or left) when they were ready. Thus the people considered them to be special. Yet the ETs knew they would eventually have to leave and allow the people to develop on their own. The ETs interbred with some of the people to create leaders so they would not be left totally without help. An example would be the first pharaohs, and in the beginning they were also worshiped as gods.

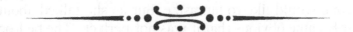

Rachel was a freelance writer for newspapers and magazines. She had a great thirst for knowledge and the unknown, yet she felt there was something else she was supposed to be doing. She knew fear was holding her back.

When Rachel came off the cloud she was in a large building that resembled a palace. "There are big columns on either side. And I'm looking out over the water. The water is a beautiful blue and turquoise, but there are little rough, white caps of water, so the wind must be blowing. However, to my right I see a rocky something, promontory? And there are some trees over there. And I can see a cove, a beach if I look down.

D: *The palace is up above the water?*

R: Oh, yes! It's up, and there's a drop to the beach. But the sun's shining and it's a beautiful day.

D: *Are there any other buildings around?*

R: I can't see anything else from there, just the water. I'm on a balcony that has sheer drapes to the side. If I turn around I know it's my bedroom. This part is open. It is very nice here. The temperature is very nice most of the year.

There were many people living in this palace, but they were mostly servants. She was dressed in light draped clothes. "It's not silk, but it's smooth like silk." She was in her early twenties, and had deep brown hair that was piled up on her head and held in place by bands. She was wearing gold jewelry: a wide gold bracelet, rings, and a wide gold necklace with a piece hanging down from it that was triangular shaped and made out of plates, instead of being a single piece. It seemed like a beautiful, idyllic existence of a wealthy woman who had everything she needed, and who was waited on hand and foot. The type of past life someone would like to fantasize. But as she talked about her life, it became obvious that it was not perfect. "The bedroom is like my sanctuary. Nobody bothers me there unless I allow them to."

D: *Do people bother you other places?*

R: I have to do things. I have duties. Royal functions. They're boring. You have to be nice to people you don't even know. Banquets. Listening to formal speeches. Protocol. Sitting for hours, it seems like.

D: *Is this done in the palace?*

R: Yes, and in the temple about a mile away. I am carried there on a litter.

D: *Why do you have to attend these things?*

R: I'm part of the royal family. I have to go. – They think we're gods, but we're not. They don't understand. It's the alien blood.

D: *What do you mean?*

R: It's in the bloodline, so they think we're gods because of that. We know more. We have more technology. It's the bloodline between the aliens and the humans.

D: *Can you explain what you mean? I'm interested.*

R: Not many know the truth, but a long time ago the aliens chose some to rule in their absence. And they mated with my ancestors.

D: *Were they ruling in the beginning?*

R: Yes, they controlled the humans. But they haven't been with us for centuries now.

D: *And they chose certain humans to rule in their absence?*

R: That was because they contained the alien blood. We're hybrids.

D: *Were they good rulers?*

R: No. They used the humans as slaves. They considered the humans to be sub-creatures, almost like an animal, but a little bit better.

D: *Do you know why they came here in the first place, or have you been told those stories?*

R: There was something in the Earth, some minerals, something that they needed. The humans had no power. They were like slaves. They used them to help get the minerals. And then to grow the food, and to take care of them. And they have left.

D: *And that is why they chose certain people to – what's the word – interbreed with?*

R: You see, they weren't gods. They weren't human, but they weren't gods. And they mated with the humans. And then the offspring were chosen to rule in their absence. There was conflict on their home planet. There were wars. They had to leave.

D: *Who were they warring against?*

R: They warred against themselves, and with others both. They weren't gods, but the humans thought they were because they could leave the Earth plane.

D: *Did those they were warring against also want things from the Earth?*

R: Yes. It's so frustrating. And the truth can't be told or we would be overthrown.

D: *But you can tell me because I'm no threat to you. I was just wondering what caused the wars. What did the other groups want?*

R: Control of galaxies. They were fighting for galaxies. The history goes back so far. Whole races, worlds destroyed, but always survivors that went to other places and then took over there. And then it started over again – more warfare. And the people of this planet, they think we're gods or descendants of gods. Ahh!

D: *They just had more technology.*

R: Yes. Plus, spiritually we're not that advanced.

D: *But your ancestors had to leave because of the wars or what?*

R: They were forced to leave, they lost. The winners made them leave. We're now an experiment. They're watching. They're protecting. They're not letting any more interference to occur.

D: *That's good. But you said now the group there is an experiment?*

R: We're an experiment. Our group. We're the hybrids.

D: *Why do you call it an experiment?*

R: We're a mixture of many races, but mainly the original race. The original ones who used the humans. The winners stopped the continuation of the experiments. They're watching to see what happens.

D: *So they didn't like it when the other ones came in and did negative things.*

R: They stopped that. They stopped the warfare. They are allowing the people to develop, but only a few know the truth.

D: *And the rest of the native people think you are gods.*

R: Yes, because a few of us are still capable of communicating. A few of us have mind power. And they had – machinery is not the right word – they had things to help build the cities and the temples. We don't use that anymore. Our ancestors did, with the aliens.

D: *How did these machines operate?*

R: It was a device that allowed the focusing of energy. It was part physical, but also very strong mental powers were used to direct it. Some of us could communicate telepathically, not all.

D: *Is this one of the reasons the machines are not used anymore? Because your people don't have the mental abilities?*

R: Yes, nobody really knows how to use them, how to start them. By focusing the mind and placing the hand in certain positions, the devices could be activated. And very frequently one would act as a focus point, and others would channel their energy through that individual.

This sounds like both the information from Bartholomew in *Convoluted Universe, Book One*, and the way the Essenes directed energy through the giant crystal in the library at Qumran, as told in *Jesus and the Essenes*. Phil was also an energy director for an entire city in *Keepers of the Garden*.

D: *This multiplied it, didn't it?*

R: Yes. There are a few in the temple who have just enough thought power remaining, and ability, to reactivate some of the communication devices, but not totally. There are other devices we no longer have the power to activate.

D: *Then the group that are watching you don't want to give you this knowledge?*

25

R: They will not help us. And as the blood line weakens the ability weakens. There is more interbreeding with the humans. Then the abilities are lessened. But some of that power, ability, is passed on to the human offspring also. – How to describe? – It's diluted, but more people have a diluted power. I think that's a way to describe it.

D: *So it's not the pure power, but it's a part of it.*

R: Yes, it's being spread genetically, latent abilities, and.... (Gasp) The victors, they deliberately shut off some of the power that we had. It was too dangerous to allow us to continue to have that power and ability.

D: *Do you think it was because you didn't know how to use it?*

R: Oh, we knew how to use it, but we did not use it well.

D: *So they thought it would be better to shut off part of it?* (Yes) *How did they do that?*

R: It's energy. I'm trying to think. (Pause) If you had a sunspot with tremendous energy that disrupts electromagnetic fields, it was as if the powerful device was beamed at the Earth. Of course, I was not born at that time, but from what I've heard it was as though you heard a sound that was too unbearable to hear. And when the sound stopped you were deaf. Something like that, but not quite like that. But as if you had lost a sense. This was how it was shut off initially.

In my other books this was described as similar to blowing a fuse. The abilities had to be taken away. They are now being returned gradually, as the people prove they now have the ability to use them in the correct way. Yet if we misuse them, as we have many times in the past, they will be shut off again. Hopefully, we will be able to keep them, as they will be valuable for our use in the New Earth.

D: *But you said in your time some people can still communicate?*

26

R: It was genetic, the ability was passed on but it was damaged. Almost similar to irradiation causing genetic damage. But it wasn't radiation, it was different.

D: *It was deliberate?*

R: Oh, yes. The winners were from a different time-space continuum because the warfare was threatening galaxies. If it had not been stopped, it would have caused unbelievable catastrophe of worlds, suns, systems.

D: *What do you mean by a "different time continuum"?*

R: The different dimensions, working with others in this time-space. But those in the other dimensions work to help regain control and stabilize universes and galaxies.

D: *They work on a massive scale then.*

R: Yes. Always being threatened, it was threatening to spill over and having a rippling effect. Yes, that's the term, "rippling effect."

D: *So the others were made to leave and were not allowed to return.*

R: Yes. It was part of the peace treaty.

The story is told (in *Keepers of the Garden*) of the original group of aliens who came to Earth to begin life under the direction of the archaic ones, because this was their purpose. For untold millennium they have traveled through the galaxies searching for planets that have reached the point where they could support life. Their job was to begin the life process. Then the developing species were left on their own because of the prime directive of non-interference.

But there were others who came with other agendas. These were the ones who were looking for minerals that their planets needed. These stayed and enslaved the primitive inhabitants so they could do the work for them. This was when the interbreeding occurred. At that time it came to the attention of the councils what was happening, and they stepped in to banish the intruders so the original experiment would not be spoiled. These were the facts I have been given through many sessions and they have been reported in my other books. Rachel's account reemphasizes and validates this information. The physic powers were allowed to become diluted until in our present time they are almost nonexistent. But they have never completely disappeared, they have just lain dormant. They are still in our genes and DNA. Now in our present time they are coming forward and being reactivated so they can be used in the New Earth. Many people have noticed that their psychic powers are being awakened.

D: *But you said you and your family still have some of these powers?*

R: It is latent abilities that come up sporadically in various individuals in each generation. I am one of them. There's just enough of us left who can do things, that the people still think we're gods. But we're not. Only some of us have these abilities. And we're not that special. We have emotions like everyone else.

D: *Which of the abilities do you have?*

R: I can tell when people are telling the truth. I sense it. So they make me go to the temple. Different types of judgments are held there.

D: *Like trials?*

R: It's different. You have your common courts, but that's just done with people without abilities. This is when they decide if the realm is being threatened in some way, whether an ambassador is telling the truth or not. They'll bring me in and I'll have to sit at the banquet and watch. I don't like to do this. It's not right. They should know what I'm doing. Not even everybody in the family is aware of everything that goes on.

D: *But that's a good thing to have that ability, isn't it?*

R: No. It's a curse. People are lying all the time and I see it. (She became emotional.) That's why they let me go to my room and be alone. It's so difficult to know there's so little love. (Crying) Most of the people are scheming and conniving and lying, and fighting for power.

D: *And you sense all of this.*

R: Yes. Here I can be away from it. My room is shielded. I don't pick up the vibrations here. I can just look out at the ocean and be healed. I'm alone then.

D: *Isn't there any way you can shut off that ability so it's not working all the time?*

R: It's so difficult. It's like being bombarded all the time. I can shut it off, but I have to work at it. If I'm tired or I relax my guard for even a few moments, I'll get overwhelmed. That's why they leave me alone most of the time. They're afraid if they press me too much I won't be of use to them anymore.

D: *Does your own family have these kinds of abilities?*

R: I have one sister, she's a healer. She understands. They use both of us.

D: *So it's not a happy place to be even though it's beautiful there.*

R: No, but I do have two children.

D: *Are you married?*

R: Yes, but he's away on political matters, thank goodness. I'm glad when he's not here. He wants a son. But when we meet I pick up all the images in his mind, and I don't want to do it. I don't want to know what's going on in his mind.

D: *Do your children have these abilities?*

R: I don't know yet, they're too young.

D: *Is this the only one of the abilities you have developed?*

R: (Pause) I know how to channel the energy through the communication device in the temple when I have to. If you saw it, it wouldn't look like anything to you. It just looks like a stone block. But there's a place to put my hand on top, and I quiet myself. And then I visualize light coming in through the top of my head and channeling. Also it grounds through my feet. And then I place my hand, and the energy is focused out from my hand into the block. And that activates it.

D: *Then what happens?*

R: Then others ask questions.

D: *How do you receive the answers?*

R: I just know. They're there.

D: *Do they come through the block, or through your body, or what?*

R: I'm not sure of the mechanics of it, but it's like I can see the pictures and I have the answer in my mind. It is always accurate. (Pause) I'm worried for my girls. They have not yet been tested.

D: *But like you said, as the blood line grows, it weakens.*

R: I hope so.

D: *Do you ever get a chance to travel like your husband does?*

R: I don't want to. (Emotional) I don't want to be around people. I want to be alone. Only my girls. Oh, I'm afraid they're going to be turned against me soon.

D: *Why do you think they'll be turned against you?*

R: Because I just know that's what's going to happen. They don't let me near them that often. It was originally my father, and now my brother. And the servants, and the high muckitty-mucks and whoever thinks it's a way to control me. They know I don't want to do it anymore, so they control me through the girls. That's one way. And they even threaten to take me someplace where I won't be in my sanctuary alone anymore. They've threatened to send me away from the palace and make me work with the people in the village far away, where they know there would be just humans and there would be no beauty in my life. And I wouldn't be able to get away from everybody else's emotions. Or they've threatened to lock me in a dungeon somewhere with all those vibrations from other people they've locked away there. They brought me down there once. (Sobbing) It was awful! It was awful! They keep on threatening me if I don't do what they say.

D: *It's good to talk about it. It's good to get it out because I understand. And that's how they control you?*

R: Yes, and not letting me see the girls. But they're getting older, and soon they'll be swayed against me. Only my sister understands. I don't know what to do.

D: *Is there any way you can use your abilities against them?*

R: It doesn't work that way. I pick up on everybody. And they use me to channel my energy with the device in the temple so I can give them information. They just use me, they want me for information.

D: *But you know if they sent you away they wouldn't have this communication. So you are important to them.*

R: But why do they keep on threatening me?

D: *Because they really need you. I don't think they would do those things to you.*

R: But they know I don't want to do this. They took me to that horrible place when I refused to cooperate. And I don't want to go back there. Now my sister, she's a healer. It's different, she doesn't pick up on the emotions the way I do. She can touch somebody and she knows what's wrong with them physically. And she knows if she can treat them with herbs and things like that. She can't give the officials information for power purposes. She can heal, so she's important to impress the humans. But she's happy with what she's doing because she's healing. So she doesn't feel used the way I do because she's helping people.

She seemed so unhappy I decided to have her leave that scene, and moved her forward to an important day; hopefully a better day. But I was mistaken, there seemed to be no escape from the torment she was going through.

R: (Deep sigh) I'm back in my room. (Pause) I've seen my girls. I took them to the beach and we walked on the beach. It was beautiful, and the water was warm. We got wet and sandy. And we had a good time. We had food with us and we ate, we laughed. And I told them how much I loved them. And that no matter what happened in the future, in some way, shape or form I would always be with them protecting them. They only let me have the morning with them because they think I'm going to a banquet this evening.

D: *And do what you always do.*

R: But I'm not going to. (Pause) Because I've said goodbye to the girls, and I'm going to commit suicide by jumping off the balcony.

D: (That was a surprise!) *Oh! You think there's no other way?*

R: I am not going to be controlled anymore. And I am not going to that place they are threatening to send me. I will go back to spirit instead.

D: *You think that's the only way?*

R: (Deep sigh) Yes. I will not be used anymore. And I will not become insane because of where they're sending me. They won't know until it's too late.

In these cases I can only let the subject tell their own story. I can never interfere or try to influence.

D: *You've made up your mind that there's no other way?*

R: Yes. That's why I did what I did with the girls.

D: *More or less like saying goodbye.*

R: Yes. I must do this. I will not be used any longer.

D: *All right. I understand. Tell me what happens. And you don't have to experience anything. You can talk about it. What do you do?*

R: I pull a stool over to the railing, and I use that. I grab the pillar and I climb up. And I am keeping my hand on one side of the pillar. I'm standing on the railing. I look out one last time, and then I close my eyes and fling myself forward. I push myself forward and out, and I fall. And I hit the rocks down below. And I see myself on the rocks, and I'm looking down on my body.

D: *You're out of the body now.*

R: Oh, yes. I could not continue to allow them to use me. It was wrong.

D: *I understand. As you watch that scene, does anyone find the body?*

R: Some time goes by, maybe a few hours, and finally the servants were knocking on the door. They knew normally they couldn't enter without my permission, but they needed to get me ready for the banquet. And when they didn't get an answer again and again and again they became frightened and went for somebody with more authority. So one of the officials finally comes and goes into the room, and see that I'm not there, but sees the stool over by the railing. And then finally looks over and sees my body below. But I was gone by then.

D: *How did he react?*

R: (Chuckle) It threw everyone into a turmoil. It threw all their plans awry. The official is afraid because he will have to tell my brother what happened.

D: *At least you're out of it now. You don't have to be involved in that anymore.*

I then had her drift away from that and had the woman's soul go to where it could have peace and quiet. Then I summoned Rachel's SC to come forth, so we could answer her questions. Of course, the first question is always why the subconscious chose that life for her to look at.

R: To explain her fear of being controlled, her fear of opening up psychically. A fear of using energy.

D: *But you know the use of energy is not always negative.*

R: Yes, she knows this. But the subconscious memory of the misuse was there. Her clairsentience, her ability to pick up emotions was being used again for negative purposes. Not to help people, but for power and control.

D: *That makes sense. So what are you trying to tell Rachel today in the present life?*

R: That was then, and she's learned a lot since then. And she'll never be used like that again.

D: *No, she won't allow it. And in our time period it is very unlikely that would happen.*

R: Correct. But there's always been the fear of opening up and picking up on other people. And not being able to control it if it was fully opened up. This time she is not afraid it could be misused, but if the ability was really allowed to open, that she would not be able to turn it off again. But she has learned. There's a different genetic mix, and different powers have been learned. Abilities that have been learned in the interim. She needs to start using these abilities to pick up on others to help them heal themselves. The ability to touch in and understand somebody else's fear. To help them verbalize the fear, and become conscious of the fear, so they may overcome the fear.

D: *Do you think the fear is what makes people sick?*

R: Yes. And fear keeps them in relationships that are no longer healthy or providing growth for the soul. Fear is negative if it is allowed to prevent positive action. Fear is good when it warns of a real danger to the physical body. It is good as a warning when emotionally a change is needed, and her ability to sense the emotional imbalances. Fear is the root of all the negative emotions. It manifests in many different ways. Rachel has the ability to help people find first the surface fear, and then work on down to what is the root fear. She will need to open up her clair-sentience in a controlled manner, so she can touch into others' vibrations just long enough to sense the problem and work on down. In other words, to touch into vibrations just long enough to get the information needed to assist that individual with their healing process, and not become overwhelmed by the other's fear and emotions. She will be able to do it with a brief touch of the hand. Initially, she will be touching their hand, later she will be touching their third eye. But it will just be a brief touch for just a few seconds, and then away. Then she will know. It's clair-sentience. She'll feel the emotions. The fear, the underlying fear. Once she knows, she'll be able to start asking the questions of the person. She will draw them out. She'll know, but she'll make them know by having them answer the questions.

D: *So they essentially heal themselves.*

R: That's the best type of healing. The Reiki is using the energy to temporarily rebalance the energy flows through all the chakras. And she can do that also, and in some instances will do that. But she will be working with the conscious to bring the subconscious fears to the surface. She will know what questions to ask. When she touches, she'll sense, and she'll start knowing what questions to ask. She'll bring them to the point where they come to the same realization.

D: *Will she begin to pick up on people's thoughts and energies?*

R: Only when she chooses to do so.

D: *It is especially important that she can turn this on and off any time she wants. We don't want it to be like last time.*

R: Very important, yes. She will be a way-shower. In other words, she will allow people to see their own paths so they can choose for themselves.

A physical question: A broken ankle, because she had said she needed a break. "It was the left one because she was holding onto the past. She was afraid of taking the step forward, so that's why the left one versus the right one. Just go forward. Don't hold onto the past."

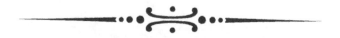

In my work the SC always supplies the same answers for physical problems. It has said many times that anything occurring on the right side of the body refers to things in this present time. Anything occurring on the left side represents things from the past, either from childhood in this lifetime or from a past lifetime. And anything dealing with the extremities (hips, legs, knees, feet) means they are afraid of moving forward. Usually they are at a crossroads and trying to make a decision. And the side of their body the problem is occurring on tells me where the fear is coming from: the present or the past. My client's physical complaints tell me a lot about what is going on in their lives. (See Julia Cannon's book *Soul Speak* for more definitions of how the body speaks to us.)

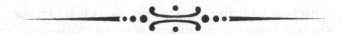

Before I close the session the SC always gives the client a final piece of advice. I call it the "Parting Message."

Parting message: Just a reminder that she now knows how to turn it on and off. She doesn't need to fear opening up. If she starts to open up and she senses something that is too much for her to handle, she'll sense it immediately and will be able to shut down. She can shut it off. No one else controls her, she controls it herself. Only when she chooses to allow others to use that energy, which she sometimes does, will it occur. But it's her choice. She is no longer controlled.

Chapter 3

DON'T REPEAT THE SAME MISTAKES

Shiela was another client who was at a crossroads in her life. She was a teacher, but felt that this was not her true purpose. She felt she was searching for something that was just out of reach. Part of her dilemma was whether she should move to another area to find what she was looking for. There was a great deal of uncertainty and she hoped to find the answers in the session.

When Shiela entered the life she saw a wall surrounding a big city sitting near the water. "Not like a fortress, but big. It looks like it would hold many people. Hundreds live there. Some of the buildings are tall like towers. Different sizes, but tall with small, narrow windows. But not for soldiers, just for light. There are no soldiers. It's old, like Sumerian old." The weather was always the same, hot. She saw that she was a young female with long golden hair wearing a long flowing brown robe and sandals. She also was wearing bracelets. "Metal, no gems, just metal with etchings with symbols in the middle. They are very rare. I only wear them on my left arm. The left is more important."

D: *Why is it more important?*

S: To create that way, that's how it flows. We create to the left.

D: *What do you mean?*

S: That's my job. You put your hand out and then the energy flows. And that's why you want the metal to draw that creative energy. It draws through the left hand. It's like healing, but it's not for your body. When you use your hand, it comes out and the metal's a conduit of energy.

D: *Like it magnifies the energy?*

S: Yes. That's why it's rare.

D: *Where does the energy come from?*

S: It comes from outside, but then you learn to channel it and give it form.

D: *Then how do you use the energy?*

S: You communicate, but not always with words. There are other ways to communicate. You use symbols. And you don't have to worry about what language if you use symbols because people understand universal symbols. They always mean the same things. So you can share messages and wisdom if you let the energy just flow. It's like alchemy because it changes form so it's not just your human voice. It's like the voice of the others... the other beings of light above that can just let it go through you, because it's pure and it's not changed by meanings of language.

D: *So the symbols hold a lot of information?*

S: They do.

D: *And you know how to read the symbols and understand them?*

S: Yes, I do.

D: *Are these like dream symbols or geometric or what?*

S: They are both. A symbol can mean more than a word because who receives it gives it their meaning, so it's not me telling them what it means. It's what they receive. If you saw a star, it would not mean what I think a star is. It would mean I am telling you to see a star, and you know what a star means without speaking my language.

D: *So everyone has their own personal interpretations?*

S: That's what they come for, yes.

D: *So you draw this energy in, then do you direct it out in any certain way?*

S: You can draw it. You can retain it. You can record it. Often I record it for later.

D: *So you don't have to send it out?*

S: No, you can hold energy. You can put it in form. You can put it in metal. You can put it in a stone tablet. You can put it in a sacred place that's protected, that won't let people take it that will misuse it. It's very pure and a protected message.

D: *I was thinking about sending that out because that's how healers work.*

S: I am not a healer. People go somewhere else for that. I am a priestess.

D: *And you said you record.* (Yes) *How do you record?*

S: You can paint the symbols. You can paint them on walls. You can put them in temples and put them on white pillars. People think that pillars are white, but they are not. They're painted on, and not everyone can read them. But the people who *should* read them can read them. Other people just think they're painted pillars. They only get information if they are ready.

She was in a temple, and she said she lived there as well as worked there. I wondered if the temple was dedicated to any certain thing, like the Roman and Egyptian temples were dedicated to various gods and goddesses.

S: No. If there are more people there it's just stronger. The message can be stronger and you can work together. I might have one skill but the next has another skill, and if you combine them it's much more powerful. You reach more people. You don't guide people if they are going to misuse it. But if they're ready, then they understand quite well.

D: *I was thinking that some temples are dedicated to gods and goddesses.*

S: We don't need them ... the God Source ... the God Source.

D: *What kind of priestess are you?*

S: I'm just a messenger. I just listen and I interpret, and I can speak languages without having to learn them. It's finding a way not to have to learn a whole new language. Just enough to give whatever message is important. It's not just for the elite. It's not for god to hide from the people. They come at pilgrimage. They come. They are always welcome. They bring food, not offerings. They bring barter, not money, fair trade. But their gift is to receive a blessing of a message or a wisdom, like a pearl.

D: *You said you live in the temple?*

S: Many of us do, hundreds. Many of all ages. Some are there to work; others to learn, and teach, everyone learns. Some heal. I don't heal. Some do. They heal broken bones. They heal hearts. They heal damage to your body. They heal damage to your thoughts. Sometimes they can't help, but sometimes they heal.

D: *Are you teaching others what you do?*

S: Yes, I do.

D: *Do you enjoy what you do?*

S: Oh, sometimes I misuse it. (She was becoming emotional.)

D: *Why is it bothering you?*

S: I think we kill people with it. (She was upset.) It's like a power. They think, "Now I have power," so they kill. I hate that. Very dark. So what do you do? Not teach?

D: *So once you teach them you have no control over it. You don't know what they're going to do with it.*

S: No. What if they kill? What if they do that? Do you take it away? Do you kick them out? To banish ... to teach anyway? To give up ... to wait? I don't like to select.

D: *Are there just a few that are using it for negative?*

S: Just a few, but it only takes a few to do damage. They can destroy. They can destroy the temple. They can destroy each other. They just want to destroy things. They want to steal things. They want to accumulate and hoard and ... I don't know what to do. We can stop. I don't think that's right though. I don't think we should stop, but if we select a few then that's just as bad. What if the healers only healed the ones they wanted? What if the gardeners only fed the ones they wanted? What is that? That's wrong.

D: *But that's not your responsibility what the person does with it, is it?*

S: I don't know. Is it? Is it my job? I don't know. No one taught me. Someone's supposed to know. You don't take a gift and give it to everybody if they are going to kill.

D: *There is no way for you to know this in advance, is there?*

S: I want to know. They come to classes. If I could read them, maybe I could separate them and just give them things that they can't kill with. I don't know how to tell. Maybe if I was older. Maybe I'm not old enough.

D: *Do you know of examples where people have taken what you taught them and used it in the wrong way?*

S: Yes. They create weapons. I teach them power, but it's supposed to be the power to create. I teach them the power to create anything, and they create bad things. They are not supposed to create bad things.

D: *What type of weapons do they create?*

S: They're kind of like a sword, but a material that can destroy with a single blow. It can destroy anything. Like a sword, like a crystal, like a sharp edge that cuts. It's like a knife, sharp edge. As if you put your hand out and energy came from your hand, but you could see it like a knife of light.

D: *So it's not a physical thing? It's an energy weapon they create?*

S: It is, because if it was energy you could channel it to heal, but they channel it to kill. It's the same energy. It's just what you do with it.

D: *But it's still not your responsibility when people do these things. The alternative is just to not teach everyone.*

S: So what do you do?

I asked for a description of the temple where she lived. "It's quite large. It has many pillars because we paint them and we paint the walls. And there are chambers and we look through them. There are openings and we can see the stars and that's a symbol as well. You look up. You use the stars. You use the reflections. You use the weather. You use the light. Everything's a messenger. It's like being in a library. If you were in a library that was not books. If you were in a library where there were people as messengers instead of books that were messengers. That's what this would be like, a library of people."

D: *Do you know how to read the stars?*

S: Yes, I do. They move and they tell you like a prophecy. They warn you of change. They warn you of opportunity, when there's a surge of energy. Stars are energy just like weather is energy, like water is energy, like the tide is an energy. The stars are energy ... not just stars, there are moons. There are many things and they are energy. And when you see something coming ... if you saw a tornado coming you'd know you'd need shelter. If you saw the Sun growing brighter you'd know to plant. If you saw dark clouds then you'd know that it could kill your plants. So you know by the stars the same thing because stars have messages and they are prophecy and they can tell you things like that.

D: *Were you taught by others how to do these things?*

S: Oracle, that was the word I couldn't think of. The stars are an oracle. I was taught by an oracle reader. You read the oracles and they tell you when there will be death, and they tell when there will be movement, like when you have to move people. And when to shelter and when to grow and when to have children.

D: *So it's very important to learn to do these things.*

S: Well, you don't have to. You can just wait, but if you knew ahead you could get the most from what you're given.

Shiela became emotional and started to cry when I asked if she had a family. "I don't think so. I think they are dead. That's how I ended up there. They took me in. It's a home. I have been

here most of my life. I don't remember being anywhere else."
She said her name was a series of vowels: My-a-yah. (Phonetic)

D: *Are the others who are doing the work or the healing having the same problem with the teaching?*

S: They seem to. They put people back together after they're hurt, so I give them knowledge that creates weapons. They harm. They bring them back to be healed. Then I send them back to do harm. It's like a circle. (Disgusted) So what do you do? Stop teaching? Stop healing? Am I giving the message wrong? Am I missing something? Do I select? What if I select wrong? There are many decisions.

I moved her ahead to an important day and she started crying. She had married, and her baby had died. "It was the birth process. Something happened. It was alright, I held it, and then it died. I don't know what went wrong. The healers did everything. It just happened. I had all the tools. I just don't know why." The child had been born at the temple. I asked about her husband and whether he was involved in the same things as she was. "He is very wise. He works somewhere else, but he is very wise. He builds things."

D: *So he doesn't use the energy like you do?*

S: No, he creates beautiful buildings.

This was a sad day, so I moved her forward again to another important day, and there was a celebration. "It's a feast day, and people come and they bring what they have to share. And you celebrate and you dance and you sing and it's a joy. It is the summer solstice, the stars tell you when. It's a time of birth. Many babies born then, and many crops are good. And the boats come in and the travelers come and it's a time of abundance and celebration." She was older now and had four children.

D: *Did you teach them?*

S: They did other things. They weren't mine to teach. They stayed at the temple and learned other things. They choose.

D: *What other things are there to learn?*

S: They build gardens. They build temples. They heal. They write. They record. They are the planners. They like to organize and they find where you fit, where your gifts are greatest. You can do anything. You can make jewelry. You can travel on the boats that come in the summer. You can go with them. They bring back spices and they bring back fabrics and they bring back people. And you can travel and bring back beautiful things and knowledge and people that are not like you, and you can be a traveler. You can use your gift free.

D: *Are there still the negative people around?*

S: They are fewer. We have our own energy to protect ourselves. It's sad to do because you have to push people out, and they can't come in anymore because they make it unsafe. And so you learn to use the energy like a moat. It's liquid. It's not like a wall. If they tried to get through, they would get sick and die. They can't get through now. If they choose to misuse it, they can't come back. We didn't know how to do this before.

D: *When did you develop this protective energy?*

S: My husband did. He's a warrior. You can be a warrior without killing. (Definitely) You can be a warrior and protect. – It's like a moat. It's like liquid. If you were at a distance and looked, you would think you saw a mirage. You know how they wiggle like wavy energy, but not solid. You see through it, but you think you imagine it. You think you see a city but you don't go because if you walk towards it you'll get sick and you'll think, "I'm crazy." So they stay away. They avoid it, and if they're meant to come, they walk right through. But if they're *dark*, it's like a repellant.

They see the city but they think they are imagining it. They don't want to go there.

D: *That's wonderful because you were very concerned about that.*

S: I was when I was young. Not now. I'm old now. I'm forty. I've learned a lot about this. I'm not done yet, but it's been very good. We're safer.

I then moved her forward to the last day of her life to see what happened to her. "You choose to go. You choose to be done and you have a ceremony like a farewell party – not a party – like a gathering, and you just go."

D: *There's nothing wrong with the body?*

S: No, no sickness. We have conquered that.

D: *You just decide it's time?*

S: You feel prepared. You get to choose. Maybe you just need to go back to review or change, but you're not sad. No, not sad. The family is okay. They know they will do the same, so everybody does it this way. It's not like you are killed or destroyed. You just kind of dissolve into the next side and just go. We have people that help you release and let go. You're ready and they help you change your bonds and then you just dissolve those bonds, and you will go out of that body. They tell you how. They teach you this. We have ones in the temple that help you cross. They are guardians of the gateway to cross. It's like birth backwards.

Instead of having her go through the death, I moved her to when it was all over with and she was on the other side and out of her body. The person can see and understand so much more from that perspective. I asked her what happened next.

S: It's like you don't leave, you just dissolve your body. You don't dissolve the rest. You can stay and watch if you want. It's not very interesting.

D: *Do you mean your real self, your spirit, can stay?*

S: It's not your spirit. It's your essence of who you always were. Your body is a vehicle. It's temporary so you dissolve it so you can be. There are things you can learn when you're not in a body, so you go. They burn the bodies.

D: *Every life has a lesson. Do you think you learned anything from that lifetime?* (Shiela became emotional.) *Why is that making you emotional?*

S: (Whispering.) I just feel so small. I just don't know about this world. It's like you have to contain this in the temple, and you can't. You have to keep others out and that's just sad because I don't know. Do you guide? Do you just give up? I think it would be better to just hide the knowledge until they get smarter. They are just not very smart.

D: *And not share with anybody?*

S: Not for a while. They're so barbaric. Why are they so barbaric?

D: *But everybody's not like that.*

S: No, but we can't just live in our little temple forever. That's not the purpose. I did learn in the temple. I never left the temple, never. I went to the shore. I went to the temple. I went to the garden. I went to the edges but I never went into the regular city. I never took the journeys because I hated that. I felt better in isolation. I thought I could bring everyone to me, but that's small. If you wait I will help them, but that is small, and I don't like small. I think I should be big so maybe I learned a lot about small. I only learned small. I think that's a good place to start. That's a very good lesson to learn, because I learned all the skills of the sky. And I learned energy, and I learned the library, but I don't know how to get beyond that. I don't know how to cross the barrier because it's so dark and I don't think it was my purpose to cross. It was my purpose to stay at the library, but it was so small. The children crossed. They were vagabonds. They left me. It's okay. I don't mind.

I had her drift away and had Shiela's consciousness return so I could bring forth the SC. I asked it why it chose that lifetime for her to see.

S: She didn't like her choice. She chose to stay. She could have followed the children like a vagabond. She could have gotten on the boat. She could have traveled. She could have left and come back. She could have been bigger. She was timid. She picked a safe place and then she regretted the safe place.

D: *She was doing good, wasn't she?*

S: She did, but she doesn't have to do that twice.

D: *Is that what you think is happening with her life now?*

S: Yes, I do. She did it. She's already been at the crossroads. She's not paying attention.

D: *Is that why you are trying to make a comparison?*

S: I am trying. Last time she was afraid of going. Last time she thought if she left she couldn't come back. Last time she thought if she went on a boat she would die. Last time she thought she would lose her children. Last time she thought she was only safe in the library. Last time she thought she needed the moat to protect her. She thought they would kill her. She thought she would be misused for killing, so she just never even tried. And now she says she can't leave it, but she already chose that. She knows what will happen. She knows. I can tell. – She'll die. She'll cross over and she'll cry because she didn't leave, *again*. We're going to make her do it again until she leaves. It all depends on how much she likes doing things over.

D: *Yes, you have to repeat it if you don't learn the lesson, don't you?*

S: We do and she can hear that. She's stubborn.

D: *She keeps being drawn to Seattle. What do you think? That's leaving the safe place.*

S: The energy is good there. The energy matches her. The energy of the library is there. The energy of those people, of the gardeners, of the builder, of the healers is there. And she knows that. She's just so used to staying that she thinks she'll die if she goes.

D: *She said her family doesn't want her to leave.*

S: The family at the library didn't care. She just assumes things. She doesn't ask. She never asks. She should ask and not assume.

D: *She said her father doesn't want her to leave.*

S: Her father went into the Navy when he was eighteen years old. He went to Guam. That's leaving. Her father left when she was born as a first child. He was gone. He was not even there. He was four thousand miles away when the first baby was born and died.

This is something I have discovered in my work. Often if a child dies at birth, and another child is born shortly afterwards (usually within a year), it is the same soul or spirit. It has chosen to come to that family, and if the first attempt doesn't succeed it will try again.

S: I think if she doesn't go to Seattle she's going to have to do this over again. She doesn't even try. I think if she doesn't try, she'll never rest. Because she's going to do it over again until she tries. It's in the contract.

D: *Shiela said a few months ago she had that accident where she hit her head. What happened at that time?*

S: She needed to come home.

D: *Was it a possibility?*

S: She could. She was finished with the sad part.

D: *She said she felt like she could have exited at that time.*

S: Shiela didn't. I did. That was just her body in the wreck. She wasn't in the wreck. The body was all that was there. It was just a body in the vehicle. I never exit. It was a way to end that body, like before when it dissolved.

D: *We want her to understand. It was decided not to let that happen?*

S: She came back to learn to *leave*. She doesn't have to start from being a baby. She can learn her lesson in her body.

D: *So it was decided she wasn't going to exit? She would come back and stay for a while?*

S: It was in the stars. Everything lined up. The time was right to try one more lesson. If it doesn't work ... go home.

D: *So it's important for her to make the right decision right now, isn't it?*

S: That's why she came back. In this body.

D: *So this body has some important things to do?*

S: Yes, it does. It's not just Seattle. Seattle will be home and she will go everywhere. She'll travel for her work. She's a teacher. She will travel to teach. She's just a messenger. Teachers are just messengers. There are many ways to teach. She will travel, but go home to Seattle. Either do that or do it over. Depends on how many times she wants to do it over.

D: *And I'm guessing, but I think if she doesn't make a decision she won't have any reason to stay in this body?*

S: No, there's no reason to stay.

Shiela had been having trouble with her eyes. Cataracts were forming and progressing rapidly, which was unusual for her age. This obviously explained it. She didn't want to see what she was supposed to be doing.

S: She created the path. The path moves backwards not just forward. It's not a crossroads. It's the same path, but paths have a forward and a backward. When you're on the path you're not on the beginning of the path. You're *on* the path. You face one way and you are moving forward. You move the other way, you're not on a different path. It's going backwards down the old path. It's one path. You've already chosen the path. You've switched forward or backward. She's not seeing clearly because she's looking backwards down the path. It's like the fog. You're not supposed to go backwards. If she was seeing clearly, she would see the path, but when she turns backward she sees fog. It's not clear because she already did that. You don't do that. That's why it's blurry.

D: *If she makes the decision to go in the right direction, the eyes will clear up?* (Yes) *And she doesn't have to worry about having operations?*

S: No, it won't happen if she chooses the forward path.

D: *They said it came on very quickly.*

S: Because she made the wrong choice. She stopped moving forward, and when she stopped moving forward her vision left her. She can do what she wants. The vision won't come back until the path is right. She was on the right path until she got scared and dropped everything. Then the vision left. There is always a message.

She had also developed diabetes. The SC said it was because she had no joy. "The diabetes is a message. She's a messenger. Her whole body is a messenger. All bodies are messengers. I know what her problem is. She won't let the message come through. If she would listen to the message, the joy would come through, but when you're a messenger and you're afraid to give the message; if you've been punished for speaking the message and you've stopped speaking the message, then there's no joy. There's just sadness. She's not listening to the message. The diabetes will also clear up if she listens." I knew the SC could cure the diabetes instantly, but it seemed to prefer Shiela to do this instead. "I would help her if she would ask. I could. I'm not going to if she's not listening. I would just have to find another message. I gave her the easy ones."

D: *So this decision is very important; everything in her life hinges on it.*

S: She's making it harder than it has to be. It's just a choice.

D: *She's worried about her family.*

S: There's more than one family. There's her soul family. It's higher. It's bigger. It doesn't have to be biology. It can be where your heart is from. You know when you see them. How will she see them if she doesn't even go?

I asked about her interest in astrology in this lifetime and whether that came from the other lifetime. "The stars are just an oracle. It's so easy to read. It's so easy. You don't have to learn a new language. The stars are the same. For every lifetime they are the same stars so you don't have to relearn a language. You just learn the message of symbols of dreams and stars and you don't have to relearn anything."

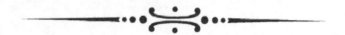

Parting message: She has to find a quiet place to reach me because I can't get through her chaos. She doesn't listen. It has to be quiet in her mind and she has to choose that place. That's the only way to get through. She has to trust when she's quiet that that's me. She'll feel it in her body. It's very peaceful. I'll show her symbols. She understands feelings and symbols and pictures. She doesn't understand words at all. I will show her symbols. You have to have more than one way to be a messenger. Sometimes you close a door and then you have to open another one. It's like an artery. It's like a detour.

Chapter 4

BRINGING BACK ANCIENT HEALING

T rina was a retired nurse who mainly wanted to find her purpose. This is what I call the "eternal" question. Every single client has this on their list of questions. "What is my purpose? Why am I here? What am I supposed to be doing with my life? Am I on the right path?" I rarely find someone who does not ask this. If I do, I might say, "There is one question that you do not have on your list." When I tell them what it is, they usually say, "That's because I know my purpose, and I am doing it." But these people are rare. The majority are stumbling through life trying to understand why they are here, and worried about running out of time. Although Trina was in an occupation where she was helping people, she was not satisfied and felt there was something more.

I had not even completed the induction when Trina began describing where she was. I had to turn on the tape recorder quickly and try and recap what she had said. She was in a beautiful, almost sacred setting, a big forest with beautiful trails and pools of water. She said there was magic in the water of the ocean that was full of fish and shells; it was healing water. "We all know how to use the magic. It keeps us alive because we take care of it. We get our food from the water. We have great respect for it." There were many people living in a village. She saw herself as a young woman with dark skin and long thick black hair wearing a colorful, pretty garment. "We get gifts from the water. We make jewelry and there's healing properties from some of the shells. We grind certain shells down to a powder, and we put them in our food. This balances our system. We never get sick because we listen to our bodies and we listen to the earth." I asked if it was a certain type of shell. "I see shiny on the outside. It's not real big, smaller than a palm. It is like nautilus, but not quite. It's a little bit more open, peacock color in the center. We grind little ones, too. The powder can also be put on wounds." She also knew what to get from the woods to

53

use for food or healing. She was not the only one in the village who could do these things; there were others who had the knowledge. "We're guided. We listen to our heart. We're not just given knowledge from word of mouth. We listen. We know what it means when our body gives us discomfort. We know what to do to take care of it. We seem to be connected to the earth. We used to remember how to heal the earth. I believe that I might be the main instrument, but I share the knowledge."

The huts in the village had an open, spacious feeling with straight walls and a capped roof with fronds. Each family had their own, but they also came together to share. "Share our stories, share knowledge, like a community." Her individual hut was this type. "It smells good. Incense burning in there, and there are pots of healing herbs up against the wall. They are in containers being grown and dried. It's all here to take care of whatever ails us." She lived alone with no family of her own. "We never feel alone. They are all my family in heart." There were other villages, but they were far away. "We collect from the shore and we trade."

D: *You said you also listen to the earth. What do you mean by that?*

T: To go into meditation to ask the right questions, and the answer's always there. We trust that source. (She seemed to be talking to someone else.) We have an answer, don't we? (Laugh) You're laughing at me ... saying, "silly girl."

D: *Who is saying, "silly girl"?*

T: The pretty one with the big, fat hair. Yes, I can see her. She's right there and she is giving me that look like ... You already know the answers. That's what she's saying. "Yes, and Trina needs to know that." I can see her right now. She's reminding me that's me and I have all these answers.

D: *As you see this woman called "Trina," do you know what the relationship is between you two?*

T: (Laugh) She's me.

D: *How do you understand that?*

T: I don't know, but I feel she's a part of me. She is reminding me that I need to do this, that I'll find the answers, and it's as easy. Just do it! (Laugh) She's giving me that little coy look, and shaking her finger like, "You remember, so do it." (Laugh)

I wanted to get the attention off of Trina and back on the woman in the village. I asked if the others in the village knew how to meditate and listen for answers too.

T: This is knowledge that I have shared with all, for there was a time where we put one person in awe that had these capabilities. The ones before. It's not so here. This knowledge has been passed down, but there was one that had this knowledge that was not shared, but is now shared with everyone. They just need to do it, too.

D: *Do you think it would be better that everyone knows how, rather than just one?*

T: Yes. For not one controls the knowledge just for themselves. It is now able to be shared with others. They just have to do it. There's much harmony here. This is the perfect place. By the meditations it has created more harmony, for people realize that we are all connected.

D: *Is there a certain type of meditation that you do? Are there any instructions you would give someone?*

T: It is quite similar to here, to go into the quiet place or to focus on the breath. And at first I'll go in with intention and the right questions, if there are questions to be asked. If there is a question I need to have answered.

D: *Do your people live a long time?*

T: Yes, in very, very good health. They seem to get stronger and stronger as they get older and older.

This certainly sounded like a perfect place, and they all seemed to be happy. I decided to move her ahead to an important day and see what was happening. Someone had come to her with a brand new baby, and they wanted her to do a blessing. There were many others gathered to watch this. She gave it a blessing with oils strategically placed on the forehead. She was also doing some chanting that was a connection to their source. "It's many vowels. Amana (?) That's what I hear or something like three sets of little vowel connections like that. A-ma-nah So-fal-ah. We are all connected and it is a blessing to remember where we come from."

When we took the story forward she had trained the baby (as it grew) to become her replacement in the village. She knew immediately that this was the one to train so the knowledge would not be lost. Then we moved forward to the last day of her life. After she had trained her replacement there was no reason for her to stay, so she consciously decided to die. She described a scene full of love, not sadness. "It's so wonderful. It's so joyful and I am there above watching them, bringing them much joy. My body is right there. She just passed, no disease, just old age. She was in her nineties, I believe. It was time. Beautiful. No grieving! We all understand. The girl will take over my hut. She's now a young lady. She's beautiful being there. I'm there above it all just watching and smiling and feeling much joy. The people are all happy."

D: *Now that you are out of the body, do you feel there's somewhere that you have to go or do you know? – You're smiling. What is it?*

T: It's so beautiful, and I'm asking, "Can I go? Can I go over to see what it looks like?" I'm asking them, "Can I go see everybody? What everybody looks like?"

D: *Who are you asking?*

T: Just all of the ones more knowledgeable than I am at this point, to give me a glimpse. "Am I at a place that I can get a glimpse of where I came from? I'd like to see where I came from. I'd like to." "You can if you're willing." Oh, I really want to. – They have me by each arm, but they laugh because they're really not arms. I need some help, I tell

them. I talked to them beforehand. I said, "If we can, I'd
like to go where home is."

D: *What are they showing you?*

T: Well, it's bright. There's a big building to the left and it's
all white and bright, but I don't think this is home.

D: *What is the building like?*

T: Vast, light pillars in white, big, tall, long steps, and the
people are all waving at me. It looks like in my imagination
what I always think the Hall of Records would look like.
And you just *think* any book you want. But they're really
not books, are they?

D: *Where are the books?*

T: Everywhere. Up high and low, and with a thought you can
have the information.

D: *Which one of the books do you want to look at? (Pause) Which one are
you attracted to?*

T: To see the one that I would learn the most from. I'd really
like to see where I came from.

D: *Ask them which one of the books has that information in it?*

T: It's at the very tip top and it's coming down ... it's on the
table. I ask it to open to the perfect page.

D: *What do you see as the book comes open?*

T: I don't know if I really see. I sense peace and love. I believe
it's a place where we don't have form, and just hearing
without being able to see anything. I am just sensing
energy. I keep hearing that I have seen what I was
supposed to experience. This other's not that important.
It's just curiosity. – But it would still be nice just to see,
since we're here. Be glorious if we could see. (She was
almost begging.) To get to see it ... because I wanna. (A
childlike voice.) Can I see it instead of feeling it? They say
that I can do whatever I want to do. Am I ready? They're
just playing with me. "If you want to be ready." I do, I
desire to see. "It's much greater than you can even

perceive." Oh, is that why I'm not seeing it? It's much greater than I can perceive? But I'd really like to perceive it.

D: *Maybe that's all you can handle at this time?*

T: Is this all that I can handle at this time?

D: *What do they say?*

T: Over here. At that big beautiful building. There I am seeing me turning the pages of this book. If I go to another page, it's all going to happen. I can see that. I'm going up to it. (Whispering) I see a pulsing white life form starting big and going in, going out and going in ... like a collective organism. Maybe that's all *us*, all of ourselves, all collectively in this huge, big corpuscle. It's huge.

D: *Maybe that's why it's hard for you to understand.*

T: Maybe so.

D: *Does that help you to understand it?*

T: Yes, maybe next time.

D: *They are very kind, and they don't want to give you more than you can handle.*

T: Now I just see lots of bright purple swirling. I don't know what that means.

D: *That's all right. This will be something for Trina to think about. (Yes) All right. Ask them, "Do we need to call in the subconscious to find answers or can they give you your answers?"*

T: Can we ask ya'll? They say, "Sure."

D: *They have answers. But do they want us to call in the other part?*

T: They say, the more the merrier. – They're the keepers.

D: *What are the keepers?*

T: They're the keepers of the knowledge.

I then thanked them for the help they had already given us. But I knew they would be limited in their ability to answer the questions. We could get more from the SC. So I then called it forth. I asked why it chose that life for Trina to see.

T: She already answered the question. It was to remember where to get the answers. When she thinks life is so challenging, to take the time and space to connect with us. Just like she did in that other lifetime.

Anything that is learned is never lost. It is stored in the subconscious mind just like a computer, and it can be brought forth if it is appropriate for the current lifetime. In Trina's case she would be able to remember how she used the herbs and the healing in that lifetime, and use that knowledge in the present one. "She will probably lean more towards the energetic medicine and the consumption of the herbs because of finding the true viable sources."

She was told her purpose: To be an instrument of peace and joy. It's an informal change agent. That she teaches by example in any form of gathering. To do meditation in the morning upon arising. To make sure she connects and is balanced in the morning. When she asks the question the first answer will be us answering. "She'll hardly be able to get the question out before she'll hear the answer."

She had a question about a physical event that happened a few months before. She thought she was having a stroke, and the other people present thought she was, too. The SC said it was not. It was just adjusting to the frequencies and vibrations of the energy shifting that is occurring at the present time.

The SC also said (when talking about physical problems) that it would be good for her to take calcium. This related to the ground up shells that she put in her food in the other lifetime, which was calcium lactate. It would be good for her to do that again, in the form of calcium.

Chapter 5

HIDING THE INFORMATION

Joanne was another woman who was dissatisfied with her occupation. She worked in real estate and was successful, but felt unfulfilled. She was writing songs as a sideline, and was interested in learning healing.

I have had many, many cases where the client went back to a past life where they lived among an ignorant and superstitious people. The person possessed psychic abilities that are now being considered normal, but in those days they were viewed with great suspicion. Every town or village had its "granny woman". Someone who had knowledge of herbs and oils and the mixing of healing potions. They had knowledge that had been passed down to them, and although they often used it for good, they were thought to be different, and this was considered a threat. The person was either persecuted or killed.

I can't even count the numerous cases I have had where the client was burnt at the stake, hung or died in other horrible ways. Maybe it was something we all had to endure as a part of our soul growth and development. This hidden memory has often been carried over into their present lifetime as an unconscious fear of developing these abilities again because the same thing might happen. This causes them to develop physical symptoms or illness, even though they do not recognize the cause consciously. We know in our present time it is highly unlikely they will be harmed or killed for their beliefs. However, in one case the SC said, "Yes, but they can be harmed by words."

In the case of Joanne there might have been something to fear because she was different. She definitely did not fit the mold of what was acceptable in those time periods. She was one of a group that I have discovered that I call the "collectors." They travel the galaxies searching for and recording information. They often created bodies that appeared to be

61

human so they would fit in. Although they are gentle, reclusive and would harm no one during their quest, they were and are viewed with fear and suspicion.

When Joanne came off the cloud she found herself in a small town, which from the description sounded like the 1700s or earlier. She heard a bell ringing. There were many people all gathered around a bell tower, which seemed like the town center. When they rang the bell it meant that everyone should come to the tower to find out what was happening. A priest was reading something from a scroll. She couldn't hear what he was reading, but she knew it was a proclamation. "I think he's talking about sin, people who sin. People to be aware of that sin against the church."

D: *It will become clearer. How do you feel about the proclamation?*

J: It makes me afraid.

D: *Why does it make you afraid?*

J: Because it's not true. There aren't people sinning against the church.

I had her look at herself. She was a very young teenage girl with long hair, dressed in gray. She saw she had shackles on her ankles. She became even more frightened when she saw that her hands were tied behind her.

D: *I can see why you'd be scared. Why do they have you tied up and shackled like this?*

J: To laugh at me. It's like a mockery.

So the proclamation was about her. "That I have sinned against the church. But I don't understand what they mean. I just told the truth. That we are each God."

D: *Who were you telling?*

J: Everyone that would listen.

D: *And they thought this was wrong?* (Yes) *Then what happened?*

J: I don't really know. It's way too confusing. These were people I thought I trusted. And they went behind my back.

I was attempting to find out what happened. She said she did not have a family in that town. In fact, she did not even live in that town. So I asked her to go backward in time to see what happened to bring her to this point. She saw that she lived in a hut away from the town in an area of beautiful mountains and valleys. There was a small village of similar huts, where several groups lived. These groups were very close, and considered themselves safe living in this isolated location. I asked what the group did. "We study. Science. It's a science you can't see, but we document it. We write it and we hide it."

I knew few people in that time period could read or write, especially women, who were normally not allowed to learn. "Can you read and write?"

J: We draw pictures.

D: *But you said it's a science that you can't see?* (Yes) *Tell me about it. How do you get the information?*

J: In our minds. We see farther past the stars and we draw pictures of it.

D: *Does the whole group do this at once or what?*

J: No. There's one teacher. We're all separate, but we're all together, and one teacher starts it. And then we all can do it. And we reach farther past than anyone can see. We get pictures, and then we draw them.

D: *How do you do this?*

J: It's like a beam of light in the middle of your head. We scan. It comes from the middle of the teacher's forehead. (She indicated the third eye.) And it shoots out. And then we all can do it. We can also send out a beam of light, but he does it first. We're not as strong as he is. He has a much brighter beam than we have.

D: *Then he projects it?*

J: Maybe that's what he does. He starts it. He projects it to us as he teaches us. And then we go farther with it, reach farther past him. Very, very powerful. We get information and we draw pictures of it.

D: *Where do you think the information is coming from?*

J: Way, way, way past the stars. I think it's a certain galaxy.

D: *So you get the information from the same place each time. Then you draw the pictures. And write the information down?*

J: That's what we do. And then we hide it.

D: *Why do you feel you have to hide it?*

J: Because it's so unusual. People would *not* understand it.

D: *What kind of information is it?* (Pause) *Because you can tell me. You're safe with me.*

J: They're showing me planets. We track things. More like a station, actually. And they get us information for the station that we need. And that's why we have to hide it because it's just for that station.

D: *What do you mean by "station"?*

J: It's like a way station. It's information for a particular person, someone that needs it, but we have to hide it. We have to keep it from the other people.

D: *Has your group been doing this for a long time?* (Yes) *Then is someone going to come that you give the information to?*

J: That's what we do it for.

D: *Have they come before?*

J: We were told they had, but we have not seen it yet.

D: *Do you know what they do with it?*

J: It's to help. And that's why we are so dedicated. I have been doing this since I was very young.

D: *And the whole group works together to do this.*

J: Yes. There's no difference between the families. But we're in the hills where we try to remain isolated.

D: *Do you know where your group came from?*

J: We were specially planted, and we're glad to be here.

D: *What do you mean by "planted"?*

J: We had to appear to be a certain way. And that's not really the way we are, so we were specially planted to work in these hills.

D: *Do you mean you don't really appear human?*

J: We have to appear the way we are. I mean, there's our form that we look like, but that's not our form. We have to take this form.

D: *So you will blend in?*

J: Yes, but we know we're different.

D: *What do you really look like?*

J: We're just light really. But we had to take this form.

D: *You were told to stay there?*

J: Yes, for a job. To take the information for the station.

D: *And collect it, and then someone would come and ....*

J: Absorb it. They just absorb it. We drew pictures so we could ... it just felt right to draw pictures. The information comes from one particular galaxy.

D: *What other kind of information do you have to save?*

J: It's coded. In pictures.

D: *Do you understand what it means?*

J: Yes, it's simple, but no one else would understand. We're taught so early. It's weird. It deals with life force and its

65

energy. I keep seeing the collective of us, but what we do is so unbelievable. Yet we look so normal. That's why we have to remain isolated. But we're busy every 24 hours. We do this all the time.

D: *Do you have to eat or sleep?*

J: I don't see us eating. I don't see us sleeping. We don't need food.

D: *What keeps you alive?*

J: Energy. The life force. It's amazing. We're in that form, but we're not in that form.

D: *But you are constantly accumulating information.*

J: I'm seeing an inverted pyramid, a pointed pyramid but going *into* the earth. They just show me how it points down into the earth. It's very sharp. They showed me that's where we store it. Files and files and files of storing it, but it goes *into* the earth. And we write with our fingers.

D: *It's at this place where you are?* (Yes.) *Is this pyramid physical, solid?*

J: Very physical. It's built into the earth. I can feel it in my body right now. I can see it in the earth, and I can feel it in my body at the same time. Across my stomach, across my chest. Like an inverted pyramid. It stores information. They want me to feel it so I know it's there. It's a little uncomfortable, but it's all right.

D: *Why is it inside of you?*

J: I think that's how they were showing it to me. It was really in the Earth, but actually maybe we all have it inside of us.

D: *The information, you mean?* (Yes, yes.) *So it was not only placed in the earth, but inside of yourself?*

J: Yes. Strange.

D: *Did your group put this pyramid into the earth?*

J: Yes, we built it. It's a very, very, very physical object. That's where we hide the information. Whoa! It's a station! It's *very* large.

D: *So it would hold a lot of information?*

J: A *lot* of information. It is a station. Oh, my! – Now they're coming in.

D: *What do you see?*

J: That's where they land. It's a station. Maybe it's a station inside the Earth, and we're above it, trying to pretend like there's nothing there.

D: *Trying to disguise it, you mean?*

J: Yes, yes. We look so primitive and poor, and stupid. But that's where the station is. The station is this pyramid. They can come in and we can see them, but no one else can.

D: *What does it look like when they land?*

J: Just light beams, flat beams, horizontal beams of light. It's strange that they'd be landing with the way we look.

D: *Are they coming in a craft or what?*

J: Yes, they're definitely in a craft. I see them all, and then they went away. Oh, wow!

D: *You said the average person couldn't see this.*

J: No. Just we, collectively. It's a station where they come in to get the information that we have for them. So they come in and exchange information.

D: *When they come in do they go down into this pyramid?*

J: Yes, they go in, but I don't know how they do that. We wait for them. They come when they need to, and get the information.

D: *How do you put the information into this large pyramid?*

J: With our minds. He gives us that light, then we reach out farther, and we get the information. And I don't know how we put it in there. I think it just happens. It just happens.

D: *But these ones that come in the craft....*

J: I'm not sure who they are. We have to take this form to live here, and then it confuses us who we are. In fact, it's very confusing.

D: Can you see how the beings look that come in the craft?

J: I don't know. They're really good energy. We know who they are, but we don't worry about what they look like.

D: But you were told to come and live here and take these forms?

J: Yes, we had to.

D: Who told you to do this?

J: We just said we'd do it. It's just odd that we're here. It's definitely our job, and we don't know why. We just said we'd do it, and we know how to do it, and we'd be happy to do it. We knew that station probably just needed our energy. It's just so different. So we don't know why we have these bodies. (Laugh) We look so stupid.

D: Otherwise people would be afraid of you, I guess.

J: Yes, that's what happened.

D: All right. Let's move ahead and find out what happened. How did you end up down in the town?

J: I was just a little too curious. I couldn't stop watching the people. When I'd come down I was very different, but the same. And I didn't act like them, but I tried to talk to them.

D: Did any of the others in your group try to go down there?

J: No, they knew better. I was just curious. But I had a way of telling the truth, and it didn't make sense to them. It was so easy for me to tell them the truth.

D: But it's not their truth, I guess.

J: Absolutely. And it's so simple. I wasn't going to tell about the station or anything. Absolutely not. I just was curious. They were so funny. I just wanted to find out more about them. I think the young boy I was friends with told his parents. I really liked him, he was so cute and funny. Then he got scared because he thought he was going to get in trouble. I was really poor, yet I didn't need anything. And he didn't understand why I didn't need anything. So he told.

D: *And you said earlier the only thing you were telling them about was God, wasn't it?*

J: Yes, that we were all God. And they were like "Noooo!" And then they got everybody together. They're going to abolish me – whatever that word is. (Laugh) They just got me and put me in jail. There was nothing my group could do. They knew that whatever was going to happen was just going to happen. These people think I'm crazy. I don't know what that boy told his parents. It was better to get rid of me because what I was saying would just scare the people. And it's just best not to have that kind of information. So that's what they do. They could make me look completely like a poor, crazy person. They never saw a person that really didn't need food, you know? They were really scared. I had a little more light than the group, and it was hard to hide. You know what I mean? But I didn't want to hide it.

In some of the stories in my other books many of these types of people had a light or a glow that emanated from them that was hard to hide. Maybe that was what she was referring to.

D: *So that's what the ringing of the bell, and the proclamation was for?* (Yes, yes.) *And what are they going to do?*

J: I don't know, but I can see my whole group watching it. Hah! I know they're thinking, "You don't listen."

D: *Then what happens? You can move ahead and see what they do to you.*

J: Well, there's not much left of me! I'm there one minute, not much left of my body after that. They torched me very fast.

D: *Was that why you were shackled and tied up?*

J: Yes. They torched me very, very fast. There were people who were sad who didn't want me killed, and so they made sure it went very fast. It was done by the bell. They wanted to get rid of me because they were afraid of me. I didn't make any sense. Never do. But my group just was like "whatever!" (Laugh)

D: *They couldn't do anything to stop it, or they didn't even try?*

J: No, they couldn't. It was so much part of a bigger picture that there was nothing they could do. They didn't have the right to change the plan, you know. So there's not much left of the body. Sad. (Chuckle) I left the body before it burned. I stood there with the priest watching it all. He didn't know it. I stood there with him, telling him I was sorry for him. It was sad. I was really sorry for him.

D: *He was doing what he thought was right, I guess.*

J: Well, maybe. No, I felt sorry for him. I think he was just a puppet. I think my mind touched his mind a little bit. I think he knew a little bit, and that he was sorry. It really is just a mind to a mind to a mind, you know? Some minds can feel it, and some can't.

D: *So some are not ready for it.*

J: Right. It's too different. And when you say it I can feel the upside down pyramid in my stomach. It's just so weird.

D: *Like you carry that information with you?*

J: Yes, yes, yes. It's like a code. But it's here on the Earth, too!

D: *Yes, it was a physical place.* (Yes) *But you were able to carry it with you even after you died and left the body?*

J: Yes. It doesn't leave.

D: *So you carried it with you on your – what, your spirit, your soul?*

J: I don't know.

D: *All right. After you left the body....*

J: Where did I go? (Laugh) Let me think. I didn't go back to the group. I couldn't go back to the group. I had to move on. I see myself shooting like a beam. I think I had to go back to the galaxy. I was really meant to do that, so that was the end of my job there.

D: *Well, you tried to make a difference.*

J: Right. And I did. I did. And it didn't matter if I died, that was the plan. I must have known it. But still, it wasn't any fun. And I see that little boy that betrayed me. He's very cute. And he's scared, though. He never dreamed that would happen.

D: *What kind of a form do you have as you're moving out into the galaxy?*

J: Not much, it's just light. I move to another place. Another time. They just give me missions. There is a place where you go to rest. It's so unbelievable. And the missions are just funny because they're so short. You go to rest, and then on to another mission. They are so short, you can almost laugh at them. You do one and then come back. And it can be anywhere. I don't know why this one was the way it was, but it was.

D: *But then they tell you to go on somewhere else.*

J: Yes, you just go so far. That's what you do! Just go from place to place. Try to learn more things, and to help.

D: *All right. Then let's leave that scene. Let's leave the being there so she can continue on with whatever it is she was doing.*

J: Not a good picture. Leaving that poor girl tied up like that.

D: *Well, we don't have to leave her tied up. You're the part that has left the body because the body's gone, isn't it?*

J: Right, right. It's just not a good picture.

D: *You don't have to see that picture. We'll just let that other part of you that went to the other side continue on its way, because that was a pleasant experience.*

I then oriented Joanne back into the body, and called forth the SC to find out why it chose that unusual lifetime.

J: She needed to know what information was with her that she forgot. She knows, but she forgot. And she always wants to write it, but she won't take the time.

D: *The information that was in the pyramid?*

J: Yes. It's coded, it's scripted. She just needs to write it.

D: *But would she understand it if she wrote it?*

J: Oh, yes. When it comes into this form here on Earth, it's very beautiful. She may not know it when she writes it, but after she writes it she knows it. She'll understand it, but she's afraid to. The information, you know, it puts her in a very tough spot.

D: *Has she been receiving this information?*

J: Oh, yes, since she was little. She doesn't consciously know it, but when she was little she was getting it.

D: *Then what happened?*

J: She tried to talk to people about it, talked to everybody. They just could not handle it. They did everything they could to make her feel stupid. She tried to tell them everything she could see, so that they could see it.

D: *What was she seeing at that young age?*

J: The magical, the mystery, the lights. She showed them, but they couldn't handle it.

D: *What did she show them?*

J: Particular spacecraft that came in back behind the house.

D: *Could the other ones see it?*

J: Maybe I just thought they could, and they couldn't. They didn't understand. It made me very ... I don't know. It was just a lot of pressure.

D: *So the people wanted Joanne to stop it?*

J: Oh, yes, yes, yes. I had to stop it. But they worked so hard to just shut me up. I don't even know where I went. I wasn't even there. I just would leave because ... I would let Joanne do that, but I would leave because it was just too difficult.

This sounded somewhat like a piece of Joanne's personality splitting off. This could be what psychiatrists call a "split personality" when one part is doing something the other main part is unaware of. If it is, it apparently did not do any permanent harm to Joanne's personality. (Refer to my *Convoluted Universe* books for more information about how our soul is composed of many pieces or shards all having their own experience or life.)

D: *So Joanne found out it was just no use talking about it. But you still want her to bring the information back?*

J: Yes, she has it! And she knows it. She keeps so busy she won't write it.

D: *She said she could feel this inverted pyramid in her body? (Yes) What is that?*

J: Now instead of the pyramid it's like a cone that goes so fast.

D: *Did it come from that other life we were watching?*

J: As far as she knows it's always been there. And it contains really, really beautiful information.

D: *When was this placed inside of her?*

J: It's weird, now I can feel it. I guess she came with it.

D: *You think she was born with it?*

J: I think so.

D: *But it's hard in this life....*

J: Very, very. Impossible. Nobody really wants to hear it. It's too good. You know? It's too pretty. People want the bad.

D: *Maybe we're getting to the time when they will listen to the good.*

J: It should be time. I'm waiting. (Laugh)

D: *In that lifetime, where did her group of people come from?*

J: Yes, they came, definitely, as a group. We all agreed to come. You couldn't just come as you were; you had to come like that. And you had to fit in. But, we didn't really fit in. I don't know what we were doing. Why they picked that spot. But it was important at that spot of the Earth to do that construction, and then put that knowledge in there. That was the spot that had to be, so we had to look like the other people just in case they found us. We were found eventually.

D: *The whole group?*

J: Oh, yes. And that wasn't a good story. It doesn't really matter because they all left. After they burned her the people in the town wanted to see where she came from. And luckily we had buried everything. So they knew that was going to happen. That was the risk. That was just the job, and that was the risk. That's the way it is, you know? I think they were all burned.

D: *Is that information still buried?*

J: Oh, yes, it is. Why do they keep saying France? France. Are there hills in France? I don't know. It's something there maybe. Yes, that's where I feel it was.

D: *But the information is still buried there?* (Yes, yes.) *But could people actually find this information?*

J: If it's meant to be, I guess.

D: *I was wondering if it was actually physical....*

J: Or etheric.

D: *That they could find it and read it.*

J: I don't know that people of *this* Earth could, unless there's something different that happens here. (Laugh) Remember, it's a *station*.

D: *Maybe it wasn't intended for the humans anyway.*

J: It was, and it wasn't. It is and it isn't. It's a place of energy that had to be there. It's a place where they reached out to bring energy. It had to be in the Earth at that place. Whether they find it, it doesn't matter. It's just energy that has to be there like a stabilizer. And for some reason the Earth was very important. And still is.

D: *Joanne's doing a lot of work with energy, isn't she?*

J: Yes. Sometimes she doesn't even know what she's doing. It's codes! She *does* know! She forgot. She's working with codes, numbers and codes, and sequences. And that's what she does. She pulls into other galaxies for it. So many depressed people come to her for help.

D: *She doesn't really know where the energy comes from, does she?* (No) *But she's pulling this sequence of numbers and codes from other places?*

J: Yes, and from herself. She has the codes. I want her to be aware of it, and then we'll show her what to do with it. She needs to know it's there. As she knows it's there, she'll know what to do with it. But she hasn't known that it's there. To become aware of it. Honor it, and don't be afraid of it.

D: *You want her to bring this back into her conscious memory?* (Yes, yes, yes.) *Will you help her bring it back?*

J: Yes. I've been trying to help her. But the time is nigh! (Laugh) It's like looking at Braille, you know? If she'll just let it come through her eyes to her hands. We'll show her like Braille, goes in the eyes, through the brain and back out from her mouth and her hands. She won't understand it, but she'll start doing it. It comes through her songs too. She's afraid to bring it out. I mean, she's died for it before, so.... (Laugh) It's a little tough. She's chosen to die many times for it. That's been her adventure.

D: *But in this present life she won't die for it.*

J: No, this is where she doesn't. If she'll just slow down, take the time, and *know* that it's there. She has to see it. She needs to know that she didn't make the agreement this time to pay with her life. Although she's not afraid of dying, it's just not a very fun experience. She's done it just a little too many times. Sometimes you can get someone to do the same thing too many times. And I think that's what we did. You get into a pattern. She needs to feel that inverted pyramid inside of her. Remember, remember where you come from. Remember why you're here. Do your job. It's like touching a little button, a little switch. Like "Turn it on." "Turn it on, you forgot. Why is this here?" "Flip it on in your head." Just don't forget what's inside, don't forget why you came. But enjoy it, this is the best incarnation that you can do this with. You don't have to pay the price. You've paid the price. Enjoy it, share it. It's nothing to die over.

Chapter 6

MANNA FROM HEAVEN

Nicole had been a nurse in a large hospital for many years. It gave her great satisfaction to be able to help people who were ill. However, she was feeling uneasy; as though there was something more she was supposed to be doing with her life.

When Nicole came off the cloud all she could see was calm water all around her. This can usually mean several different things. The person might be in a boat on the water, or in some cases they might be a sea creature. I always let them tell their own story. I have found that I cannot influence them anyway. They will always report what they see or are experiencing. In this case she said she was not *in* anything, just kind of floating on top of the water. I asked how she perceived her body. "It's like I don't have a body. I am just a thought. Not a body, just a thought."

D: *Do you feel like you're part of the water, or just on the water?*

N: Just on the water. Kind of floating because that's where I decided to be. No reason, just wanted to be closer to the water. It's very calm and soothing. There are no waves, just little ripples. But there's nothing else I can see, just water.

D: *Very peaceful. That way you don't have anything you have to do, do you?*

N: No, I don't have to do anything. I never have to do anything anyhow. I just be. Just experiencing. Just feeling. I don't have any goals.

D: *What do you experience?*

N: The warmth. How warm it feels. A little bit of rocking of the water if I want to sit down on the water. Come down a little closer, I can. I'm kind of floating. Right now I don't have to do anything else. It's so nice. There's nothing to do. That's all I am, just a thought.

D: *Do you think you have to go anywhere?*

N: No, it doesn't occur to me I have to go anywhere. Just enjoy. It's what I'm supposed to do right now. The Sun is shining and it is warm. There's nothing else. It's just water. I can see a fish or two. Sometimes the Sun glints off the water, so it's hard to see. Just relax and be and enjoy.

This could have gone on for quite a long time. And even though Nicole was enjoying it, I decided to move her by condensing time to when something was happening. I didn't know if she would continue to be a thought, but she suddenly announced, "I'm a man. I have clothing, but it's unusual, rough and tan. It's what's supposed to be worn, but it doesn't feel comfortable to me." She had medium long dark hair and was young and healthy. Her shoes were, "Leather that's constricting, but it doesn't provide support. They're just loose leather things on my feet. They protect against the sticks and the rocks some, but they still bruise my feet sometimes. I much prefer going barefoot, but then you get your feet hurt." He was in a dense forest walking up a hill over rough terrain. "There are trees all around. I love the trees. I feel like I'm a hunter, but I'm hunting something that isn't to eat. I'm going somewhere." He was carrying a brown leather bag over his shoulder. There was some dried fruit in the bag, but also some other small things. "Rocks. Some of them are shiny, and then there's one very black one. I use them for my health, so I don't get sick. To protect me against things that could happen to me."

D: *Did someone train you how to use these things?*

N: Yes, an older man. He told me how to use different things for my protection, for other people's protection. That's what I'm doing. I'm going somewhere to find somebody to teach. I'm going to show them how to use the stones too. That way I'll pass on the information. It was passed to me, and then I'll pass it on to others. I also work with crystals.

Shiny, different angles. I don't have any with me this time. And feelings of the night somehow come into it, but I don't know how. How the darkness is. What's in the darkness somehow goes with the stones. I don't understand that.

D: *You'll remember more as you talk. But I guess you're used to the woods. It doesn't bother you walking out there?*

N: No, it's very friendly. I love the woods. I know everything that's in the woods. There's nothing to be afraid of.

D: *You don't have weapons with you?*

N: (Indignant) No! Why would I?

D: *Oh, I was just thinking of animals.*

N: No, they're my friends. They don't hurt me. In fact, I help heal them, too! I do! I help them when they're hurt. For some reason they're not afraid of me. I put an energy around them somehow to help them heal so they're not afraid of me. They get hurt sometimes.

D: *So you know how to transfer energy? Would that be a way to say it?*

N: Yes! I do! But I use the stones, too. The man told me how to use them.

D: *You're smiling. You must like what you're doing.*

N: I do, I do. I really do. I help everything. Health is important to animals.

He lived by himself. He didn't live around other people. "It contaminates. I do better without a lot of people. It's much better."

D: *I was thinking of the man who taught you.*

N: I visited him often, but he lived by himself, too, up on a mountain.

D: *Do you have a family?*

N: No. My mother, she lives where the other people live, but I don't. They live in the village, but I left so I could learn.

Other people bring in bad energies sometimes. So it's best to be by myself.

I am always trying to determine a time period or location, so I asked about the type of houses his people lived in. "They're made out of sticks. Sticks on the roof, and sticks in the walls. Small, brown, no light. Dark. They're damp. I just live outside wherever I happen to find a place. It's better to be out in the forest. It gives you energy. In the houses it takes away. Outside is where we're taught. Anyhow it is best that way."

D: *What about when the weather turns bad?*

N: It's not a problem. The weather is our friend. It doesn't bother me. I don't mind being wet.

D: *Doesn't it get cold?*

N: No, not where I am.

D: *That sounds like a perfect place. What do you do for food?*

N: Whenever I need some food, it's there. I can find it or it just comes out of nowhere.

D: *I think that's miraculous.*

N: No, it just happens.

D: *What kind of food do you eat?*

N: Whatever comes. I don't know what it is, it just comes.

D: *I thought maybe it was something that grew in the forest.*

N: No, I can eat that, and it's good. But usually this other food is just there. If I want it, it comes. It is white. No form to it, it's just a lump, but it's very good. It's everything I need. If I'm very hungry more comes. If I'm not so hungry, if I just want a little bit, it's just a little bit that comes. And it's just right there. I just have to want it, and it comes.

It sounds very much like the mysterious manna that sustained Moses and his people during their wanderings in the desert. *Exodus 16:13: And in the morning the dew lay round about the host. And when the dew that lay was gone up, behold, upon the face of the wilderness there lay a small round thing, as small as the hoar frost on the ground. And when the children of Israel saw it, they said one to another, It is manna: for they wist not what it was. And Moses said unto them, This is the bread which the Lord hath given you to eat. – 16:31: And they called the name thereof Manna: and it was like coriander seed, white; and the taste of it was like wafers made with honey.*

When Nicole awakened she had a partial memory. She said she saw the food she created by thought as looking similar to a solid pile of rice. It could taste many different ways, but was very good.

D: *What about the rest of the people in the village?*

N: Oh, they have to work for theirs. They have to grow things. They put things in the dirt, and they make food out of that. Or somebody goes out and kills little animals. I don't have to. All I have to do is want something and it's there. It's food that tastes so good.

D: *Has it been that way all your life?*

N: Yes, but it wasn't supposed to be. Somehow I wasn't supposed to know I could do that because nobody else could do it. Except for the man. He could do it. But my mother didn't like it. My mother said the food wasn't right, because it didn't come the way they made it. It was different, and nobody else wanted what I had.

D: *They wanted to work for it.*

N: They didn't *want* to work for it, but they thought mine wasn't right. They were so thin! They were so thin because they had to work so hard for it, and I didn't.

D: *Did you always have that food, even when you were a child?*

N: Yes, all I had to do was want it. That made me different. And nobody else could do it. Nobody except the man. He lived way up on the mountain. But I would go see him. I think he was my father! I don't know why he didn't live in the village.

D: *Did he look like the rest of them?*

N: No, he didn't. Everybody in the village was dark. Dark hair. He had blonde hair. Light hair. And his skin was lighter. I don't know why he looks different. I look more like my mother.

D: *But he lived by himself up in the hills?*

N: Yes, it was a hole where he had a fire, but it was nice in there. It was warm, and he had whatever he wanted. And I would go see him. Everybody else was afraid.

D: *Did they know he was there?*

N: Yes. They knew, but they weren't supposed to go see him. He was the one with all the information, but everybody was afraid of him, except me. He could have helped them, but they were afraid. He taught me many things, but not everything he knew. He taught me I could do things. I always knew how to find the food. That was easy for me. He taught me how to keep myself healthy. He taught me what it was going to be like later, beyond ... beyond this time.

D: *What do you mean?*

N: Beyond when I was going to be here. He told me what was going to be.

D: *What did he tell you?*

N: There wasn't going to be anybody anymore that could make the same things I could. There wasn't going to be any more food like that because everybody was going to be afraid, and people were going to be mean to each other. Not like when he was there, or when I was there. I don't want to be there then. People are mean. They don't take care of each other like my mother and the villagers. They don't do that. It's beyond that time. After I'm gone away forever.

D: *What did he teach you about keeping yourself healthy?*

N: There were some stones to keep away hurt. And some stones to heal hurt places when you fall down against a rock and hurt yourself, and it would make it go away. Or you could, if somebody hit you and made a mark, it would make it go away. Or hit you with a sharp stone and make a split, make a place in your skin, the skin wasn't there. It would make it go away, and it would be fine.

D: *That's wonderful!*

N: Oh, it was. I thought it was! But everybody else was scared of it.

D: *Did this man come from the village originally?*

N: No, no, he didn't come from there. I don't know where he came from.

D: *Did he ever tell you?*

N: He did, but it was a secret.

D: *Are you allowed to tell me?*

N: I feel I can. He came from farther away than we could ever, ever, ever walk. He came from a star. He showed me which one. And I tried to tell my mother once, but she wouldn't believe me.

D: (Laugh) *Naturally.*

N: It was his mission. That's the word he used. It was his thing for his life that he needed to do. He needed to do it to help people. This is where I got my desire to help people.

D: *Did he say how he got here from the star?*

N: A thought. He came by a thought. He didn't have anything, just a thought. That's all he had to do. I can't do that yet.

D: *But he's in a body that you can see, isn't he?*

N: Yes, and he's very nice looking to me. I like the way he looks.

D: *How did he get a body if he was just the thought?*

N: He could do that, too. He *can* do that. He can do whatever he wants. If he thinks about it he can do it. Like I can think about food and I can do it. But other people don't like that.

D: *You said you felt he was your father?*

N: He is. I think he just thought me into my mother. I didn't know people could do that. He just thought me! But I was the only one. He knew I would be more like him. Somebody else needed to be there to watch over the people.

D: *And he gave you that job?*

N: Yes. I am special.

D: *Is he going to stay there and help, or do you know?*

N: No, not after a time. He leaves.

D: *After you have learned everything?*

N: For some reason he had to leave early. He had to leave before I learned everything. It was unexpected though. He had to leave before he wanted, for some reason. Don't know what the reason was. He didn't tell me. He told me he was going to have to go. And I'm sad because I wanted him there.

D: *He must have thought you'd learned enough anyway.*

N: As much as he could teach me at that time. But I wasn't that old. I could have learned more. I wanted to learn more, but he had to leave. He just thought, and he was gone. That's all. He just thought it. That's the way of it. Everybody who can do it, can think it, and it's done.

D: *But you know how people are, the majority of them don't know they can do these things.*

N: That's because they can't do these things. They're not from that place.

D: *And you were different. You weren't like the others.*

N: Right, because he thought me. I like being able to do these things. But there must be more like me somewhere. I think there should be.... They live in another place quite a ways off. I don't know where they live, but they're through the forest somewhere. I'll know them when I see them. I will. I'm always moving. I always have to go somewhere else. So I don't stay long in a certain place. I have to go help somebody.

D: *Will they accept you helping them?*

N: Yes, but people are still afraid of me because they don't know how I helped them. So I don't stay long in a certain place. I'm always moving. I always have to go somewhere else. I don't get to stay.

D: *How do you know when someone needs you? Do they contact you or what?*

N: I just know. I know when it's time to leave, and I just go somewhere else. And there's always somebody there that needs me. There's never any one place I get to stay. But that's all right because I like the forest. Everything is provided for me, and it's so easy that way. I don't have to do anything. I just take care of other people. I always feel good knowing that.

D: *Are you supposed to teach anyone?*

N: When the time comes, I will think somebody. When I'm old enough and have been enough places, then I get to think someone. I will find somebody special that listens to me. Then I will think someone into them. And then I will teach them.

D: *Otherwise, if you're the only one, you don't want the knowledge to be lost.*

N: Oh, it won't be. It won't be! I will have a son. But just one, just one. There's too much knowledge to pass on.

D: *So you couldn't have a class.*

N: No. It's got to be one. Too much to learn. Not enough time for as much as there is to give.

I thought we had pursued this as far as we could, so I moved him forward to an important day.

N: I've hurt my leg. And it's not the day I die, but a few days before I die. It's too soon!

D: *What happened?*

N: Something fell on my leg and hurt it. And I can't move. I think it must be a tree. It's something big and heavy. I can't push it. It hurts. It has my leg trapped. I can't get it out. I could heal it, but I can't. I don't have my things, and I'm stuck. I should have known this was going to happen.

D: *Why should you have known?*

N: Because I'm supposed to know everything. But I didn't know this.

D: *Well, I don't think anyone can know everything.*

N: No, but I knew everything. I knew so much. But I didn't know *this* was going to happen!

D: *You can't be prepared for everything.*

N: No. And I don't have my bag. I don't have my stones. I could have helped if I'd had my stones. I left those back there.

D: *Would you have been able to lift that tree if you had your stones. Does that make you strong also?*

N: It would have fixed it, and I could have got it off. Yes, I could have got out. I didn't have it. I'm supposed to always carry my stones. That was a silly thing to do, to leave them.

D: *Did you ever find someone else to teach these things?*

N: I was already doing that. That's where the stones were. I was supposed to find more stones.

D: *So you were able to think someone who you could teach?*

N: Yes, my son. He's very young. I haven't taught him everything yet. There wasn't enough time.

D: *Did you find a woman you could do this to?*

N: Yes, she was very sweet.

D: *Did she understand what was happening?*

N: No, because that wasn't the way of it. But she understood enough so I could have my son. And she let me take him. That's very unusual! Most of the mothers keep their children. But she knew I could do special things. She wanted that for her child. And I had been training him. But he's not with me. He has the stones. But that's okay, I'd rather him have the stones. He'll need them.

D: *Does he understand enough to know how to use them?*

N: Probably not. But maybe he'll learn. Maybe he'll have enough of what I gave him to be able to do that.

D: *Did you teach him how to make food appear?*

N: He knows how. I didn't have to teach him that. He knew that already.

D: *Maybe there are other things that he will know. Maybe he'll be able to learn by feelings, intuitions and instincts. And he'll be able to figure out the rest.*

N: Right, right. He's a smart boy. I've given him enough. I hope that he'll know the rest. – So I guess it's going to have to be my time. It wasn't going to be my time, but it is now. I was supposed to stay longer. I was supposed to stay until I was an old, old person. – I just get weaker and weaker. Nobody finds me.

I moved him to after the death had occurred, and had him look back at his body from the spirit side.

N: It's a sad body, all crumpled up. It wasn't that old. It could have been older, but it wasn't. It was all crumpled underneath that tree. I don't know how that tree fell on me.

D: *Sometimes things are meant to be.*

N: Must have been it.

I then asked him what lesson he thought he learned from that lifetime, as he looked at it from that perspective.

N: By traveling I learned not to be afraid to stay in one place. I wasn't supposed to stay in one place. Traveling was what I was to do. And to learn new things as I went. I learned not to be afraid and stay in a village like everyone else. Some people are afraid of the unknown. They just want to stay with what they know is safe. I'd already done that a long time ago. I knew better. I was supposed to go and try the new.

I then left the man there and had Nicole drift away, and then called forth her SC. I asked why it chose that life for her to see.

N: She needs to know it's important for her to keep healing. She needs to be aware of the abilities that she does have, and that she has so many more that she doesn't even know about.

D: *She uses some of the abilities to heal as a nurse.*

N: There's more to be learned. More to be done.

D: *But in that lifetime he used stones, didn't he?*

N: Of course. You have to progress through the lifetimes. You have to use whatever materials you have until you get to where you don't have any materials, but you can do it instinctively.

D: *So she doesn't need any tools now?*

N: No. She thinks she does, but she doesn't. These are crutches that we learn with. We use these stones and crystals. But you get to a point where you don't need anything. You use thought. Thought is very powerful. Thought is all you need. It's the lifetime. The lifetime is still here in Earth, and it's so grounded in Earth that people don't realize that you can just use thought. They think they have to use material things, but you don't. This is how we progress.

D: *People are always asking me for rituals they can use.*

N: Rituals are more like baby steps. You use baby steps to get to where you can do what you need to do. And you don't need the rituals anymore.

D: *You mean Nicole has progressed beyond that?*

N: Yes, but she doesn't know that. She doesn't know how to get there yet. She's supposed to be healing and teaching. But I don't know the way to show her. She will just have to develop.

D: *But she works as a nurse, so she's around the healing environment.*

N: That's not enough. There's something else that she's going to have to do.

D: *Is she supposed to use her healing abilities in the hospital?*

N: No, that has passed. She's supposed to advance, but we can't tell her how to advance. She wants to know, but it isn't time yet. It will come. She is working with babies and children, and that was important. But they're baby steps to where we're going, to where we need to be. She needs to do more, think more, be open more. And these things will come. There is no school. The knowledge will come from above, from beyond, if she lets it. She wants school, and this is not something that can be taught. This is something that comes into your life from beyond.

D: *What do you mean by "beyond"?*

N: From places not here.

D: *Not of Earth?*

N: Right. Other realities. Realities? Is that right? Other places that are not here. Not physical. Not heavy. It's another place, but it's not heavy.

D: *It's not a solid physical place?*

N: It is, but it's much lighter. It's very, very more thought than physical. This will come, but in its own time. She wants to hurry it.

D: *Everything has to happen in its own time. But can you tell her, should she be doing hands-on healing or some other type?*

N: It helps if you touch people. But it's more thought as when that man was thinking food. It's the same type of energy. The thought will help. The thinking will infuse the ability.

It doesn't make sense, but that's what happens. Thoughts infuse and the abilities happen.

According to the dictionary, infuse means to instill or extract certain qualities.

D: *But you know we humans like to be taught and shown things.*

N: Some things, there's no telling. They are learned by thought. Which is good because you're helping with the thought process. Allowing expansion of ideas to open up the mind. The more open the mind the more easily it is to infuse the abilities into the person. She knows these things are coming to her. It's just going to take a while. She's in a hurry. She's afraid something is going to happen to her to stop her life before she learns this lesson. She doesn't have to worry about that. She will be here. It's just going to be a while. The only way is to trust her instincts, intuitions. There's no book, there's no school. Nothing anybody knows right now is true, exactly. It's just going to have to come. She'll know these things. It's stronger than intuition. It will be a knowing. She'll have to allow it and not be afraid of it because the human condition is to be afraid. To touch people will heal them. There are so many who say they can do this, but it's not true. Many of them can't. The ones on the ... communication device ... ummm....

D: *You mean television?*

N: That's it, that's it. They say they can do that, but that's not right. They can't do that yet. There *are* people out there that can do that, but these people *say* they can do that. They're hurting those people by lying to them. But there will come a time when there will be more people that can do that. By touching and thinking, they can heal the people.

D: *You said there are some who are doing it. They probably are in the background anyway.*

N: You would have more knowledge of that than I would.

D: *I mean they don't let people know.*

N: Only a few people like you that they're not afraid to talk to. They tell you everything. But you have to listen to know who can do it, and encourage them because they feel afraid, too. But we're trying to send the language of the healing through and infuse the abilities. But everybody is feeling alone, and they're not going to be alone. But they do not understand they have this ability. These people are lost because they don't know of anyone they can talk to. They are afraid people will not understand and accept them.

D: *But this will become natural by the time Nicole can do it?*

N: Yes. There will be more people doing it. It will happen before she's gone from this life.

D: *Should she continue to work at the hospital for now?*

N: She can, it doesn't matter one way or the other. She'll receive the infusion when it's time. Everybody who is supposed to do this will receive it about the same time.

D: *But you can't tell us how long it will be?*

N: Oh, a while. It will be while you're still here. Nicole's still here. But it won't be for a few units yet.

D: *So it will happen in our lifetime, but it won't be right away.*

N: Right. Somehow fear has to leave people, and there's going to be an opening of knowledge. There's going to be a wave of knowledge that will start infusing. And along with this will be the healing.

D: *So we're supposed to be involved in all of this.*

N: Everybody will be involved, but only those who really care about it will be the healers. Everybody on Earth will be involved in this wave, but people are so afraid they can't open it. They will be too afraid to open to it. But the healers and the ones like you will be on the front end. They will be the ones who get the most out of it, the afraid ones won't. It will take special abilities. But there will be enough people that they will be able to help the others progress.

D: *I have many people coming to me who are told they are to be healers.*

N: They are, every one. Yes. As much as possible we need more healers because there's going to be such a sickness over this planet.

D: *What do you mean?*

N: A terrible ... it's a bad sickness. It could hurt it so bad it won't recover. The sickness, it will take a lot of healers thinking positive to countermeasure what could happen.

D: *Is this a sickness that will affect the people?*

N: Yes! Oh, oh, everybody will be sick! Oh, that's not good!

D: *What kind of sickness?*

N: Environmental pollution.

D: *Something from the air?*

N: From the ground, and the ground is supposed to be healthy. But it hasn't been for a while, and it won't be. It is going to take so many healers to help people get over that, if they can. There have been so many warnings, and nobody's listening. It will happen.

D: *Will this happen through the food we're eating?*

N: The food, the water. The water's the worst. But the food, it comes from the ground. And there's nothing to do to save everybody.

D: *Do you mean it's being contaminated?*

N: Yes, and it's going to take everybody thinking positive, and doing positive to even get around this. It's so massive. It's over everything. (Shocked at what she's seeing.) Oh, my!

D: *I wondered what was going to happen to require that so many people be healers.*

N: Oh, there's going to be more healers needed than there's going to be! Oh, my – how sad! So many people are going to die!

D: *Is this happening gradually now, or will it happen all at once?*

N: It's happening now, but the effects will become – ten years. In ten years the effects will be known fully.

D: *As to what it's doing to the body?*

N: Yes. I need to say "ten years." (This session was done in 2005.)

D: *Will this affect people more in the cities than those that live out in the country?*

N: That's the sad part. It affects everybody the same. It's the stuff you put into the ground, it seeps into the water. There's going to be nowhere safe. The healers are going to have to come and cleanse the people and the land.

D: *Then the healers will be protected from this sickness?*

N: No, not necessarily. Some of them will die, too.

D: *That's why there has to be so many?* (Yes) *I was thinking if they are to help the others, they will have to be protected.*

N: There's no protection for this. It's everywhere. The only protection will come from somewhere else.

D: *Do you think that will happen?*

N: If we're lucky it will. They'll take pity on us. If we show we really want to do right, then they'll help us. If we continue the way we're doing, they won't. There are so many out there that will if we'll just start by cleaning up what we have now. Otherwise they're just going to let us find our own path. They can't interfere. If we're already on the path they can help us.

Chapter 7

JUST WEARING A COAT

Pamela had been working for an environmental company. She had recently been fired over issues and conflicts with her boss. She had discovered dishonesty within the company and felt compelled to report it. She now wondered if she should go in a different direction instead of returning to the corporate world. This was the purpose for the session. I always trust that the SC will take the client to the most appropriate time and place to explain the problems in their life, even though to me it doesn't make sense in the beginning. I know it will all be resolved before we are finished because "they" can see the bigger picture.

Pamela saw herself standing on a hill looking down at a small town. She saw that she was an elderly man with a long grey beard, dressed in simple long cloths draped over his body. He was carrying a staff so I thought he might be a shepherd. But she said no, that he was a wise person, an elder, healer. He lived in a small hut on the edge of the woods above the town. The hut did not contain much, but the main focus was a pot over the fire where he prepared herbs and medicines. He grew some of the herbs and he gathered others from the woods. He said he had not been trained in this work, but instinctively knew which herbs to use to help the people who came. He lived alone, but seemed to enjoy his work because he felt he was helping people. He not only used herbs, but also his hands. He could heal by touching certain parts of the person's body.

I have had many sessions where the person was a healer using natural substances. Many of them had come by their knowledge naturally, and others were taught by some wise person. Yet even though they did a great deal of good for the people, they were still viewed with suspicion and feared. They usually lived in isolation because people did not think they were normal human beings like the rest of the community. These past lives are good examples of the role of fear in the development of humanity. People have always been afraid of what they do not understand, and they cannot trust the unknown, the strange and unfamiliar. We have come a long way since those times. At least we don't kill people for their beliefs. But still I find remnants of that fear even in modern times.

D: *You said no one taught you to do this. You just knew how?*

P: Yes, I just always did. I learned this from the animals in the forest.

D: *Are there any other ways you heal people besides the herbs and touching them?*

P: I talk to them. Sometimes that's all they need. Sometimes it's very simple. Sometimes it's not. Sometimes they need to take the medicines with them to remind them to heal. It doesn't really do anything. Sometimes it does. It can. They don't really need it, but they need it to remember. It scares them to heal without it.

D: *You know they can really heal themselves. Is that what you mean?*

P: Yes, but sometimes they're afraid. They want someone else to do it, and that's alright. And sometimes they are fearful of me, but they come anyway. Sometimes even when I help them, somehow that makes them more afraid that I am something to be feared. Because they don't think they can do it when I tell them "they can." It's easier to be afraid.

D: *There's no reason to be afraid, but that's how some people are, I guess.*

He had discovered the basis of what I teach in my classes. That everyone has the power within themselves to heal themselves. Yet because they do not believe they could possibly have this natural power, they think they need someone outside themselves to do the healing.

I decided to move him ahead to an important day, and he said, "I see them coming up the hill. They have torches. I knew they would. They're coming to burn my house."

D: *Why would they do that?*

P: I heal people. No one's supposed to do that. Only God must heal. I'm not of God, they say.

D: *But they came to you, didn't they?*

P: Oh, of course. Someone convinced them that it was evil. It makes no sense. They don't make sense. I'm not of their group.

D: *You're not originally from that town or what?*

P: No, I look different. I look very different. They are very simple. I'm not. I'm from a different place. I came to help them. – And they will burn and they will think that they killed me, but they didn't. I simply leave.

D: *You came from a different place? – You're smiling.*

P: It seems I came from the Stars because I won't die. I try to explain when I come, but they won't listen and they think if they kill me I'll be gone.

D: *But you said you came to help them?*

P: Yes, but you can only help so much.

D: *Did someone tell you to go to that place?*

P: I could choose. I chose. It was a possibility of helping and some growth was made. I thought the people could learn. I thought I could teach them and some did learn. Many of them were taught, but this will make them fearful, too. They won't be able to do like they would have, but they'll remember for a while.

D: *They won't lose all the knowledge.* (No) *But you said you came from the Stars?*

P: Yes, it's a different place.

D: *Tell me about that. You were smiling like it must be a good place.*

P: There are many of us that come down and do that.

D: *Did you decide to come as a group?*

P: In different places, we usually go alone to each place.

D: *But then you're away from the others in your group.*

P: Yes, but it's a short time. Just come and try to help, leave a little knowledge.

D: *Tell me about this place that you came from?*

P: It's a ship.

D: *Did you have the same kind of body when you were on the ship?*

P: No. We're different. We don't have the same bodies, but we adapt some to come down. We have to. The body has to be adapted to the place and the visual to make it. It's okay that we're different. It's important to be different, but not too different.

D: *Otherwise, you might scare people?* (Yes) *So your normal body looks different?*

P: Yes, it's shaped somewhat different.

D: *Did someone tell you to come and do this?*

P: That's just what we do. The evolution of the group is to try to move things forward. Or bring bits of information to them, bits of technology. Otherwise, it takes too long. Some groups do better than others. Some groups are not as fearful. It depends on the belief system of the group. If the group is already fearful, it's more difficult to overcome. But if they have moved forward, then more progress can be made without having to work so much with the fears.

D: *Have you been working with this group in that village very long?*

P: Oh, no. A human lifetime perhaps.

D: *Did you develop this body as a full grown body?* (Oh, yes.) *You didn't have to start from a child then?* (No) *You decided on that type of body so you would fit in.*

P: Yes, but different. The people, their skin tone, is different. So the skin tone I chose was different, lighter, to draw attention. But because they are simple in their evolution, it can go both ways. It can become a god-like thing and then come into conflict with what they consider to be their gods, and you never know how it will go.

D: *You never know how they are going to accept you.*

P: No, but enough learned about the herbs that do work, and some learned to use their minds. Others don't want to believe they can do it themselves; they want a god.

D: *So some will be able to take that knowledge and use it.* (Yes) *But in this case they thought you were not working with their gods?* (Yes) *So they thought you were evil?*

P: It's all about the power and the medicine, and the village felt they were losing their power. That's really all it amounted to.

D: *So they saw you as a threat?*

P: I tried to work with them. This one learned and then he thought he could do it himself and progress would still be made. It was very special for him at first because I worked with him first. But then the others came, and he wasn't as special. And he wanted all of the knowledge for himself, so he turned the others against me.

D: *So he is responsible for sending the people up the hill with the torches?* (Yes) *How do you feel about him doing that?*

P: Oh, that's okay. That's just what they do.

This was good that he did not carry anger towards them because that creates karma that could be carried forward to this present life.

D: *Well, you said they were coming up and you thought they were going to burn the house. What happened?*

P: They burn the house and go.

D: *What happens to you?*

P: I suppose that body does burn.

D: *What do you see?*

P: Just sitting there in the house and getting burned.

D: *You didn't try to escape?*

P: No. There was no point.

D: *But you're out of that body looking at it now?* (Yes.) *What are you going to do now?*

P: Go back and choose another body and do it all again. I will still help.

D: *Are you going to go back to the ship?*

P: Yes ... whatever it is. That's where I get the other body. I can choose.

D: *You said, "Whatever it is." It doesn't look like a ship?*

P: It did. I do see a metallic type object, but I don't know.

D: *You said that's where you go back to to get the bodies?* (Yes) *How does that happen?*

P: It's almost like a shell.

D: *You're back there now and I guess you're getting ready for the next one. You said you want to go out and do it again?*

P: That's just what we do. It's our job.

D: *It doesn't discourage you when something like that happens?*

P: I don't feel emotion at all.

D: *How do you get the next body? What's the procedure?*

P: Just choose the place and take what was learned from the last experience and shape accordingly. Maybe it was shaped too differently, so I'll have to try the next time to ... it's like the mind can create the body. It's easy. So take the lessons learned and make them maybe more similar; maybe more different, but you try.... It's like just a shell. You just change it. Then you just walk in. You just appear. It's not a full life. It's not that you're born. You just put on the shell and walk in.

D: *Do you create the shell on the ship, or do you put it on where you're going to?*

P: It just sort of happens when you appear.

D: *When you decide where to go?*

P: Yes. You just walk into it.

D: *You always come into it as an adult?*

P: Yes. You can choose not to, but it works better.

D: *You don't want to waste time being a child.* (Right.) *You also don't forget your plan that way either.*

P: No. This is a different thing than an incarnation. In an incarnation they have a plan. This is a task.

D: *It's something you decided to do to help.*

P: To teach.

D: *So the next time you'll pick another place and you'll heal them and teach them?*

P: Oh, yes. And sometimes it lasts longer than others. And I'll learn how to deal with them better. We are a small group that does this.

D: *Did you ever have incarnations?*

P: Yes, this is just one, and the task is to go serve this purpose many places.

D: *Did you have a physical life on Earth before?*

P: Many. This was just a task. A choice to spend that period of time teaching, helping. I teach. I learn, but it's different than many of my incarnations that I will learn from. But the bodies and the tasks are simply parts of that life plan. Then go to a different life. But for this life the job was to go down to a particular group and help them for a period of time. And put on a human coat to do that, and then go back. And I can do that as many times as I want until I choose to incarnate as human again. I just wanted to go try it. It always seems to end the same though. There's a point where the fear kicks in and they don't trust anymore, and then I have to leave.

D: *That's not your job to try to change the fear?*

P: I do, and some do well with it. But it's after I leave that they don't always go in the right direction or it will fade over time. It's different with everyone, but there are many who will. But overall, progress is made even when the fear comes. Progress was still made. It's okay. I have no emotion one way or another in any of it. It does not matter.

D: *Because you're not really that person.* (No) *You're just having the experience.* (Yes) *But do you have the knowledge of what happens that you can carry with you?*

P: Yes, but because it's not human, there are no human emotions.

D: *Okay. But now you're out of that one, and you said you go and choose another body.*

P: But it's still not human. That's still *that* life.

D: *Are you aware that you're speaking through a human body that we call Pamela?* (Yes) *Is that a different case?* (Oh, yes.) *What happened?*

P: I wanted to try it from the human side. It's very different.

D: *You decided to live a full life?*

P: Oh, yes, many. We've had many, many lives when at times it was very hard to be human.

D: *But when you chose to come into the life as Pamela, did you make a plan?*

P: Of course.

D: *What was the plan when you came in? What did you hope to accomplish?*

P: Everything ... everything. To tie up all the loose ends and understandings. To resolve the human lessons that had been gathered through all of the lifetimes. To clear that and this, to learn what needed to be learned.

D: *When you made your plan, did you set up that there would be obstacles?*

P: They have to be.

D: *Why does there have to be obstacles?*

P: How do you prove you've learned anything?

D: *I was thinking it would be nice to come into a life with no problems.* (She laughed.)

P: We can choose that, but it's not as much fun as it would seem. We don't have to have big problems. If there is no dark, you don't recognize light. If you don't do it for yourself; if it's all laid out and everything is easy, you can choose that and just experience the human experience, but there is no growth in that. It's the challenges that are the growth. It's quite easy to understand in spirit. It's quite another to make it happen as a human.

D: *So the whole idea is to grow?* (Of course.) *To learn more?*

P: Master the human emotions. It would be very difficult as a *human* seeing them coming with torches. That's why I didn't want to do it anymore.

D: *But you know when you come into the body you forget your plan.*

P: Yes, but when you've been through it and you choose to make another plan, you choose to still do the work but not have the emotions. That was the choice. Then after that, try at some point the human experiences again and to be able to understand even with the human emotions.

D: *Combine the two?*

P: Yes. In the other life of being able to choose the bodies and of going to teach, there is no fear and no emotion of satisfaction either, so you lose both. You can experience and gain knowledge and share knowledge, but you get no satisfaction or fear of people killing you and such because you get neither. So you don't get the joy that you would of sharing in the human, but you also don't get the fear. So then the next challenge is to try to get that in the human form, experience the joy and limit the fear and do it anyway. It is important to learn to *overcome* fear. It's very difficult when people are coming at you with torches in the human form, because you know you will lose the human form. In the other, it was just a coat. It didn't mean anything. The task is to learn in the human form. It's only different.

D: *It sounds like you must be very advanced when you try to do these things.* (Yes) *Someone, in a human life, who is caught on the wheel of karma going round and around, wouldn't be that advanced to make that separation, would they?* (No.) *So it sounds like you've been doing this a long time.*

P: Yes. This was to be the last time. I can choose differently if I want. We can always change our minds.

D: *You think this is the last time you will experience being a human?*

P: It was the plan, but the plan can change. And then free will and choice come into this life, and maybe one that was very gentle would be very nice to experience.

D: *Do you think you've probably learned everything you can?*

P: Much has been done, yes.

D: *There wouldn't be any reason to come back again?*

P: Only for fun.

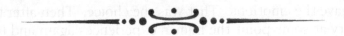

In several of my books, even those written over twenty years ago, shape shifters are mentioned. However, they are never referred to in the negative context such as some modern writers are saying. They are the type mentioned in this chapter and others in this book. They are always beings who have come or been sent to help the struggling species on Earth. They have been coming for untold numbers of years. They do not come through the normal procedure of being born and living a physical life. They form a body that will fit into the culture they will be living in. They do this so they will not frighten those they will be living amongst. They are always there to help, to teach, so they try to work in that capacity. Many of them, even today, are working in the medical profession, the teaching profession, so they can help by giving their knowledge. They do not influence, but simply share and teach. They are forbidden to take an active part in the governing of a society. That would go against the first rule: noninterference. So they remain in the background. Many people, even today, have probably been in contact with one of these people and did not even know it.

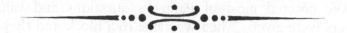

I thought it was time to get to the therapy and ask Pamela's questions. I asked if they could answer the questions or if I needed to go to somebody higher. They said they thought they could try to answer some questions. "You seem to know a lot about Pamela," I said.

P: There are many here who do.

D: *Well, the present life she came into was not fun. It was not a pleasant life that she set up, with her difficult childhood and everything. Why did she make such a difficult plan?*

P: It was to have all of the issues cleared in one life. It was very complicated. All of the remaining lessons and karma from all the lifetimes were to be arranged to be cleared.

D: *All the leftover stuff?* (Yes) *And she could only do that by having a very bad childhood?*

P: It wasn't all that bad, but there was damage done. It was balance in karma and by choice because the issues that were there were ones that needed to be faced again and overcome.

Pamela had experienced sexual abuse as a child, and her parents weren't very good to her. "She chose to be a woman and chose that energy and to be attacked in that way." That seems cruel, and there are times that I have difficulty believing that a soul would choose such circumstances. Of course, on the spirit side it seems very clear and easy to work out. I asked if she had any karma from past lives with these people in her life. They said there had been, but it was now all cleared. Her marriage had also been a bad experience, and they said she could have been done with that quicker. She didn't need to stay in it as long as she did. They agreed that all the leftover "junk" had been cleared, and she didn't need to come back again unless she chose to.

We covered most of Pamela's questions and valuable answers were given. Then we came to a block and they said they did not have the information, so I asked if it would be all right if I called in someone else who would be able to answer the questions. They agreed, and I thanked them and called forth the SC. The first question is always why it chose that particular lifetime for Pamela to see.

P: So she can see it's the same.

D: *Is it the same?*

P: Yes. She's only wearing a coat now, too. It's just a human coat.

D: *Yes, just a human shell. I always call it a "suit of clothes."* (Yes) *Why did you want her to know that?*

P: She forgets. (She was smiling.) It all seems very real because it is. The humans have the feelings and it's very real, but in the end it's the same. It's all spirit. It's all one.

D: *Of course, in that other existence there were no emotions involved.*

P: Yes, that's easy.

D: *He was helping people but he didn't have to feel anything.*

P: No, but you miss the good when you miss the pain. That's the lesson. Emotions are very important. You can't just do away with them.

D: *Pamela did choose a difficult life this time.*

P: Yes, and it was more difficult than it needed to be. There were to be tasks, but it became difficult. The tasks were the same, but she was hampered.

D: *But she learned a lot, didn't she?* (Oh, yes.)

I then asked the question that the other part could not answer. Pamela had had a hypnotic session with a friend who had taken my class, and something came out that neither one of them understood. They were told that something happened when she was a baby or very young that caused a piece of her soul to be taken. This did not sound correct to me.

P: The trust. It was trust.

D: *Let's explain it to her. What did that mean? How a piece of a soul could be taken? Did they have that information correct?*

P: "Taken" is not the right word. It wasn't supposed to happen that way. The trust, the bond, was broken; the bond with caregiver. The mother could not, did not bond. They did not bond. That part of her soul did not develop. While the mother could not show physical affection, there was still a suffocating neediness from the mother.

D: *That's what it means. It wasn't taken away. It just did not develop. That makes more sense because I've been taught in my work that you can't take a part of the soul.*

P: It didn't develop and it was set aside, and that has made it difficult. It was difficult to have a caring, loving relationship with anyone because she did not get that as a child. That was to be done and the mother could not do it. But it is a very similar story. The mother's focus was on the husband and her own pain was too great. She couldn't show love to Pamela. And as a result, that portion of Pamela's soul didn't develop, and that affected her the whole life. The mother's lack of affection carried through to each of Pamela's mates.

This affected Pamela's marriage and she never felt safe, so she couldn't show emotions. She now had a man in her life that was influencing her in a good way. He was providing a safe environment for her to learn to express and feel emotions. Most of her karma had been worked out except some with her daughter. "There's nothing she can do and she knows that. She must forgive herself. The mistake she made was very similar to her mother's mistakes. The development was not there. She couldn't give what she didn't have. She's learned much in spite of it. She could have made different choices, but it was because part was missing, so to speak, was not developed and she was not capable. Because even in a bad situation, if that loving connection is developed, the soul can overcome many things. But without that development, it's very hampered. She's done well."

D: *That shows the importance of childhood, doesn't it?*

P: Yes. She remembers very little of it and it's best. – She literally wanted to die. Many times. She didn't want to be here without love. What was the use of feeling the human emotions if you only felt the pain? She came into this life to feel emotions. That was what was not according to plan. She was supposed to be able to feel love. And it was not returned to her in the way that she needed, wanted, and gave, and so she shut down. And came up with other behaviors and techniques that would resemble or make it seem as though it was love.

D: *Did she ever try to kill herself?*

P: No, but many times she didn't want to be there.

This was the main reason for Pamela's physical problems, especially sleep apnea, the shutting off of the breath. "It was a shutting down."

D: *She didn't want to be here if she didn't have love.*

P: No, and it was very sad. In her childhood, the people around her showed her love in certain ways, but because of the abuse it was a mixed bag. It was on the surface one way, but behind the scenes it was another. And the lack of affection from the mother. The mother just did not know how. She was very distant. Her mother had many, many problems.

D: *She didn't know what love was either.*

P: No, and when it was arranged, the potential was there, but by the time it occurred, she couldn't do it. So Pamela knew that pain was all she equated with love because she had nothing else to equate to. Thus her marriage was much worse! The pain was much greater.

D: *Did she know him in another life?*

P: Oh, many, many. He had the potential in this one to make it different, and he chose not to. He could not do it.

She seemed to have finally turned the corner with her association with the new man in her life. He was totally different and a very good influence on her. So it appeared that her life could finally be turned from negative to positive.

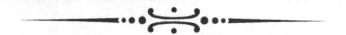

The subject of healing came up. I have had a few people who said they wanted to be healed, and they were but they would not accept it and became quite angry with me. They said, "You should have fixed me."

P: They want their illness. It serves them. They have to be ready. There are only so many that you can help, and it is up to them. And some of them might relate to Jesus telling them in the Bible, to cast out the demons first. It's not a real demon. It's the beliefs inside of them. They can't heal. There's no point in bothering to heal them until the demons have been cast out, and the demons are of their own creating. Ask them if they are really ready and willing to be healed, and don't come if they are not! There are many who need you. You don't waste time on those that won't.

D: *I had one woman who was yelling and screaming at me on the telephone because she said I didn't heal her.*

P: You aren't the healer. She is.

D: *I know it goes back to her. When she walked out of my office, she was fine.*

P: If someone wants to stay in lower energies, you must honor that. You have done your job. But healing was done on many levels. And even if they don't move into higher energies in this lifetime, it will be acknowledged, otherwise. Growth did occur. It was still worthwhile. The energy is so important. To waste it on ... you said it's swine and pearls.... That is true. Your work is very valuable. (They started laughing.) Oh, we love working with you! You make such a difference because everyone that you teach, it has an exponential effect across the globe. They won't all do it, but they're aware. Everyone that you touch still has an effect because everyone talks and every seed is planted everywhere. It has made a huge difference.

Chapter 8

THE EMERGENCY CREW

S hani was originally from Africa. Now living in America she had her own financial business. She mostly wanted to know about her relationship problems, rather than her purpose.

Shani relived a strange life on another planet trying to help people who were in hopeless or desperate situations. She would create a body similar to those she found herself among so she would not cause attention or suspicion. It was a difficult job because of the emotions she sensed from the people. "I want to help them. I don't like it. It's very, very uncomfortable here."

D: *Did someone tell you to go and help these people?*

S: Yes. I came from another place to help them. I was assigned to do this.

D: *What was the place like that you came from?*

S: Oh, it's beautiful! The people are happy. They are very, very nice. We have a lot of energy.

D: *What do you do in that place?*

S: My job is to help others from other planets. They sent us to that place. They just know where to go.

D: *So where you started from, did you live a life there?*

S: Yes. I lived a life there on another planet. I was sent out on an assignment to help. This is a very, very bad time. They tell us where to go and how to advance.

D: *Do you have a choice?*

S: Not much choice. But you can't say no because it's what you do. You just have to go and do it. It's my job. They can't see me, but I have to be like them. I can't be myself and come down. I have to look like them.

D: *Are you sent on these assignments very often?*

S: Yes, I am. All different places. Where I come from everybody is working, going to different places in the galaxies, the planets. And so I go there and do some work.

D: *They never know where they're going to go until they get their assignment?*

S: No. We just wait. Something needed very badly. We're the emergency crew, we call ourselves. (Laugh) It's so funny.

D: *But you're not like Guardian Angels?* (No) *They do emergencies sometimes, don't they?*

S: Yes, they do. But we're like energy, and we live in this space. Not a planet, just a space. And our energy is very high and we go and help other people on other planets.

D: *And somebody else knows when these emergencies come up?*

S: Yes. We have a station that gets all of that information. The information goes to that station, and then we are given this information and we are assigned.

D: *Is there one person over it all like a director?*

S: No, there's no such thing as a director. It's like somebody is assigned to do that, but not a director. He's just a person who is assigned to get information for us.

D: *But they know what's going on in all the different galaxies and planets?* (Yes) *That's a big job.*

S: It's a very big job, and now is a very important time also.

D: *Why is it important?*

S: Because there is going to be many changes going on.

D: *Where are the changes happening?*

S: Everywhere, all over the universe, all over the galaxies.

D: *What kinds of changes are taking place?*

S: I think it's going to be a disaster. It's going to be drastic changes, going to be a change to evolve, to grow. To go to the next level, to all of the planets.

D: *So it's time for the entire universe to move?*

S: Yes, I think so, yes. Some of them are moving very fast. Some of them are slowing, but everybody is moving.

D: *Does this affect everybody and all the planets?*

S: Yes, it does.

D: *Does this affect in different ways?*

S: It all depends. It's just so different. It's so much and so huge and so many other things. It's very difficult to explain this to you right now.

D: *But it does sound like a big job. There must be many others like you then?*

S: Yes. We have different crystals. Some of them have this blue crystal, some of them have the white crystal, some have yellow ones, some have the purple ones, some of them have the green ones. All have different crystals, but the crystals are not what do the job. It's the energy in the crystal, and I have one really bright and light red one.

D: *Do the colors have different meanings?*

S: They all have different meanings. If you have the red crystal, you go to different places where the red crystal is important. All of them have energy, but if you have the red crystal, like I have, it will be a healing crystal. It heals everything it comes to. It heals the body of a human being, or even a planet. It's powerful. It doesn't have to be very big. Just big enough so you can carry it. You can put it on your neck like a necklace.

D: *So the other colors have different purposes?*

S: Yes, different purposes. The blue one brings all knowledge. If there is a place where they need the knowledge, whoever has the blue crystals goes there to bring the knowledge. And if you want to have a big construction or building, you go with the white crystals. It helps with the construction and with the architects in planning. If you go with the yellow crystals it will bring the flourishes to grow the flowers or the trees. All nature. And the purple crystal is the most powerful, and we use that to bring people to a higher level of spirituality or to evolve at a much higher speed. It's very powerful. The green crystal is used for traveling, when you go from place to place, for power, for speech and things like that. And of course, my red crystal is used for healing.

D: *So each individual has different assignments and missions?* (Yes) *Does it have to do with their evolvement, which crystals they use?*

S: Yes, and also their interests. They have to be interested in doing those things. All of them are important.

D: *How do you go to this place to do this assignment?*

S: I just go. I just get there. I don't know how I get there. Just by thought, I guess. (Laugh)

D: *And when you go to do your assignment, you have to create a body so it will fit in?*

S: Yes, we have to fit in with our environment. We have to be that person, otherwise, people won't accept you. You have to have the body or whatever it is where you are going.

D: *Otherwise they'd be afraid. They have to have something they would accept.* (Yes) *Have you been doing this for a long time?*

S: Yes, a long time. I love it. It's beautiful, but I do other things too. I also go to places and live there in that body or that place.

D: *You mean you stay for longer periods of time?* (Yes) *So you don't just go on assignments and leave?*

S: We do both, assignments then go. Some are just for a very short while. Just to send them the light and the energy, then go back. Some places you need to stay longer. For example, if you go to heal a place. You can heal the planets. You can heal something that was destroyed. You can restore. When that happens, I go with a group of others. It needs a lot of energy. We did a lot of work on *this* planet. We have to heal the planet, the Earth planet, so it will evolve and grow, and the other groups are coming also.

D: *Do you ever go and live something like a life?* (Yes)

I was trying to get her to the point that we could refer to her present physical body.

D: *Will you stay for a long time?*

S: No. I don't like to stay for a long time. I don't like it there because I live in this energy. And this light is so high that when you live someplace, you lose that power and become like them. So I don't like to stay there. You lose your power and you become powerless, and I'm not used to that. I'm used to this power all the time, and when you become human, it's like the power is not there. I get so confused.

D: *But you are told to do that sometimes?*

S: Yes, for a reason, of course, for a purpose.

D: *Otherwise, you just stay in that beautiful place and go on assignments?*

S: Yes, I do.

D: *Do you know you are speaking through a human body right now?*

S: Yes, I know. (Laugh)

D: *Is this the body you were told to go and live in for a while?* (Yes, yes.) *Tell me about that. Did they give you this assignment?*

S: Well, there are many reasons for it. Number one, I was born in that place in Africa to heal that place. Just being in that place would help because of my energy, that portion of energy to heal that place, and for the family, also. They had past life issues with each other. And I came to help.

D: *To help them sort it out?*

S: Yes, not in the way of sorting it out. It was just by giving them my energy, they get healed. I don't know how to explain it in words, but it's there.

D: *Yes, but when you entered the body, you forgot all of this, didn't you?*

S: Yes, and that's the most unpleasant experience. We come here and forget everything and have to start all over. But the power is still there. It is very minimized. You don't bring all this power. You can't do that, but you bring some of it for that reason. This is my assignment now, to live in this one body.

D: *To help? But you're not in Africa anymore.*

S: Yes, I came here because there are many humans needed in this area too, in this place.

D: *Now you're living in Washington DC.*

S: Yes, that was the purpose. I have to be there because they are making all kinds of decisions to destroy the world, destroy the Earth.

D: (This was a surprise.) *The government there? They're making decisions that could hurt the world?*

S: Yes, and I have to send my energy there to change that. It's not just me, there are so many others.

D: *But as a human, you don't know those things, do you?*

S: Oh, no. Everyone is just a vessel ... to just be there and do the work inside.

D: *How do you know about these decisions and the things going on?*

S: Like I told you, I have information. We have a store of information where I came from, so they tell me the information when I come for the assignments. They put that information in me, and I know exactly what to do. I have to send energy to the government, to the White House, to the Capitol. To all those places in Washington. All the time, all the time, I send energy and light.

D: *But Shani doesn't know you are doing it, does she?*

S: She has no clue. She doesn't know she does this. I do it in the evening at night mostly. There are many others helping because it is the work that has to be done quickly, and we need a lot of help.

D: *Why does the work have to be done quickly?*

S: Because otherwise, there are many bad things that are going to happen. People are making bad decisions all the time, so we just want to help with that.

D: *You mean to keep those things from happening?* (Yes) *The new President (Obama) is not as bad as the old one (Bush), is he?*

This session was conducted in May 2009, a few months after the election.

S: No, the new President is a light bringer. He is chosen.

D: *The old one was creating a lot of negativity, wasn't he?*

S: Yes, he was not a light. He had bad energies, and he believes in war and he believes in destroying life unnecessarily.

D: *But now he is no longer in a position to do these things.* (Yes) *Do you think now things will change with the new one?*

S: It's not so much that the new President will make a change. It's that so much of the consciousness has to be raised for everybody in the government. There are people who are really trying to do bad things still in the government. He is just one person, but it's very important for him to be there. Many people don't know it, but he is also one of the light people. He doesn't know it, but he is very powerful, too.

D: *So people like Shani who are occupying bodies, are able to influence... send energy to other people who are negative?*

S: Yes. When you send energy, it's not just to change their mind. It's sending the energy that's floating around the environment. You just change that energy to the higher energy, and people start thinking differently.

D: *But isn't this interfering with their free will?*

S: That's why we can't go and influence individuals. You can't go against free will. We just leave the energy out there for them to get it free for free will.

D: *But you try to spread the energy so it will raise their consciousness, or whatever?*

S: Yes, it's already created. The bad energy is already created from bad thought, bad ideas. We try to move past that with new ideas, with new energies so that people can start getting that information.

D: *So there are many of you that have come to live in physical bodies?*

S: Yes, but more than that, many of us are in spirit forms here. All of them are working for the same cause. I am both spirit, and I am living in a body. There are others who came as a spirit, as energy. They didn't have a body. They are working on that level. It is more difficult to work in a physical body. You are limited in your power.

D: *And she doesn't have a clue. She doesn't know what's going on.* (Laugh)

S: No, she doesn't.

D: *Does this mean that she hasn't had past lives?*

S: She has had past lives, but most past lives have been mine for assignment purposes, for work. It's not to evolve, to be born here and to evolve here. It's not that kind of past life. Normal past lives are very different.

D: *I'm used to exploring lives where a person just goes through their life and they have connections with people.* (Yes) *So this means there wouldn't be any karma accumulated, would there?*

S: No. No karma for her. She doesn't have to return. Just go back on another assignment.

D: *So if she were to remember past lives, they might be similar to imprints. Do you know what imprints are?*

S: Yes, of course, I know what imprints are. Sometimes we do imprints, yes. But her memories are from assignments, not imprints. With her there is a difference.

For more information about imprints, see my book *Keepers of the Garden.*

D: *Okay, I'm always finding out new things I didn't know.* (Laugh) *But she's here in this life for a reason, and she doesn't know she's influencing the government.*

S: No. (Laugh) No clue, no clue. But she's very, very important in Washington. To be in that place and that position. We were lucky to get that place for her, the house she lives in. Everything is arranged so the energy can go in a certain way. It is a location where she can send her energy in different directions and it all gets there in the same time.

D: *And she didn't know that. That's why you picked the house and the occupation, so she would be right there?*

S: Yes, everything. It's so funny that we chose that house for her. She was made to go there and buy that house. So she is like a beacon going out. She loves it. It's a perfect house for her, the energy and everything.

Among the problems that Shani wanted to find the answers to was that she was afraid she was going to lose the house. She was afraid she was going to lose everything. "She is not going to lose anything." Yet she had lost her business that she was doing out of her house. "The business had to go. It's time for a change and she knows it. She's going to have an assignment. We call it assignment in our world, but it's called a job?"

D: *Yes, that's what we call it.*

S: Her present job is gone. We don't want her to do that anymore. It's an assignment, and we're going to send her all over the world this time. She's going to go to different places. She will keep her house, but she's still going to be traveling all over the world. She will be talking to people. She's going places sometimes thinking she's going to be talking to people, but she's going there to send energy to that place, especially the government. Her energy is going to be in places where an important government is at the time. For example, if Russia is doing something and a decision has to be made, we will take her there and she will use her energy there. For the governments and also the people. There are many people suffering in this world and we sense it. We feel that people are coming asking for help all the time and she's one of the people who volunteered to do this, so we use her to send out the energy to all these places to heal.

They also assured her that she would have plenty of money to do these things. She was worried about that because she needed a large sum to pay some debts, and she needed it soon. They didn't seem concerned. "I will arrange something for her. She will have money. We will have a way for her to get the money. It will come in time, but we cannot give the details." The money would not come through a job, but that was all the information they could give, except a time frame that everything would be taken care of in three or four months. The traveling would start in a year or two.

D: *I have to ask a question. You know I've been sent to more and more places all the time all over world. I think I have a different purpose.*

S: Yours is different. Your purpose is to bring information to people. That's why you are here.

D: *I also go to different countries.*

S: You're taking information to people and you're bringing information from one place and sending it to another place. That's what you do.

D: *So you are a different kind of energy?*

S: Yes, it's a different kind of energy. Ours is stored in a higher place than this planet where she comes from. It's a place that stores all that information and we can access that information and use our power and energy to influence people.

She was also having difficulty attracting and keeping a man in her life. They said her energy was so strong and the man could sense this, and it would cause him to leave. She would have to find someone of the same energy, but they felt having a relationship would interfere with her work because it would interfere with the energy being sent out. "She can have someone in her life, but it must not interfere with her assignment. It's very important what she does. She doesn't know. There are very few people like that in this world. If she found someone like her, either she or the other person would have to move to another location. They can't do that." This was also the reason she was overweight. They didn't want her to be attractive. But now the weight could come off because she was going to be traveling. Her symptoms of heartburn and gas were just the energy, also when she thought she was having heart problems. At times the energy was too powerful for her body. "Doctors couldn't find anything in her because there's nothing there. When she calls upon the energy to use it, it's too powerful for the body. And we try to use it slowly because it's too heavy for her, but she's going to use that more often now." I asked if it could be turned down so she wouldn't have any physical discomfort. "I can turn it up or turn it down. Whenever she channels energy, she gets more energy to channel. It goes through the body and she gets more. And she's been doing that a lot since the turn of this year. It's going to Washington. There are many changes with the government and, as you've heard, the economy is changing. It's her assignment. She knew that before she was born. We always give her what she can handle."

D: *Can she handle this information?*

S: Yes, she can handle it. She's very powerful, more than you think. She's going to be surprised, and at the same time excited, I am sure. She doesn't know why she feels the way she does, and what she's doing. She has no clue. She's very healthy. Her body is rejuvenating as we speak. Yours is rejuvenating, too.

It has been stressed many times in my work about the power of the mind to focus and create. It was said, "If the power of one man's mind is powerful enough to change circumstances, imagine the power of group mind. If you can get groups of people focusing on one thing you can change the world and truly create miracles. Because the power of group mind is not only multiplied, it is squared. The power is tremendous." I was encouraged to spread this message at my lectures and classes everywhere I went all over the world. I was told to tell people if they can take just five minutes at prayer groups, meditation groups, metaphysical gatherings, etc. and ask everyone to focus on peace and harmony; we could change the course of the world.

Chapter 9

ANOTHER TRAVELER

Peter was a young black lawyer. One of his main reasons for coming was to find out if he should change his job. The one he had was successful, yet monotonous.

When the session began Peter was just being an observer, watching scenes of nature: horses running in a field, then he was floating over a beautiful countryside. He didn't want to come down, just to continue to fly and observe. Then he came to a scene that he began to describe in detail: a river running through a valley between two mountains. There was an encampment where people were moving around doing work. "This is where the people are. That's where the people are staying. They're working, but they're waiting for me. I'm still flying, but they know I'm there. I want to see the people. I want to check and see if they are safe, from the air. I'm meeting the people and protecting them as they travel through this valley. I'm making sure it's safe for them."

His job was to watch over these people and to guide them. No one had told him to do this. "I just knew. I'm their leader. I've always taken care of the people." This was confusing because it sounded like he may have been some type of guardian spirit. Yet when I asked him to describe himself he sounded physical. "I am a male human being, but I can fly, though. I'm very strong. I can change forms, too. – I can travel through space."

D: *You mean you have the ability to change into anything you want? (Yes) What about the people? Can they see you as a human being?*

P: When I want them to.

D: *I was wondering, if you have a physical body, can they see you flying?*

P: They can see me when I want them to.

D: *Otherwise, you'd be invisible?*

123

P: Yes. I travel through space though, where I have no form. I just know I'm going places. I've come to Earth and I have human-like characteristics and can fly.

D: *You said traveling through space. Do you mean the space of Earth?*

P: No, through space to different planets. I'm always moving from planets.

D: *So you have the ability to just go anywhere you want to?* (Yes) *Those are wonderful talents. But right now you feel your job is to watch these people as they are traveling?* (Yes)

I asked for a description of the people. "They're just like Indians. They don't have a lot of clothes on, but they have coverings. They are connected to the land. There are hundreds of them all traveling together."

D: *Have you done this before, taking care of people?*

P: It's always been my responsibility to look after people, no matter where they are.

I condensed time and asked him to see where they were going, and if there was anything he had to do. "Do you remain in the air over them or what?"

P: Yes, I am flying over them. They're traveling. They're going somewhere and I'm making sure that they're safe. These people always travel. They don't stay in one place very long.

This could have taken a long time so I had him move ahead and see if there was anything he had to do. Even though his job was to protect them, he now saw himself in a physical body holding a spear. I asked for an explanation. "I decided to mix with them. When I come with them, I'm always physical. When I'm not on Earth, I'm not physical."

D: *Was there a reason you decided to become one of them?*

P: So they would know me. I could be with them. They could see me. They would know who I am. So, I take on a physical form when I come to Earth.

They would listen to him more if they saw him as a physical person. He was leading them to a safe place. "I travel with them, but I give them the direction."

D: *You tell them where to go and then you don't have to have a physical form anymore?* (Right) *Do they think that's strange when you are suddenly gone?*

P: They know I'll come back.

D: *Do you go and take care of other people, or do you just watch them?*

P: No, I do other things. I go to other places. I have many jobs, but it's always to help people.

D: *Is this what you have always done?*

P: Yes. I don't like bad things.

D: *Have you ever lived in a physical body where you had to stay? Do you understand what I mean?*

P: Yes. I don't remember any physical body except when I come to help people.

D: *Then you become physical when you want to?* (Yes) *That way you're not trapped in a body. You can just form it and dissolve it at any time that you want?* (Yes) *So you stay with this group for a while and help them to go where they are safe. Then you go somewhere else?*

P: Yes. I'm going to a planet. I'm in flight. It's different. There's a light. There are squares of light on the planet ... technology. The squares are just lying on the planet.

D: *The squares of light are the technology?*

P: Yes. They are used for energy. It's an advanced culture. People live in them.

D: *Is this a planet you have lived on before or are you still exploring?*

P: No, I know this planet. I am going down.

D: *When you come down, do you take a physical form?*

P: No. My form is like an energy ball. This is where I live.

D: *Are there people on that planet?*

P: Not people. They're different. Balls of light.

D: *But it is consciousness though, isn't it?*

P: Yes. We're workers. We go to other planets. I am getting this energy. I'm getting these energy squares and I'm taking them with me to another planet. I go into these squares of light and I get energy from them, and then I fly off.

D: *Where are you going to go now?*

P: I just travel. And help people.

D: *Have you ever thought about becoming a physical being?*

P: Yes, when I come to Earth.

I was trying to bring the session around to Peter, the physical human lying on the bed.

D: *Have you ever thought about staying in a physical body?*

P: No. I visit.

D: *Have you ever thought about just staying in a physical form and not having to go back and forth?*

P: I like going back and forth.

D: *You have never had a desire to stay in the physical?*

P: No, I'm only here visiting.

D: *You have complete freedom that way, don't you?*

P: Yes, but I do work.

D: *Does anyone tell you what jobs you are supposed to go to next?*

P: I automatically know.

D: *Well, let's see where you go next. Are you going to stay on that planet or are you going to float somewhere else? What feels right?*

P: I'm on Earth now and I'm looking at a building. It's dark.

D: *Do you have another job you're supposed to do?*

P: I don't know. I'm watching this building. This time it feels different. I'm *dragged* back to Earth. When I come to Earth now, I'm backwards. It's like I'm being sucked back to Earth and I'm looking at this building. I've been drawn here against my will.

He suddenly found himself in a body, but not the kind he normally created. He was now physical, but was he incarnated?

P: I can help the people actually as a human being but I have to learn more. I have to make them believe that I can help them. That I can heal them. That I can help their lives.

D: *Do you think you could heal them better in a physical form than the other form that travels?* (Yes) *Why did you decide to become physical? You were doing a lot of work out there, weren't you?*

P: Yes, but they needed my help here. I was sent here to help.

D: *So somebody told you to enter a physical body and become physical?*

P: Right. At first I thought I was going backwards, and then I just set out to do what I have to do.

D: *So you chose to come into the body that's known as Peter?* (Yes) *Did you enter the body as a baby?*

P: Yes, but there's something that happened. I don't remember what it was, but I was a baby.

D: *But you did come into the body when it was a baby?*

P: Nine years old.

D: *Stayed in the body as it grew?*

P: At nine years old.

This might sound strange, but I have encountered this in several of my cases. When this type of energy first tries to enter a physical body it is too strong and so radically different that it clashes with the physical. It can cause an abortion or miscarriage because it is too much for the fetus to handle. In these cases only a small portion of the soul energy is allowed to enter the baby's body during development and infancy. As the child grows more energy enters in small amounts. For some reason the majority of the soul is allowed to enter at the age of eight or nine. I have had clients who say they felt they were not physically in the body until that age. They usually do not remember anything about their childhood before that age.

D: *Do you like being in this body?*

P: Yes, but I want to improve it. I want to make it perfect. I want to understand. I want the knowledge.

D: *But Peter has the knowledge of the Law, doesn't he?*

P: That's not enough. This is bigger. It's bigger than the Law.

D: *That's one of the things he wanted to know. Is he supposed to be doing something else in addition to his work?*

P: I'm supposed to explain things to people ... get them to know. There's a reason. I want everybody to be healed.

D: *This sounds like this is the first time you've taken on a physical life. Is that true? (Yes) It's always a little strange, isn't it?*

P: I want to tap into the subconscious. I know that there's all the knowledge and I want that.

D: *All right. Then if it's okay, I'll call in the subconscious to answer questions. Is that all right? (Yes) I have enjoyed talking to you, and I thank you very much for the information you have been giving us.*

I then called forth the SC in the hope of gaining clearer explanations. It said it hadn't taken Peter to past lives because it was more important for him to know about this part. It agreed that this present life was his first time to be in a human, physical body. He had always been an observer and a helper.

D: *Did someone tell him it would be better to be physical?*

P: Yes. There's work for him to do on Earth. Transition ... help with the transition.

They explained that this had to do with the shifting into the New Earth. He was one of the many people who were coming here for the first time. The ones who had been on Earth for a long time were not going to be able to help. They were still caught on the Wheel of Karma. New pure souls were needed to come in and help. This is explained in more detail in my book *The Three Waves of Volunteers and the New Earth.* Peter was one of these new souls. Even though he was doing a good job with the Law, they wanted him to do more. "Teach people how to heal themselves. Teach people about the mind. He knows what to do."

D: *Do you want him to take any kind of classes?*

P: Yes. He knows what to do, but he'll have to take classes to let them know that he knows what to do. He is also to work with energy. He has the power in his hands.

D: *He just has to awaken it?*

P: Yes. He can heal with his hands over the spine. The energy is all at the base of the spine. There's a ball of fire at the base of the spine.

I knew that the Kundalini was located there and was a great power, but a person has to be careful using it. They kept insisting that Peter knew what to do. He was not to touch the person, but to work within their energy field. They said there was a small blockage in the small of his back that was keeping him from awakening the energy that he was to use. He needed to visualize this block being dissolved so that the energy would be free to move upward. He was supposed to take a class to learn how to use this power. "The women are supposed to teach him. It will happen soon." This energy had not been allowed to be opened earlier because it was too much power for him. But now it was time and he would be able to handle it. "He can't waste the energy. He has to always use it correctly. He can't do it for selfish reasons."

D: *Does the person have to want to be helped?*

P: He has to convince them of *their* own power.

D: *Does he have to ask for the person's permission before he works on them?*

P: Always!

D: *Then he won't be wasting it, will he?*

P: No. That's correct.

He was to continue to work as a lawyer at his regular job because it was to put him in touch with the people he needs to know. "But you said he is here to help with the transition?"

P: Yes, this is it. He has to follow his path. He wasn't ready until now. He has to tap his third eye.

D: *We don't want him to have any problems in his job. Do you want him to be careful?*

P: Always. But he has to continue to explore and search and learn. When he works on people they will know. He will help many people during this time of transition.

D: *So he'll have two things he'll be working on: his law career and his healing.*

Peter was clearly one of the second wave of volunteers (born 1958) because he seemed to be an observer. He had been one for an extremely long period of time, so what could be more natural than for him to continue it in his present life?

Chapter 10

COLOR AND SOUND

Erika was already involved in energy work, in the field of Kinesiology. (This is the study of the movement of the body. In other words, how the body works and the influence energy has on it.) So the use of energy was not new to her, but she still felt she needed advice.

When Erika came into the scene it was dark, but she knew it was not night. It was dark because there was volcanic ash in the air. "The air is thick black. The ground is crispy like it has been burned." The air felt hot and smelled of burnt ash. As she became aware of her body she saw that her feet were black from walking through the crinkly ash and burnt soil. She was a young man wearing rags, and his body felt skinny as though he was starving. He knew he had lived there before this disaster happened. "There were the fields where we had our sheep. I had a little house, a sod hut. Not very big, but it was mine. – The house is burned down. It's nothing. I don't know how it could burn because it was made out of sod, but it burned." He had lived there alone because he did not have a family. Yet he did not feel lonely because he had his sheep and a dog. "This is up on the high mountain. And the valleys were where all the people were."

D: *Where were you when the house burned?*

E: In the stream. I was in my house when the ground started to shake. The sheep started running around and making a lot of noise, and the dog was trying to round them up.

D: *Like they knew something was happening?*

E: Yes. Then the ground started to shake. I ran out. I saw the ground shaking and my sheep were scattering. And the dog was trying to calm them and get them together, but they took off and the dog went after them. And there was a plume up on the mountain and of course, lava and spewing stuff all over the place. And I was getting burned so I ran to the stream.

D: *Had this happened before?*

E: No, not while I lived here. The people talked about, I mean, in stories. – I stayed down low in the stream and everything burned. I stayed there for a long time. Then, I don't know. I must have been unconscious for a while. I think I woke up and the world was black, and there was no house, and no sign that it had ever been there. And everything was crunchy and I was starving.

D: *What are you going to do now?*

E: I've got to find my sheep and my dog.

D: *You've got to find something to eat too, don't you?*

E: I've got to find my dog first. I think I have to go down the mountain, where the village was. I can't imagine the sheep would have rushed up. They must have gone down. It seems like they would have gone sort of to the northeast and up a little bit and then down. There's a big lake down there.

D: *That would have been the smart thing for them to do, wouldn't it?*

E: Yes, and sheep aren't very smart. (Laugh)

I condensed time to see what happened.

E: The dog is down by the lake. And the dog is overjoyed to see me and managed to save about a third of the herd.

D: *Are you going to stay down there?*

E: I think we have to go because it's too much smoke or ash from the volcano.

D: *Are you going to go to the village?*

E: That's all ash, too.

D: *Oh? It was destroyed, too?*

E: It wasn't destroyed, but it's impossible to live there.

D: *Are you going to try and find those people?*

E: I don't like them.

D: *Hmm, why don't you like them?*

E: Because they don't like me. I'm different ... just different. I'm not like them, because I talk funny. I think I have a cleft palate or something. Look funny ... talk funny. Too ugly.

D: *Did you ever have a family?*

E: I don't think my family wanted me either, or some taboo against people like me. Some kind of "thing" that people like me couldn't live with the rest of them.

D: *Like an outcast?*

E: Yes. I see a woman. She wasn't my mother, but she made sure I was all right.

D: *Then you decided to live up there by yourself with the sheep?*

E: I think, somehow, that she was the one who made it possible for me to do that. I was happy.

He had no choice now but to leave this land and look for another place to live. He started walking with his sheep and his dog, even though he didn't know what was in any other direction. I condensed time again to see where he went.

E: We've been going for a long time, but there's another valley and it's beautiful. It has a river going through it. And there's another village there. It's really weird because the people there don't have that taboo. (He sounded happy.) They heard my story and they are very willing to let me bring the sheep there and heal them. And actually, this is really funny, but there's another one there like me. And this person is really good at healing sheep wounds. They have all these burns. So we just trade sheep lore and they invite me to become part of their community.

It seemed that he had found an ideal situation. I asked him to move forward to an important day, and he was confused.

"Am I a different person?" He saw that he was on a granite mountainside; a different mountain than he had seen before. At first he thought he was wearing something white, and then he discovered he was a being made out of light. He was talking with someone that he called "Spirit" who was giving him instructions.

D: *What kind of instructions?*

E: About light. I'm getting instructions on how to use it.

D: *To use physical light or what kind?*

E: It must be the spectrum you can't see. Like the rays. I can see them. Different colors.

D: *How are you supposed to use this?*

E: Embody them. Each ray has an essence.

D: *Each color ... a different color ray?*

E: And if you embody it, it changes whatever's around you.

D: *What do you mean "embody" it? It has to go into a physical body?*

E: No, not a physical body.

D: *I am trying to understand. You said to "embody" them.*

E: Whatever I am, I become the ray.

D: *You mean you become the individual color?*

E: Or a combination.

D: *For a certain length of time?*

E: For different uses. It's like I walk through earthly situations embodying a ray, and then things change consciously. A conscious embodiment.

D: *You mean you're like a light when you enter a physical body?* (No) *You talked about "walking through."* (Yes) *I thought you meant when you become physical.*

E: No. It's just walking among people. They don't necessarily know I'm there.

D: *They don't have to see you?*

E: No. Some can sense me.

D: *If they saw you, would they see you as light?* (Yes) *So you take on the ray of essence, the color, and then you are on Earth walking among people. How does this affect the people when you're around them?*

E: They change or they resist. Either it exacerbates them or they suddenly change.

D: *For the better?*

E: Always.

D: *Then when you're doing this, do you take on another color?*

E: It's many different colors within short periods of time. You can switch back and forth according to the situation you're in. The place and the environment of the people. You take on different colors for whatever is needed.

D: *That would be very important. By just your presence, walking among people, you could affect them greatly, couldn't you?* (Yes) *And they don't even know what you're doing, do they?*

E: It doesn't matter.

D: *Were you told by someone that you were supposed to do this?*

E: That was my instruction. That was what I was taught on the mountain.

D: *That you were just a being of light?*

E: No, I always knew this.

D: *And you were given the instruction to go and spread this and help people?*

E: I had all along been doing stuff, but this was a particular lesson.

D: *Have you ever been in a physical body?* (No) *You've always been this being of light?* (No) *What do you mean? Tell me about it.*

E: I've been a light form other places, but not on Earth.

D: *Other planets?*

E: Other places. Other layers.

D: *Other dimensions?*

E: I guess you could say that.

D: *So what were you doing on the other layers?*

E: Learning. Learning about light.

D: *What was it like on the place you were learning?*

E: It was all light. It was variations of light.

D: *Were there others there like you?*

E: Yes. They were all learning about light.

D: *Light is very important, isn't it?* (Yes) *Do you think you learned everything needed about light?*

E: No, that's why I had to come down and walk around people. It's amazing to see what light does.

D: *What does the light do?*

E: If a person has an open heart, it just opens the heart more. And if they have a closed heart, it's like being hit with something terrible because the person is more agitated.

D: *They don't understand what's happening.*

E: No, and they continue acting more like they were acting. They try to lash out.

D: *They think they are being attacked, and they're not. Is that what you mean?*

E: They're not being attacked. It's coming from inside them. It is my job to let them experience the light. It's up to them whether or not their heart opens. There are different colors of rays and they have different uses. I am still learning.

D: *That sounds like a wonderful thing to teach people. You can help many people with just your presence.*

E: Yes. That's really all anybody can help a person with.

D: *They don't know you're there. They do have free will, don't they?*

E: They have free will, absolutely!

D: *So you can't make anybody do anything.*

E: No, no, no, but that's the free will, if their heart is open or not.

Color and Sound

He was really enjoying doing this and helping people in this way. He had no desire to enter a physical body. He felt he could do a better job as a light being.

D: Do you have to go back to that layer to learn more?

E: I can go back at any time. I can go back and forth. But I can get more information on Earth, too. I go up to my mountain. But I can be anywhere. Beautiful places. I can open up and ask.

D: Beautiful places with good energy. But the instructions always have to do with light?

E: There's another part of it. This is the newer part that I don't know much about. Sound.

D: I've heard that colors and sound are very, very important. (Yes) What are they teaching you about sound?

E: That light and sound are the same thing.

D: What do you mean? I look at them as being separate.

E: They're the same. Every sound has a vibration. Every sound has a color. Every color has a vibration. Every color has a sound.

D: People don't think of colors as having a sound.

E: I know they don't, but they do.

D: We keep them separate. (Laugh)

E: That's because we like to split and divide on Earth.

D: Yes, we like to make divisions. What are you doing to do with the sound?

E: That's what I don't know. I don't understand this all yet. It's part of my training. I think there's another layer where you learn that. And know how to use light and sound as one.

D: I can see how you can use the light energy when you're among people. How can you use the sound?

E: You can't hear it, and you can't see the light. But people receive the sound the same way they receive the color.

D: *They're not aware it's happening to them?*

E: No, except if their heart is open. Some people need more – I don't know how to say this, but they need more sound than others do. It depends on the person.

D: *Does it also depend on how developed they are?*

E: Yes. People know and can feel it either way and receive it as a whole. But the ones whose hearts are closed need more sound.

D: *To help them open up. More sound instead of more light? You think that's more powerful that way?*

E: No, it's just what they need. I think they'll feel better.

D: *So you don't intend to go into a human body?*

E: No, too limiting to go into a body. Why would I want to do that? (Laugh)

D: *Are you aware that you are speaking to me through a physical body?*

E: Oh, yes, I know that. I don't like it. I could give you information without having to feel physical.

I explained that this way Erika could hear the information and understand later. "Do you have a connection with this physical body in any way?"

E: She's an old friend. She is a tricky one, very resistant, not mean, but resistant and stubborn. (Laugh)

D: *Let's tell her about it. She wants information, doesn't she?*

E: Well, maybe she needs information, but she doesn't want it. She wants to figure everything out by herself.

D: *But that's hard, isn't it, and you feel all alone?*

E: That's just the way she is. That's why I enjoy her.

D: *In that lifetime that was shown to her, she was alone there, wasn't she?*

E: Yes, she liked it. She thinks she needs to figure things out on her own. She *likes* to. She thought she could handle it and figure it all out by herself. She's wrong, so that's why I'm around.

D: *When you come into the body you forget all these things, don't you?*

E: Oh, you sure do. That's why I don't want to do it. No way! So I try to slip her a little bit of light, a little bit of sound.

D: *Is there something in particular you want her to know? Now's your chance to tell her.*

E: Just for her to remember she's light and sound. Very positive energy. That's all she is. She also works with energy.

D: *Why did you want her to know about that young man with the sheep? Why was that important for her to know about that lifetime?*

E: Because of the house. (The one that burned.)

In her present life Erika had moved over thirty times. She had been unable to settle down in a stable environment.

E: She needs to understand that wherever she is, it's her house.

D: *She takes it with her, you mean?*

E: No, there's no "taking it with you." It just is.

D: *Do you mean the human body?*

E: No. In other words, wherever we are, it's our house. It's not a place. There are no confines. It's not walls. It's not a body. It's wherever we are... it's home. Kind of like Dorothy.

D: *"The Wizard of Oz?"* (Yes) *It's always been there even when she was looking for it elsewhere. Erika said she would like to have a house. Do you think that's possible?*

E: She could have a house. She could, but just realize that the house is not *her* house. The house isn't what she's looking for. In other words, she can have a house and she can be happy in a house, but her real house is the Earth and the

139

universe, this big bubble of cosmos. She was limiting it, which is why she couldn't find it.

D: *She has created a lot of problems for herself. Isn't that true?*

E: It's just resistance. She's resisting the light and the sound. Blocking it out because she wants to do it herself, wants to figure it out all by herself. She's scared. She kind of forgot me and she forgot the other layer and she's scared so she doesn't want to open her heart. She couldn't respond the way she did on the other layer. She couldn't play with the energy in the way that she did. She didn't know how to use the light. She didn't know how to use the sound. She didn't know how to use the energy to make it. She didn't know how to do it and she forgot and she got confused. And she hated moving around in the body. She knows she's made problems for herself. She knows that part but she just can't remember how to step out of it. I've been with her for a long time. In fact, a number of lifetimes. We go back a long time.

D: *Are you like a guide or guardian angel? Those are terms we put on things.*

E: I'm her friend. She is very stubborn and it's a stubborn thing that she came here to learn about. So she keeps inventing the wheel because she won't relax and allow the fact that once she asks how a wheel is made, we can then make more wheels. So that she can actually do more and be more and live more, experience more and learn more. So she's very slow. It's like each breath goes back to the beginning of cave man and slowly develops forward.

D: *She's making it too difficult.* (Yes) *She has many talents. She has the abilities to do anything she wants to do.* (Yes)

I turned to some of her questions: "What about these night terrors where she wakes up at night screaming? What's the cause of that?"

E: I don't know how to say it. She's been carrying ... like resistant cells. Maybe you could say that they're codes in her DNA that are "hard" energy in her fields. They're like mirrors so that when life comes in and Source energy comes in it gets reflected back, but doesn't become part of her being. She's reflecting. It's like these DNA protons are little teeny, teeny, reflective mirrors that are reflecting back Source energy, and not allowing it to be part of her system.

D: *Does this come from other lifetimes?*

E: Yes. She has added them to her DNA.

D: *But they don't apply to her life now, do they?*

E: No. They are active right now. And they don't need to be. All she would need to do is flip the code on. In other words, she could have all the code switched on so she could be living fully and have full physical immunity as far as her health is concerned. So that germs and bacteria and viruses and all those things just don't need to be part of the scene. I don't think she knew what she was doing. I think she was kind of tensing in a cosmic way, resisting. Saying she wanted to do it by herself and that caused this "switch" to happen. She can flip the "code ons." She can talk to her DNA and ask it to draw the "code ons" to be on.

D: *Can you do it?*

E: I can't do it, but the Light can and the Sound can.

There had been a terrible loud thunderstorm going on throughout the session. It had not interfered with the communication. In fact, the SC said it liked the storm. "She can use the storm."

D: *All right, do that. The storm has plenty of energy.*

E: She can allow that Sound of the rain to enter her system along with the lightning. And allow it to wash on through and as it comes through and the Light comes through, it's blue ... blue. White light.

D: *And this will push the switch?* (Yes) *Is that what you're doing now?*

E: I'm not doing it. She has to do it.

D: *Give her instructions as she flips the switch.*

E: So you're letting the lightning, the blue White Light, to pour through your system like liquid. And it pours through every cell in the body, from your head to your feet, vivifying every single strand of DNA with blue White Light and this liquid Sound. There's no need for resistance anywhere. (It moved it through all the parts of her body.) I'm just anchoring it for her. She has to do it for herself. The resistance is leaving. It's washing out. She doesn't need it.

She was given an exercise for her to sleep without being afraid: "She needs gold light to sleep. When she lies down to go to sleep, to visualize a gold womb, a gold egg. And see herself inside of it, enclosed by the womb or egg. Then she will feel protected, and she can decide each night how much sleep she wants. Some nights she'll need more and some she won't. That would be a fun thing for her. It puts her in charge ... which she likes. And tell herself she will awaken refreshed, relaxed, invigorated and enthusiastic. And with abundant energy to connect and move forward in this new phase of her life."

Parting message: Spend time with her heart every day. Just put her hands on her heart and when she does that, she'll be connected with me.

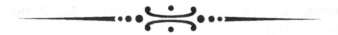

In another case, the SC gave me another healing technique that could be visualized by the client in the privacy of their own home.

The SC sent a soft, flowing heat all the way down the spine and into the shoulders. And down into the arms and fingers. And down into the legs and the knees. "It's a loving, gentle heat.

It's a healing heat. She needs to visualize that heat coming in all the time and do that visualization a couple of times a day. Coming in through the crown chakra and just floating all the way down through her body. And it's more than a heat. It needs to be a healing, flowing, almost like a lava heat flowing down through her body. She has to visualize this two times a day, morning and night. When she wakes up in the morning and when she goes to bed at night. Visualize heat like flowing lava going all the way down. It is coral-colored and green with little specks of white."

Chapter 11

PROTECTING THE KNOWLEDGE

A ndrew came to me to get guidance as to if he was on the right path.   He has had the feeling all his life of pain and uneasiness; like he didn't belong here and this caused him to not be able to enjoy life. Andrew worked as a healer with people and animals as well as with the grid. He also taught science combined with metaphysics in addition to being an artist.

When Andrew came into the scene there was confusion because he felt there were chains on his feet and legs.   Then he realized it was chain mail or armor of some type.   He kept saying he was feeling much pain.   He was a young male in his thirties standing outside in the dark.   I asked why he had pain. "Because I'm being betrayed.   I have done the best I could and I was betrayed.   We were doing what we were supposed to do and they didn't want us to do it, so we are going to be tortured and killed."

D: *What were you supposed to be doing?*

A: Protecting ... protecting knowledge. I know they are coming to take me. I am just waiting for that. They are going to come to get us.

D: *How did they betray you?*

A: They knew where we were so they told where we are.

D: *Is this someone that you know?*

A: Yes. They were afraid anyway. If they did not tell, they would be tortured and killed too, so they didn't have any choice.

D: *Where are you waiting?*

A: Somewhere ... there's a place ... like a castle or something.

D: *Could you get away if you wanted to?*

A: They would find me anyway. I'm one of their captains of a very high rank. I am one of the main ones they are looking for.

D: *You said you were protecting knowledge?*

A: Yes, but they were envious. They didn't want us to have the power.

D: *What kind of knowledge were you protecting? You can tell me what it was, I won't tell anyone.*

A: Ancient knowledge. It's knowledge from the ancient times. It was also protecting the people and they knew that. Actually those were going to be safe, so the knowledge can go on when the right time comes.

D: *So it's not going to disappear?*

A: No, it's not going to disappear. We are taking the heat so they are protected.

D: *What was the knowledge about?*

A: Blessings for everyone ... powerful, but I was just the keeper of those who need to be protected.

D: *Were you practicing the knowledge?*

A: No. I only knew it was important and my duty was to defend and protect. And to hide and also to be the friend. I am the one that is to be taken and I am afraid. They are also going to be killed and I am afraid. I am going to be tortured and I am so afraid, and I know what they are going to do to me.

D: *What good would it do to hurt you? You don't know the knowledge.*

A: They don't know, but we are going to tell them that we know so we protect the other ones. We are going to confuse them so we are going to protect the other ones.

D: *The ones who know how to use it?* (Yes) *Is this knowledge in the form of books?*

A: Yes ... records and places. Books and people that know how to use them. It is not all recorded.

D: *Is it supposed to be passed down to the right kind of people?*

A: Yes. And I am the one to be the shield for them.

D: *Do you know where it is kept?*

A: Yes, but it's all done in a way that I don't know the whole thing. But I know that I need to do certain things to protect them. So even if they torture me, there's nothing I can say, and what I will say will confuse them. I will tell them, but it's not going to be the truth.

D: *Did someone come to get you?*

A: Yes. They've come to get me and they are going to torture me.

D: *This place where you are, the castle, is that the place where you live?*

A: It's a place where we gather.

D: *Is this the place where the knowledge is?*

A: No. The knowledge is not there. They think it's there. It's not.

D: *Are you the only one they are going to take?*

A: No. Many, many. Some don't even know they will be taken or what will be done to us. Some are here, and others are at other places. I am alone right now.

D: *Is this something you have been doing for a long time?*

A: Yes. I believe in the knowledge and there has to be someone to protect, and I am here to protect. I am the first line to protect.

D: *But you said that even though they hurt you and the others, there will be other people to carry on?*

A: Yes, yes.

D: *It can never totally be destroyed, can it?*

A: No. I am so afraid ... so afraid.

D: *Is this ancient knowledge on certain subjects or do you know?*

A: Yes, it's ancient ... very ancient ... very powerful. It is on many things. It is healing. It is many things for humankind to pass through. We are protecting that. They think it's witchcraft. But it is not. We know a little bit ... enough to make them think it's witchcraft, so we are going to be taken as people that do witchcraft. So they are going to torture us.

D: *Why do they want to know it if they think it's witchcraft?*

A: Because they want it for themselves. They want power. They are very ignorant, but they want the power.

D: *Are these people part of an organization or something?*

A: They are the government. The church is the government. They are afraid that knowledge can take from their own power. They don't want anybody to have power by themselves. They want to be all powerful. – They know where we are. They know where to find us. I am just to keep, to defend, to protect.

D: *Have you hidden the knowledge somewhere in the castle?*

A: No. No. We made believe to them to distract them until everything's safe. They will look there but it's not there. They will torture us and they will not get much because we don't know. We only know a little bit ... just enough for us. We knew it was going to happen, but now I am so afraid. I am so ashamed. I am so ashamed of being afraid.

D: *If no one has all of the knowledge, and these people only have bits and pieces, it could survive.*

A: Yes, it will survive ... as all will survive. – I'm afraid. I know I just have to go through it one way or another, but I don't want to. I'm afraid of the torture ... very afraid of the torture ... afraid they are going to do things to my body. (His voice sounded very scared.) They are going to put me down because I am a captain. They are going to really pull me down.

D: *Is there any way you can escape before they come?*

A: No. I will not escape. I have to go through it. That's what I serve to do. It is not my duty to escape. It is my duty to stay. They have to take me.

I thought it was time to move the story ahead and find out what happened. I condensed time to when they had come. "You have control over what you see." I suggested that he watch it as an observer if he wanted to.

A: (His voice was trembling and hard to understand.) I just don't want to go there. – They come and they take all of us to their castle ... just hundreds and hundreds of soldiers everywhere. They take us and they torture us. – I don't see any more. I have a hard time seeing so much.

D: *Did you tell them anything?*

A: I don't have anything to tell. They made me tell things ... tell them what they want to hear. They tell them everything they want to hear. They have pleasure torturing us because they feel powerful. They see our soul diminished.

D: *What was the final result?*

A: Just to kill us after they tortured us. I am so ashamed. They did things to us. They shamed us so much. (Misery) I am so ashamed ... so ashamed.

D: *You don't have anything to be ashamed of. You did the honorable thing. They were the ones doing the dishonorable things.*

A: I don't regret it. ... Everything that I loved, they killed and tortured everything. So much hate ... so much hate. ... But they won't find the knowledge. – They burned us.

I then moved him to where he was out of his body and could look at the scene from a different perspective. "Can you see the bodies?"

A: Yes ... charred ... just charred bodies into the fire and then just throw them into holes ... just nothing.

D: *Every life has a purpose. What do you think was the purpose of that lifetime?*

A: It was my duty to test my courage. I did what I needed to do, but I felt ashamed of what they did to me and my body.

I don't know why I feel so ashamed.

D: *Every life has a lesson. Do you think there was a lesson to be learned from living and dying like that?*

A: I was too proud of who I was ... too proud of my duty. I felt superior. Such a duty. It was important to me my whole life. Maybe I was too proud of my own manhood and ... (Stops) Maybe it was a test for me to be loyal to that knowledge.

D: *Maybe it could have been a test.*

A: Maybe it was just that ... just that. Maybe it was also that I was too into my body because I was so affected when I was tortured, when they did those things. I was too attached to my body.

D: *But humans get that way, don't they? We live in the body and we get attached to it.*

A: Yes, it's true.

Rather than call forth the SC at this point, I decided to move him through time and space to find another lifetime. That way we could take him away from the horror he had witnessed. This time he saw that he was a woman looking at herself in a mirror. She was very beautiful with black hair and green eyes, in her twenties. She was in a beautiful building. But the thing that was different about it was that there were beautiful crystals everywhere. They were all sizes and colors from some that could be held in the hand to those that were ten inches in diameter and four or five inches thick. "I just put my hands on top of them (the large ones) and can control their energies. I can manage energy with them. I can use them for healing. I activate these chambers where people get into to heal. And the crystals give energy and colors and create an energy field where the person can be rested and healed. I have that power."

D: *I know you can use power in many different ways. Do you use the healing power for positive?*

A: Yes. I use it for positive. I know my power and so I am proud of it.

D: *Do other people know how to use this same healing?*

A: Yes, other people know, but I'm the one who really knows the most. My own body resonates with that energy so I am part of them. I synergize with them.

D: *And the people get into the chambers and you work with them?* (Yes) *Do many come at a time?*

A: They come one at a time. It's like seeing a doctor. I can use that. It's part of my duty ... part of my work. We have that technology. I was trained from when I was little by those who have the power to do it. They know who can do that, and who to train.

D: *So not everyone can do it.*

A: No. People are very advanced and we know what person can do this. We guide them to become what they are. They already know what they can do. People can fully develop themselves and do what they like. They have free will to do what they want, but everyone is born with specific skills and we can do that.

D: *You were taught or trained how to use the crystals then?*

A: I was just remembering.

D: *And you said you are very proud of what you can do?*   (Yes) *Are you also proud of being able to help people?*

A: Yes, but also you know, I am very beautiful. And sometimes have people to be with me because I want attention ... and that's not good.

D: *Are you married or have a family?*

A: No. I just can be with whoever I want to be with.

I asked her to look out her window and describe what she could see. "They are all beautiful buildings. There are domes and columns and just a beautiful city. And the landscape is mainly crystals and stones and gardens." I then moved her to an important day and asked what was happening.

A: I'm being judged. They say I didn't do right. I used some of my power to attract men to be with me. And I shouldn't have done that.

D: *Why did you want them to be with you?*

A: Just for the pleasure. And I shouldn't have done that.

D: *Why is it wrong to use the power in that way?*

A: Because then you can influence their will. You go against their free will. It was not complete. I never did anything to hurt anyone, but I knew I had the power to attract and I shouldn't have done it. Somehow I manipulated their will to be with me. – They find out and they are asking me not to do any more work.

D: *Because you were using it in the wrong way?* (Yes) *But you were also using it positively.*

A: I know. But they consider this a negative use of the power. They don't want me to use it anymore. I have to leave this place. I want to stay, but I cannot do that anymore. I will be a common person. I have to leave the building and stay in the city. They can block my energy.

D: *I was wondering if you could use it without the crystals.*

A: I can, but they are blocking me. They just can prevent my energy to flow.

D: *They have ways of doing that?* (Yes) *Do they have machines?*

A: No, they just get together. They are powerful beings there. They have power over the energy. They do it to protect others in good will.

D: *So they block you and you have to live life as an ordinary person?* (Yes) *What do you think of that?*

A: I feel that they are right. I even realize that I shouldn't do that. Maybe one day they will forgive me and call me back again.

D: *But isn't it hard to just shut it off after you've done it so long?*

A: Yes. It's so hard. It's so hard.

D: *What are you going to do now?*

A: Just live. Just an ordinary life. Now I don't have any more of the power. They say I can teach. I cannot use my power but I can teach. I am going to start teaching. – They could have been much harder with me, so that's good.

D: *At least the knowledge will not be lost.*

A: It will not be lost. There are others that know about that, but I can just teach.

I had her leave that scene and move forward to another important day and asked what was happening. "I'm meeting someone. It's a man I am meeting. I am meeting someone that is coming into my life. I am older. I've been alone all that time because nobody trusted me because they didn't know if I still had that power to use, even though they stripped it from me. The other people didn't trust me anymore. So this is the first time that someone approached me, but I know they are trusting. They know that I am not going to do that again. I feel happy. Maybe I didn't know that someone could be with me without trying to manipulate them."

D: *Is he interested in the healing energy also?*

A: No ... just in me. He trusted in me and who I am and that's nice. He is one of the teachers, too. He teaches history. The history of this place ... the world.

I condensed time moved her forward again to see if she stayed with this man or what happened. She had remained with him and now had a daughter. She could see the girl had inherited the same power that she had. She had the power of the crystals and was being taken to be trained. "I am happy because I taught her and I am sure she will never make the mistake I made. I tell her that she doesn't need to do anything like that because she needs to be accepted the way she is. She is going to be a good healer, and she is being taken to be trained. She will

153

do beautiful work." I thought we had learned as much as we could about this life, so I moved her to the last day of her life and asked what was happening.

A: I'm dying and I'm very old. I've been here many, many years ... hundreds of years. My daughter is here in the chamber. They put me in here so there is no suffering. It's like I'm going to sleep.

D: *They put you in the chamber when you are dying?*

A: Yes. This is a special chamber so people can die very peacefully, where there is no suffering. This is different than the healing chamber. This is a chamber for the ones who are dying. There is nothing to reconstitute now. It is time for the soul to go, so all we can do is help the soul go to a place where there is no pain ... a place to go to sleep.

D: *So there's really nothing wrong with the body?*

A: The body is just old. Worn out from living hundreds of years. It was very healthy and strong, but it's a choice to help when it is necessary. And my daughter is doing that for me. It's so beautiful, and I feel at peace.

D: *And did she take the knowledge and use it in the correct way?*

A: Oh, yes. She has been doing that for many, many years already. She's in the same place I was. They put her in the same building. She took my place, so she was the one that was doing that.

D: *So it didn't bother you that they made you stop doing that work?*

A: No. It was necessary. I needed to pay.

I then moved her to when it was all over and she was on the other side. I asked what she thought she learned from that lifetime.

A: That when you have power, you must always be careful what your desires are. Sometimes you think that you need to unequalize things to get what you need and sometimes that's not always necessary. Sometimes I thought that the way I could only be safe was to control who was being with me. And I controlled it using my power. I have to learn that lesson that I don't need to control things.

D: *That is a valuable lesson. If you were given the power in the future, in another lifetime, do you think you'll know how to use it?*

A: Yes.   I have to be sure that I don't use my power to control anyone.

D: *But the ego gets in the way, doesn't it?*

A: Yes, that's what I'm afraid of.

D: *That's the human part.*

I then had her drift away from watching it, and called forth the SC. I wanted to know why Andrew was shown the two lives as the man and the woman; because there are always so many that the SC can choose from.

A: Because he needs to know that he has the courage to do anything he needs to do. He has the power to do it.

D: *Because that man gave up his life to protect it, didn't he?*   (Yes) *What is the connection between that life and his life now?*

A: He needs to use the power that he has. He needs to know that he doesn't have to go through the same thing. He doesn't have to suffer anymore. He thinks he has to suffer. He thinks he has to be tortured over and over. He never let go of the torture. He needs to let go of the torture.

D: *That was just the one life when that happened.*

A: Yes, but he's torturing over and over.

D: *Because he thinks if he has the knowledge he has to have suffering to go along with it?*   (Yes)   *Is that why he says he has pain inside his body all the time and the uneasiness?*

A: Yes, yes. The pain and the shame because he was abused so badly. He was abused in many ways.

This also explained sexual problems that were affecting him in this life because that was the part of his body (sexual area) that was tortured the most. They (the Church) had to completely humiliate the person.

D: *But nothing that happened was his fault.*

A: Yes, but he was so ashamed.

D: *He was very courageous that he stood and did it. He could have tried to escape.*

A: Yes, but he cannot let go. He cannot let go of the torture dreams he has over and over.

D: *Can we leave it with the man it happened to?*

A: We need to because he cannot do anything anyway. He cannot handle it. He's going to die if he doesn't do it. He thinks he has to suffer.

D: *It serves no purpose to have him go through it again and again in this lifetime.*

A: Yes, he tortures himself. He brings so much suffering to himself. He's trying. He doesn't know any better.

This took much work before he finally agreed to let it go. The SC said loudly, "We will leave it with the other man. He leaves it there. It stays there. We leave it. He's not going to see it anymore. He's not going to see it because he keeps bleeding. He thinks every time he does something good he will be tortured again." Andrew began to cry as the SC worked with him to release it. This took much work. "He wanted so much to know that knowledge and we are bringing that knowledge to him. He deserves to know that knowledge in this time. The suffering belongs to the other man."

D: *So you are separating the two and allowing him to have the knowledge?*

A: Yes. He has to have the knowledge he needed back. He

deserved to have the knowledge.

D: *Is that why you showed him the second life?*

A: Yes. She had the knowledge. She knew all the crystals. She knew their power.

D: *The first man protected the knowledge, but didn't know how to use it. The woman knew how to use it.*

A: He knows much more. He knows so much. He has the power. He has more power than he thinks. He has had many other incarnations where he learned many things.

D: *So that's why you showed him the second life, so he would realize he has this power? (Yes) But he did misuse it in that life.*

A: Yes, but he needs to know he doesn't have to be afraid. He's not going to use it wrongly. He is not going to manipulate anybody. He keeps punishing himself. He is free now. We free him. We free him now! He's going to be happy. He's going to be proud but happy, and his pride will not hurt anybody. He's going to be proud in a beautiful way. He's going to feel joy in helping and serving. He's not going to abuse it. He doesn't have to be afraid to use it. He's going to feel more things than he ever thought he would feel. He's going to enjoy life. He's going to see himself differently. People are going to see a spark that was not there before. – There are many here. There are others helping others. They are as one body. Powerful. He has more power than even he imagines because this is the time. There is not much time. There is much to do in such a short time. There is no more fear. He will go to other places because we need him many places. He's totally protected and his body is so strong, and keeps getting stronger. His body, his immune system, every part of his body is protected at a level that is not human.

D: *That was one thing he was wondering about ... his body.*

A: His body is not completely human. His body is here; his other part is not here. It is being reconstituted on another plane. He has a lot to do. When his mission is done, his body is just to stop. He is going to have a perfect body and when his mission is finished, then he can go on. He has other missions to do after this planet, but that will be later.

We did a lot of work going through the body and healing everything that he had complained about. "His body is now strong and healthy. It will be kept this way for him all his life on this planet."

D: *That's wonderful. Let me ask a question. He said when he was born he had blisters all over his body. Why did that happen in the very beginning?*

A: There were several things. The blisters came from his incarnation when he was burned. (Another lifetime.) And also he needed to accelerate his karma to do what he needed to do, so he had to live many, many lives in this lifetime ... condense it so he had to suffer losses. He has to suffer pain because the only way he can do his healing to others is through resonating with the reality in his lifetime. So he needed to live many, many experiences in a short time to be ready to help others. He needed to understand others. He could not understand the pain of others. We allowed him to suffer that pain. We make him learn hard, hard experiences because the experiences that humans are going to learn now are very hard. He can collate and understand. If you don't experience you can't understand the pain of all of this. It's all for a good reason. It's all beautiful when you see the whole picture. It all makes sense in the universe.

I wanted to ask some more of the questions he had listed. "He said there was a twin that was supposed to be born with him. Can you tell him about that?"

A: The twin was another being that needed to be with him to help him to come here.

D: *But why was the being born dead?*

A: Because its mission was to be only through the time of its evolution in the womb of the mother.

D: *I was thinking that maybe the other being changed its mind and didn't want to come.* (This has happened in other cases I have explored.)

A: Actually it had already decided it was only a companion before the birth.

D: *One more question. He showed me the strange writing and strange figures he has been drawing for a long time. Can you explain what that is?*

A: This is an ancient writing. It is from ancient times when he was living in an incarnation. He used to write about science and the things he knew in those times. He thinks he came from another planet, but he's from another dimension. The writing is not from another planet. The writing is from an ancient time that will be known and discovered soon.

D: *Is it a civilization we don't know about?*

A: Yes, it's a civilization. You may know a little bit about it, but this is a civilization that goes back to many, many thousands and thousands of years.

D: *That's why it's a language that we will not find evidence of?*

A: We might. There may be times that this will be found. Everything will be found. There are times coming up that humans will find out about their past even when they don't want to believe in it. They will find things that will startle them.

D: *I believe that. So that is what it is and he just had a compulsion to write it?*

A: Yes. He wrote so much about it. He used to write so many things because he wants to write about science now. But the truth is it's just something that he did before. In that other life he wrote and actually he wrote records about ancient knowledge.

D: *It seems he's been involved in knowledge in many, many lifetimes.*

A: Oh, he has been involved so many times.

D: *There is a certain symbol that he draws a lot. What does that mean?*

A: It's the flow of his energy. It's the way his energy is received and emitted. It's actually the pattern of the energy of his body.

D: *I've had other people show me strange writings they have done and we're trying to find a resemblance between the writings.*

A: You can compare. You will find similarities because its connected to other writings. The evolutionary display in this history of humankind.

D: *You've told me before there were many civilizations that developed to a very high degree. (Yes) They were destroyed.*

A: But the knowledge is still there.

D: *It's in our minds.*

A: It's in many places, yes.

Parting message: He always needs to see himself in the light. Just see his light ... his pure light. If he sees himself in the light, he will be happy. Light is what he is. He is just light. – He will know whatever he needs to know from now on. He will be amazed at the synchronicities that he is going to defeat. He needs to get accustomed now that everything is easy. That will be his challenge to get accustomed that everything is easy. And that will be amazing to him. It will take him a while to really, really adapt to this new reality.

Chapter 12

ORBS OF INFORMATION

Betty was an energy worker and teacher. She came for a session wanting to better understand her personal relationships and most importantly to know her purpose in this life.

Betty came off the cloud into an elaborate setting which seemed out of place in a desert. There was a roll of green carpet spread out on the sand, similar to the way we put down a red carpet for someone important to walk on. The carpet led to a small pyramid that had an awning over the entrance supported by two marble pillars. Betty saw that she was a dark-skinned man dressed in gauzy white clothes that would be typical for wearing in a hot climate. She was also wearing elaborate golden sandals. There were many others there, and he was busy as a coordinator organizing the expected arrival of some type of dignitary. "This is a special place. Not everybody could walk up to this place. I feel this small pyramid is a house of ceremony, perhaps knowledge. Only special people are allowed to come here. I am not a servant, that sounds too lowly. I am arranging this event. And whoever is coming, they don't normally come here. They are coming from afar. I'm wanting everything to go right." She suddenly slipped into the observer mode: "This man that I am, he's a very uninteresting person. He's a little too fussy, but efficient. I'm not even sure I would like this person. Not that he's disgusting; just ... I know what it is. He's a fussy little hen." Then she returned to participating in the scene: "There are people in the background that would be considered true servants, to arrange food and cool drinks. I do see platters of food that seem to be a special delicacy. But I have to coordinate everything, the timing, who does what, who would

161

sit where. It has to be done correctly. This pyramid is small, but it is considered a House of Knowledge."

Then the people that the affair was for began to arrive. "They're coming. They're very special, very dignified. I think they might also be worshiped. They are extremely important. They are two people, both very tall and *narrow!* One has rings on her neck. Their heads are small, and they are very exotic looking, like of the desert. I don't know why I would say this, but she is of Nubian. It's like they had to make an official pilgrimage to this, perhaps this is a shrine. They are under the awning, and they have on a long, narrow cloth, so stylized. What is interesting is that you almost can't see them walk. It almost looks like they float in. And there's a gentleman attending, same narrowness, small head. Their heads are not shaved, but they're cropped close. Their skin is olive, goldenness about their coloring, and her eyes are grey and gold. The one lady is the most important of the two. She is very quiet."

D: *How did they arrive?*

B: I don't know. There's nothing like a chariot or a horse. I don't know what kind of vehicles they came in. It's almost like they just appeared. In modern times I think we would call that "teleportation". They just appeared. But in my watching there's nothing that startles me or is unusual for me. – I tell you, one of her pets is actually a lion, and her skin is beige looking, and almost grey-green eyes. They're *very* unusual eyes. They look like normal human eyes, but it is just the coloring. That's very startling. She carries herself like royalty, or a worship hierarchy type being. – I think they've seen me before, and they know that I'm efficient and will take care of preparations. I'm like the coordinator, the first greeter. I think she can communicate very well on a mental level. She's quite special. I believe this male with her is her brother, but she's the most important. And I've actually seen, they make vases like her, this is what is odd. They are so narrow with bands on their neck and their small head. But there is a long vase that's almost in the same style. – I know she has something to do with Isis. It's their official role to visit the shrines, which I believe are dedicated in some way. They're pretty high, whatever they do. The funny thing is I can't see their arms. They have on a beige piece of cloth and it is a swath over the shoulders, but it just contains their arms, too. That's why I can see the vessel, vase look about them.

D: *Are they going to do something inside the pyramid?*

B: Yes, they came to bless it. It's a ritual where they have to have food and drink. There are bird eggs and some fruit on the platters. Everything is very specific. Protocol, that's the word. Protocol. Master of Protocol. And the eggs are laid on peacock feathers. So they have to partake in a certain way. She uses her left hand, he uses his right. They have to drink. – (Whispers) That's really odd. There is written knowledge contained in this pyramid. The pyramid is like a book, literally. And each year this is done. I won't say it's done on the elliptical, but it's done at a certain time with astronomy. And when it's a particular time, they come. They know where to read. I don't know how this works, but as if you had strips on the wall that had words or art.

D: *You mean it is carved into the wall?*

B: Right. And it's a particular one, the proper one. She knows where it is, strips. It's like it comes out of the wall like a shelf? And it's codified. And she reads it like prophecy and announcement. This is very, very ancient, ritualistically stylized. Like on the New Year you would prophesize how the crops are going to be, and any unusual astronomical things. It is huge.

D: *She just reads one part then?*

B: Right. But it is codified. She's the only one that knows how to read it. That's what's interesting. I don't know why I'm getting to see this, but the strip is about (hand motions) four or five inches wide. And it comes out like a shelf, and this huge book is lying on the shelf. The book is about three feet tall with cream colored pages. It's about three feet wide with both pages open. She's tall and narrow so she doesn't need to take the book off the shelf. She can stand and turn the pages. But the two pages are so huge. When something's in a certain order they know what will happen that year. I get to view this, but I don't know how or what's in there. How it works or how it comes about, but she does. I think she's highly, highly educated. Bred for this, she's studied this; she knows how to do this. She understands it, and she's a real symbol for whatever, if this is a religion or a culture, or a way of knowledge.

D: *What is she going to do with it after she looks at it?*

B: It's pronouncements for the year. How the year will be, or the prophecy.

D: *But she is the only one who can make the drawer come out?*

B: She's the only one I've seen. It has to be here because it's very specific. I think it will be read in front of many officials, and then it goes out to the people. It also has something to do with Sun worship because there's Isis in there. And she has a wooden type of long pen. This is very, very formal. Part of the page is like soft copper or bronze. She has to formally make her mark and notation.

D: *To show that she has read it.*

B: Absolutely. It's very formal. I think it's done with calculations that are in astronomy. She won't come back for a while. I think they see what's going to happen.

D: *When she is finished, what happens to the book?*

B: It goes back in. She's the only one that can open it. I don't know what she does.

D: *So it goes back into the wall?*

B: Yes, of the pyramid. Where the shelf comes out of the wall it is a soft copper. There is something else she does that is *very* interesting, while she has it out. From some place on her body, or a pouch or something, she takes a specific jewel. It is oblong and what we call emerald cut. And when the book is out she places the jewel in a codified place. It activates something. There's a little slot for it on the right side.

D: *Maybe that's part of how she can open the drawer in the first place.*

B: I think it might be.

D: *After she puts the book away, what happens then?*

B: That is pulling the knowledge out, and making the pronouncements, the formal part of the ceremony. They have to go to other places. I don't think she leaves; I think she talks with officials. I don't think she talks much, I think she listens. She has great mental powers, it's amazing.

D: *She had to give the message to them.*

B: Correct. It's very formal to do this.

D: *Then your part is finished with this?*

B: Yes, I have to do the protocol. I just make sure everything runs smoothly.

D: *Do they leave right after they've finished?*

B: They leave, and that's funny again. They're so stylized I don't ever see walking. It's almost like they float. Very interesting people. And very mysterious, and it's all been that way for a long time.

D: *Then how do they leave?*

B: I've seen them. They (astonished) travel by night! I even wonder if there's a ship they get on, not a sea ship, either. I wonder if they travel by – oh, today we would say ET ship, but it's a craft.

D: *So they don't travel with camels or caravans,*

B: No, they're too advanced for that. That would be a common person thing.

D: *So after they leave, your job is finished?*

B: Right. And I don't even, if you would say, lock up the pyramid. Somebody really higher closes. I don't know how the door is opened or closed, really. It kind of slides. It's absolutely seamless. – But I make sure the awning is taken down and stored with the carpet.

When his job was complete he returned to the city. "I don't think I live with anyone. A very silent person. I'm not even sure, now that I think about it, that I can talk. There may be a reason for my silence. I don't think I can speak. I don't know if my tongue is gone. I'm a very silent person. Good for them to trust with secrets." So this was why they didn't mind if he watched everything. There was no way he could tell anyone how it was all done.

In one of my *Convoluted* books there was the story of some survivors of Atlantis who came to Egypt. They hid their sacred artifacts in a pyramid wall, and made it invisible to everyone except those who were of the correct vibration. Those were the only ones who would be able to open the part of the wall where they had placed them.

The man worked in a library in the city. "I think it's symbolically like our architecture. It is not really a pyramid, but has some shapes and arches, and it's a place of light. It's a store of records and knowledge. I have to check to make sure things are coded right. It's a job I love, but somebody else might not. It's almost a job that one person could think they're very important doing, but this male is just very efficient at it. It just is what it is. I keep track of it more like a librarian. It's very busy work, and it's constant work. I actually do see myself in a room at night. I have candles lit, there's a nice plate of grapes and fruit. A solitary life."

D: *Do you know how to read what is in the library?*

B: I don't indulge myself in it because there's enough work in the organization of making sure things are in their proper place. It's very busy, time consuming work, and I do like my quiet. I sit at a table. I have a nice candle and I'm enjoying my evening with fruit and bread, and a little solitude, not to be so busy. It's sparse, but not unadorned. It's nice. It's almost like, as a librarian, I am a monkish type person. It's an important job taking care of the information. Very busy, important, get it done, work all day, and have enough special events as coordinator to be an important job.

I decided to move him forward to an important day because it seemed like he did not have much variation in his job. When I did he leapfrogged. This is what I call it when the subject suddenly jumps from one lifetime to another. She was in a different body in a different locale. She saw that she was a young girl standing with others in front of a temple which was located on a platform on the top of a flat-topped pyramid. She was looking down at crowds of people who were gathered at the bottom. One man with her appeared to be a priest, bare-chested with red paint all over his body. She said he appeared to be Mayan, with the Mayan nose and straight black bangs and hair plastered to his head. He was very dramatic, passionate, making angry gestures, trying to appear frightening to the people. She was standing next to a man who was a dignitary, but also her father. There was a lot of shouting going on, but she said it was all part of the ritual. "The priest is supposed to be fiery and emotional, but if you didn't know it, it could probably scare you. I am being trained so I will go into the priesthood."

D: *Do you know what the ceremony is for? What it signifies?*

B: I think the timing is everything. It has to do with astronomical things, so the timing is important. But in this case there is a sacred object that is brought out. It is kept in a little hand-carried wooden chest. It's an actual hand of a revered person, and the flesh looks dried and black. Now they're holding something that looks like a turquoise orb. Odd, revered though. In this culture their lives are ruled by ritual. This culture, if it is Mayan type, is extremely ruled by it. Also orbs rule here.

D: *What do you mean?*

B: In the other life you have pyramids, but in this one there are orbs. I can see them coming from the sky. Glass orbs. Orbs are very important and they do multi things. They can transport messages. The ones I see are small like the glass orbs you see in fishermen's nets. But they can transport messages. I see them floating across the sky. I see their hand holding an orb. But then I'm seeing the whole scenery area where there's nobody there. It's the first break of dawn light. The orbs are coming across the sky, and there's a chill in the air even though there's greenery everywhere. There's a little chill at dawn. And there's a courier there to receive and take the orbs.

Research shows that glass fishing net balls were once used by fishermen in many parts of the world to keep their fishing nets, as well as longlines or droplines afloat. Large groups of fishnets strung together, sometimes 50 miles (80 km) long, were set adrift in the ocean and supported near the surface by hollow glass balls or cylinders containing air to give them buoyancy.

D: *What do they look like when they're up close?*

B: They look like clear glass, or coke bottle glass. They have a transparent to greenish, whitish green look. There is nothing that you open. The message is written on glass. You have to hold it up and turn it and you can read it. It's incoming, and has the message on it. And the courier takes it. They don't read it. They just take it to the place where it's officially read, which would be a higher up person. And that's interesting because this man they take it to uses a reddish light. And you can easily read it with the red. They turn the orb and they read it. It's back-written looking. I think it's in words, and also I think it's in formula. I do not see anything I recognize.

D: *So the person, the higher up, reads it and understands it?*

B: Absolutely. He's like an elder, sage, scientist, something like that. But the room he works in has a red glow, which makes it easy to read.

D: *It makes it visible, I guess.*

B: Yes, that's it, thank you. Because they look like glass balls, transparent whitish or coke bottle green. You use the red light and then you can see what's there.

D: *What happens after he reads the message?*

B: He's like a scientist. He calculates and it gives him the information he needs. I think that it has to do with mining and government business. I guess ores or minerals. It's the regional business. You can see that the society's a well-off, orderly society. I also think that in the region there is mining for the sake of mining and commerce. I think *he* uses it more in an alchemical way. That would be a very good word for it. I think the balls come from whoever his agents are in the mountains where the mines are. I think they write on them and then turn them loose. I don't know how they're propelled. I can't even imagine it. The balls are records, and he has wooden shelves where they are stored.

D: *So he doesn't send them back. He just keeps them.*

B: Right.

I decided it was time to bring forth the SC to try to understand these two lives and their connection with Betty. I asked about the first life with the pyramid and the woman who came to decipher the information. "Why did you choose that life for Betty to see?"

B: We know she needs to do research and we send her research. And she needs to codify what she gets and present it in written form. So we want her to know she has background in this. She coordinates this. She's efficient at this. She can do this. She took care of high knowledge. She organized it all. She has a background in another thing, to see that these are jewels, just like the woman used, and are placed before you. They are jewels, so bring them forth. These are colorized, and remember they're on the codes of the DNA of the person, too. So they're richly codified already. And the body is able to receive this. Body receives and restores as a vessel also.

I believe it was referring to Betty working with crystals and various stones in healing. "It is easily done, so her vessel is properly prepared to receive it."

D: *The woman who could do the deciphering, where did she come from?*

B: She had a similar star background that Betty has. I think it's a star family.

D: *Because the man didn't see her come or go. She just seemed to appear.*

B: Yes, she just appeared, floating like. I think she probably had ET background.

D: *Then you mean that Betty comes from a star family?*

B: She comes from a codified star family.

D: *Can you explain what you mean by that?*

B: It's a historical background. It's codified in a particular quadrant of star system. Star system is what you should say. Star system is more accurate. We have planetary families, and so her background is in one sense specifically designed to handle the knowledge that she's given. It's very easy. And also she can do the same job as the decodifier – that's the word – same job.

D: *So each of these star families have certain jobs they do?*

B: There are certain jobs they do. They are programmed, in essence, to report to a Star Master, which is a person who is in an area or quadrant of star systems. It has to do with codification of knowledge. And it is not an unusual method. It is the librarian method. That's a good way to describe it. And there are couriers of people, souls, entities born, who carry something similar to containers. They have certain jobs to do. Betty in essence needs to come out of the closet. She doesn't know this consciously, but she reports to the Star Master.

D: *What do you mean?*

B: A branch of ascending and caring. It's almost on a cellular level, too. A bloodline. An ascent. A trained messenger who knows how to receive and write and report, but who has some of the specialized bloodlines of Star Master.

D: *When does she report to him, at night when she's sleeping?*

B: Yes, nothing conscious. The person is not conscious at all of it. The freedom of contacting the unfettered mind is where you get your information to report at night.

D: *Why did you show her the second life? It looked like South American, with the orbs. What were you trying to tell her about that?*

B: Second was again the research. They had higher knowledge of astronomy and they had a good message system. They were saying that the mind knowledge is easily sent on coded little bursts of cycled messages, easily sent through the atmosphere. So in this culture it was physically sent on glass balls, but they are also sent into the codes of the mind, easily sent bursts of knowledge.

D: *How were the orbs transported?*

B: These were on energy currents. It's the same way that you would throw a baseball, but these could travel long distances. And so you basically will them. You just will them.

D: *So they would just put the message into the balls with their minds?*

B: It's actually written on there, but intent and will is what sent them. And they had learned they were very good at that. It wasn't something the common people did. Intent and will. Some of the orbs dropped out of the current. But that was the beauty of it, if one was dropped and landed on the ground and it didn't crash, you couldn't read it. Several found them, but even if you held it up to the fire you couldn't read it. It had to be in the red glow. Like today, what do you call it? The red spectrum. They might think it was a very special or even magical glass ball, but they would just keep it.

D: *Were you trying to show Betty again she has to deal with knowledge and information?*

B: Yes. We wish to show her she receives contained information. It is contained information that she is equipped to read. That she may just wake up with brilliant ideas not knowing where she gets them. And we do send her specialized transmissions.

D: *So these brilliant ideas are actually coming from you. Is that correct?*

B: Absolutely. And she is a descendant of our star system family, so when we say there are bloodlines there are bloodlines. She is part of the family, and this is one of her multitasking roles for us. She sends transmissions back, but she's unaware of them. And we check where she is and how she is, and this is over very, very long distances. The energy lines are connected. So she is teaching what she needs to teach. We wish to speed her up a bit. (Betty was already teaching how to use energy.) There are other things we want her to do. She is doing one thing we want to intensify and this is why she has aches and pains over the body. It would all flow easier if she would not hold back. She's resisting.

She was told she was to write, and to travel extensively, especially to Scandinavian countries where she would use the energy to work on balancing and cleansing the water. They were urging her to get started.

B: You two have one common thread. It is the message that you carry, but it is also the energy that you carry. It is called "connect the dots." It is called "stand in front of people." It is called "where you stand you are a temple unto yourselves." But you are also standing in front of people giving them codified knowledge and energetically connecting them at the same time. It is why the two of you could conceivably stand in front of two thousand people and energetically connect them. When you get better you can stand in front of ten thousand people. And you project a wave of energy through the audience connecting everyone. They listen to your words and they learn. But the real way they honestly learn is energetically. It is a common thread that people like you have. And you very easily open up amplifiers in people's encoded sites of their body, and you amplify into them. Everyone hears a slightly different frequency and they think they're getting something a little bit different, but it adds onto the next index card of their information. Even as you think you randomly travel, you are spreading energetically across a geographic landscape in the patterns that you fly on airplanes. She can mine her own information out of her information that is already codified. Information can be mined inside of her, and there are no hierarchy barriers. Her youthful fear of failure is not a block anymore. That log no longer burns on the fire. It is just ashes. They are old, useless tapes that are not to be played anymore.

Research revealed that there have been many strange spheres located in Costa Rica. There are all sizes, but they are stone balls, instead of glass. There are many myths surrounding their origin, including that they came from Atlantis. Their roundness is so perfect that there is no explanation of how they were constructed.

Chapter 13

CRYSTAL SKULLS

I was in Virginia to give a hypnosis class, and this was my demonstration on the last day of my class. In those days I would always pick someone from the class to be the one for the demonstration. I never knew in advance who I would pick, so I had no idea how it would turn out. It is usually difficult for the person because it is what I call a "goldfish bowl" setting. They can feel nervous being in front of so many people and not being prepared in advance. I am nervous too, but I have learned to trust "them," and they always lead me to pick the most appropriate person for the class to learn from.

When Deb first entered the scene it was sundown and she had difficulty identifying anything, yet she had the feeling it was South America. At first she thought she was in a cave, and then decided it was a tunnel, a passageway, with sheer cloth draped over the entrance. "It leads to a metal door. I have a key. I carry it around my neck on a rope."

D: *Are you the only one that has the key?*

Db: One of the only ones. No one else can have it. They're not allowed. There's a large, heavy lock on the door. It's very special, very ornate. The key is big. It fits the large lock, a very heavy door. It's made so that people can't break in. It's a secret place. Most do not know.

D: *You've probably been there many times.* (Yes) *But I'm allowed to go this time, aren't I?* (Yes) *Then let's unlock the door and open it. What's on the other side of the door?*

Db: It's a room that's kept for treasures. It has different things that are special and sacred. Writings like ancient text. Parchments and scrolls. And that's not all though. There's a human size crystal skull. It is sitting in the middle of the room on a table like a pedestal.

D: *Did you make this skull?*

Db: No. I'm a keeper of it. I have to protect what is in this room.

D: *Do you know who made this skull? (Yes) Can you tell me about it?*

Db: It was given to us. It was carried down from ancient times. It was carried from a city that was destroyed. It was kept safe though.

D: *Do you know how this city was destroyed?*

Db: Yes. There were different Earth changes, and then there were eruptions like volcanic.

D: *Was this in the country where you live now?*

Db: Sort of. Part of land that went under. Only parts of it are still above water. Most of it sank. This wasn't that land, a different land.

D: *Is this where the writings came from also?*

Db: Some of them from there, some from more recent.

D: *Are you the only one that's protecting these things, or is it your people?*

Db: No, there are a few that are trained. If it was just one person it could be lost. There are a few, but it's carried down. It's not given for many to know about. It's very powerful.

D: *What is the purpose of the crystal skull?*

Db: Communication. Storage. Information and history.

D: *How is it stored, if it's just crystal?*

Db: It carries an energy. It has the ability of lots of storage.

D: *And this is carried within the crystal itself? (Yes) Do you know how to read it?*

Db: Yes. You have to place your hands on it, and you have to connect your mind with it. And it stores what you put into it.

D: *This was how it was put in there in the first place?*

Db: By those who knew.

D: *And you can retrieve it by putting your hands on it?*

Db: Yes. It's like a telepath. The information to those who are trained, and how to access it when they do put their hands onto it.

Deb saw she was a female in her thirties. She had been trained for this since she was a child. I assumed there must be more to this place than just the tunnel and the secret room. She said at one time there were more people than they had now. I had her go outside the tunnel to see her surroundings. She said the tunnel was in a mountain, and outside it was very, very lush, very green, in a mountainous area. The place where she lived was near there. "There are structures, there are temples. There are the flat-topped pyramids. They're used for ceremony, and they're also used as teleports."

D: *What do you mean by teleports?*

Db: It's a landing platform for the ships to come.

D: *You mean the ships land there on the tops of the pyramids?* (Yes) *What kind of ships?*

Db: Ones from the other places, ones from Earth. It's other galaxies. It is said that the skull was passed down, several of them, not just one. That many had come originally from the other cultures, not from Earth. They were a gift.

D: *Were the ships coming before the cities were destroyed?* (Yes) *What is their purpose when they come now?*

Db: Trade. One of the places where the information can be stored because of the skull. We give them goods, fruit.

D: *And they trade knowledge and information?*

Db: Yes, and other things. Their own, different goods, different items.

D: *Then they are good people.* (Yes) *What do these people look like?*

Db: Much like us. Some have different features or coloring; different tones of the skin. It's more like shades like we have our shades. Ours is more like a little reddish, darker skin tone. They have their color, their shades. Some blue, even.

In my book *Keepers of the Garden* it was said that in the beginning of life on Earth there were many different skin colors, even blue, green and purple. Most of these eventually died out, or were absorbed into the genetic structure of the human race. These tints are still occasionally found in humans today, especially the port wine birthmarks that are a genetic carryover from the purple race. So when Deb said there were blue people that came to their city, it did not surprise me. It just added more verification to the information I have been accumulating for many years.

D: *It sounds like these people have been coming for a long time.* (Yes) *Do any of your people ever go back and forth with them?*

Db: They have, yes.

D: *Have you done it?* (Yes) *Tell me about it. You're smiling, so it must have been a pleasant experience.*

Db: It was very interesting. It's like they know who we were.

D: *You were?*

Db: They know who we were. They know, they read your soul. They know who was who. It's like there's a destiny for each person. They know who you were, so they know when you come back. They know when you're born again. And it's entrusted each time to those who return who knew from the beginning.

D: *So they more or less follow the soul. Is that what you mean?* (Yes) *Or they can read your soul to know where you originated from?*

Db: Both.

D: *So they have trusted you to protect the information and travel with them to their places. What was that like?*

Db: The buildings, the whole cities, are built of crystals. It's very interactive, very much operates on thought and projection.

D: *It's all mental and telepathic?*

Db: Not all, but a lot. It's like the whole environment is interactive with the crystals. It is very beautiful. We go there to visit for rest or vacation. It's a very well-developed society. Very fun, too. Just very advanced.

D: *Your community sounds like it's isolated.*

Db: Yes, because they won't come anymore just for the regular public. They remain more secretive.

D: *You mean they only come to places that are isolated?*

Db: For the most part, yes. Most people, they don't believe anymore. They don't remember enough and they're not always kind to them. So they're very selective of who they will see. There are leaders on our world that would misuse the knowledge.

D: *Could the leaders harm them?* (Yes) *This is why they only come to a select few, and to select places?* (Yes)

I decided to move her forward to an important day.

Db: Someone important has arrived. They haven't been here before. It's like royalty of sorts from their planet, and a whole little entourage. And they've brought one of the other crystal skulls. They want to put them together in the little room at the end of the tunnel. It's as if one of the crystals is male and the other is female, sort of.

D: *They have that energy.* (Yes) *Why are they giving you another one?*

Db: It's not being given for permanent, just temporary, so they will share the information from one to the other. They will put them together and they will communicate. It's very special.

D: *If it's only temporary then they will take the new skull back?* (Yes) *After it has communicated its information to the other one.*

Db: Yes, and vice versa. And royalty has come to watch, to observe.

I moved her again to another important day, and she saw herself teaching. "The instruction is carried on to other generations, too. And some of the Keepers are male, and some are female. And I'm passing on the knowledge, the training."

D: *Is that what they call you, the Keeper?*

Db: It's similar, but it's almost like a different language. A different word that means the Keeper. I am passing the knowledge on to others, so that it won't be lost. One is my own daughter, my own child. And it's her first time of being able to communicate with the skull. This is after the other one had come, after the communication.

D: *That is very important to keep the knowledge alive.*

Because this was a demonstration I was giving for the class, I couldn't spend as much time exploring this as I would have liked to. I also had to get to Deb's questions so the class could see how this part of the session was done. So I moved her forward to the last day of her life in that lifetime.

Db: It's like transitioning in the sleep state, the dream state. It is very easy.

D: *Then you just slipped out of the body? (Yes) But you had so much knowledge and training that it was easy for you, wasn't it?*

Db: It's like I knew. I was older. I prepared people. I told them that I would be going soon.

I then moved her to when she had left the body and was on the other side, so she could look at the entire lifetime and see its purpose, its lesson.

Db: The mission was to keep the knowledge safe.

D: *Do you think you learned that lesson?*

Db: I lived it.

D: *The preservation of knowledge was very important.*

I then gave instructions for the SC to come forth, and I asked it why it chose that lifetime for Deb to see. She had told me before the session that she knew about many of her past lives, and she didn't think we would find anything of importance that she didn't already know. But after the session she said this lifetime was something new.

Db: It relates to the current endeavors of spreading knowledge, keeping knowledge. And safeguarding knowledge.

D: *And you were trying to show her another time when she did this? (Yes) Because now she is also involved in the same thing, isn't she?*

Db: Very similar, very similar.

D: *So you wanted her to see that she had done it before. (Yes) Was this after the time of Atlantis?*

Db: Yes. It was in South America. The people look like the forerunners of the Maya.

D: *So they were before the Mayans. We've always been told that the Mayans were the ones who built the pyramids down there.*

Db: Some of them were built before the other cities were destroyed. They were built by some of the Atlanteans. And Lemurians, even older. Some of them were ancient. Some of them survived the Earth change. Others were rebuilt.

D: *She said the flat part was used as landing places.*

Db: Yes, and ceremonies.

D: *I am curious. We've always been told that they performed human sacrifices there.*

Db: Not in this land. That came later. That was after the fall. That was a later culture. That didn't happen in this time.

D: *In our history we've always been told this is why they were built, for ceremonies as human sacrifices to the gods.*

Db: Not these.

D: *Then what was the original purpose of the building of the flat-topped pyramids?*

Db: For what they were used for. For the landings of the crafts from other planets. And for public ceremony because many crowds could come around and hear important announcements and see from all sides.

D: *Then in later years it became distorted, and that's when they resorted to the sacrifices? Were the ships still coming in the later times?*

Db: For the most part, no, they stopped.

D: *I don't think they would have approved of the sacrifices, would they?*

Db: No, that's part of the reason they wouldn't come. They would have been in danger, too.

D: *Why did the people resort to human sacrifices, do you know?*

Db: In later cultures it was more of a power play. It was more of a way of warring. Mostly it wasn't their own people that were sacrificed. It was those of warring factions, the warriors who were killed. It just kept getting worse. But see, it was not only the past that was put into the crystals. The future was put in there, too.

D: *So they knew what was going to happen?*

Db: Yes. There was prophecy in it.

D: *The tunnel where she saw the hiding place of all of this knowledge. Is that still there?*

Db: It is.

D: *It hasn't been discovered yet?*

Db: There are still Keepers.

D: *Even now, living back in the jungles there are people who still protect the knowledge? (Yes) That's wonderful. Then maybe it will remain.*

Db: It will not be revealed until the time is right.

D: *We're being told the time is right now for some of the knowledge to come back.*

Db: Not yet.

D: *But it is still hidden in that tunnel.* (Yes) *Are both crystal skulls there?*

Db: No. Just one. It is hidden there in the tunnel, and is still protected.

D: *Then the wrong people won't get their hands on it, will they?*

Db: That's why it has to wait.

D: *It has to wait until the right time. You know in our time there are many other crystal skulls that have been discovered.* (Yes) *Do the ones we have today serve the same purpose?*

Db: Some of them. Some of them don't. Some of them are replicas, just to give the people something. Some of them work, and the replicas don't. Some of the ones are genuine, and some of them are not.

D: *So many of them did come from other planets?*

Db: Yes, and Atlantis. They were from other places. Each one from a different planet, each one from a different place. And that's part of the way of communicating the records from each place, so that it's carried within the skull.

We then went on to ask the questions that Deb had written down before the session. One of the questions dealt with Deb's connection and fascination with the dolphins.

Db: Part of the connection goes back to other planets, more water-based ones. The dolphins are not totally from here, they were brought. They were not originally from this planet.

D: *I've heard of the water planets, where everything is so free and easy. Is that the planets you mean?* (Yes) *So that's why she has the connection with the dolphins because she goes back to a time when she was on those planets.* (Yes) *And one of these creatures?* (Yes) *Dolphins are very special, aren't they?*

Db: Yes, they are. They're not just smart mammals. They're like us, but they never forgot; they never devolved. They never forgot the connection with Creator, and they never forgot the connection with each other.

D: *And that's why she is able to communicate with them, and feels at home with them.*

Db: Yes. And the fragment, that's why it went there. – They are guardians also. There is one of the skulls, at least one, under the ocean, and there are those among the dolphins who are the guardians.

There is much more about these unique and remarkable creatures in my other *Convoluted Universe* books.

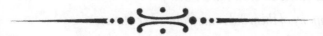

The following information about crystal skulls came from another client that was omitted from earlier books. I waited years until I was able to get more information to explain this phenomenon more fully.

D: *Collette was wondering about the phenomenon that we call the "three skulls." (I was confused.) I'm sorry. I don't know where the word "three" came from. I meant, the phenomenon that we call the "crystal skulls." Are you familiar with what I'm talking about?*

C: Yes. And the number three was no mistake. There are three sources for crystal skulls. Three planets from which they began their descent to the planet Earth. Those planets are made from a crystalline source, as Earth is.

D: *Do you mean the planet itself is crystalline?*

C: As the internal part of Earth is made from a crystalline substance, the human body is also made of a crystalline substance. The planets from which the three original skulls came from are also of a crystalline substance.

D: *In other words, they are constructed very similar to the planet Earth?*

C: Not in the same form. It just has some of the same components of crystallization. As a quartz crystal is shiny and bright, and sometimes you can see through it, and sometimes it has a cloudy look. This is the source, the substance of the energy of those planets. It is not something you can see visibly at all times. Such as with the planet Earth – what you would look at as a globe or a ball – the internal part that you cannot see with the human eyes is made of a crystalline substance. If you were to go to the caverns, such as in New Mexico, and Arkansas, and Brazil and Siberia, and other places on the planet where the crystals are mined, you would see that the internal part of the Earth is a crystalline substance. The *whole* of the Earth is a crystalline substance. It's an energy. We came from a crystalline substance. The technology today on the planet Earth is just beginning to see the sources and uses for the crystals, such as much of your computer systems. Even the watches are made of quartz crystals today.

D: *Yes. But I've always thought that the magma of the Earth is like lava. But you're talking about part of the crust?*

C: Part of the crust itself is made of a crystalline substance. It's almost in disguise because it is not time for that knowledge to be known by everyone. Because the energy of it is so powerful, it might be used in a negative way.

D: *I always think of the dirt, and the elements, and the minerals, and that crystals are just scattered here and there.*

C: They are scattered, but there is much more crystal than most people know.

D: *But you said there were three separate planets that these skulls came from?*

C: No. The number three represented three planets from which crystals came from, which the skulls *could* have come from. Not necessarily *did* come from. But there are three other planets that are of crystalline substance like planet Earth. So you started to say "three skulls." And I said the number three did not necessarily mean three skulls, but three planets that were crystalline based. The number three also is significant because we see these three planets as a trinity. And a trinity is very powerful in all aspects of all knowledge, of all technology, of everything that is.

D: *Is this the source of where some of these skulls came from?*

C: Initially, yes.

D: *We're curious about the skulls and how they were made. Were they made on these other planets?*

C: The ones that were found *here* were not made on those planets. They were made on this planet by ancient civilizations. And the knowledge of "all that is" is contained within the skulls.

D: *I thought maybe they were made on those planets and brought here.*

C: No, they were not *brought* here from the other planets.

D: *And the skulls were all made by ancient civilizations?*

C: Yes. And the knowledge that *they* knew, and that was channeled through them from the power of our Source, the Source of *all*. That is within the crystals.

D: *Then they were not taught how to do this, or shown how to do it by someone else?*

C: No. It came directly from Source through the hands of the ancient ones who touched the crystal. And with the hands of the ancient ones, Source *molded* the crystal into the human skull. As the hands of the ancient ones touched the raw crystal the hands were as though they were tools. It began to take the shape of the skull. Tools were not necessary. It was Source moving through this human being.

This sounded very similar to the way the people in Atlantis evolved to where they could use their minds to make stone malleable. This was one of the ways the ancient monuments were created. They carried the knowledge with them when they escaped the destruction. This is expanded upon in my other Convoluted Universe books.

D: *There have been many arguments and discussions about how they were created. Some people say it was with tools, but it would have taken an incredible amount of time and energy to do it that way.*

C: It is very significant that you use the word "energy," because Source – and some call Source "God," some call Source "universe," some call Source by many names – Source is energy. And the energy that was connected through the ancient ones who held the stones, their connection with Source was so powerful and so directly connected, that with the combination of the two and the stone, we have a trinity. So when we have the three together, anything is possible. Everything is living. Everything is alive. And with the ancient one holding the stone, which is a living being, and connected directly to Source, anything is possible in the shape of the skull. Form came into being, came into physicality, simply by the energy.

D: *You said these were ancient people. How far back were these skulls created?*

C: In linear time, in Earth time, thousands and thousands of years. Twenty thousand up to a hundred thousand years. And there are many skulls on different continents on the planet Earth. Some have been found, some have not. Some *may* not be found.

D: *They say that certain ones were connected with the ancient Mayans.*

C: That is correct. Not *all* crystal skulls go back to a hundred thousand or more years. Some are more recent. The Mayan civilization, in terms of linear Earth time, is a long time ago. They existed in your time fifteen, twenty, twenty-five thousand years ago.

According to experts, the Mayan civilization began about 3000 BC, but there is much debate still going on about this and they cannot agree. So it is possible it had been around much longer.

C: However, in the time infinity, there is no time. And in the universe there's no time. It's only space. How can I say? (Big sigh) There are Mayans today who practice in small groups. It is a civilization that is not totally destroyed or gone away, as many people think. There are still Mayans around. The ancient knowledge still exists in the Mayans. And they did in fact have a skull that is very famous. And the skull is very much revered because it does give out great knowledge for those who know how to access and retrieve the knowledge. And it will be given *only* to those who use it in love and light and in the highest good of all.

D: *So the skulls they created would be more recent than the older ones you're talking about?*

C: Some of the older ones have never been located. The time for them to appear has not come about at this point in time.

D: *I guess I'm thinking of Atlantis. Would they have any connection with that?*

C: Of course, definitely, yes. But not a skull that you know of, that exists in this time.

D: *Did they pass the knowledge on to later people, like the Mayans?*

C: No. The Mayans are more descendants of Lemuria than Atlantis.

That would definitely place their origin much older than the archaeologists think because Lemuria existed before Atlantis.

D: *But there was the knowledge of how to create the crystal skulls as far back as Atlantis. (Yes) Why were these objects made in the shapes of skulls? What is the significance?*

C: In the human physical body the head or the skull houses the brain, or – to put it in modern terms – the computer. The biological computer. It was a place to house the mental, the intellect, the knowledge. And a crystalline structure is very powerful in holding knowledge. So the significance of it being in the shape of a skull is that a human can associate skull with knowledge, with the mental, with the most important thing. People who are non-spiritual think everything comes from intellect, from knowledge, from the brain. And so that association with the brain and the crystal; the crystal being that it would just store knowledge. The brain stores knowledge as a computer does on disk. Therefore a crystal in the shape of a skull is very powerful to a human being. Also, let us say, that a crystal skull, especially a clear quartz crystal, can store the knowledge of *all* universes. And for one to find the access, is to be able to tune into – not the skull – but into the energy of the crystal, of the gem, of the stone.

D: *There are many who have studied the crystal skulls, and they think they relate to death and negativity.*

C: Yes, there are many stories like that. And that is for a reason. There are those who are not prepared to use that information that can be stored in a crystal skull, or any type of stone that's carved in the shape of a skull, as many might use that information in negative ways, in ways that would harm people. Therefore there is an appropriateness in that being known as the "skull of death" or "skull of doom." Because the people that would look at it in that way might, had they the knowledge of how to use it, use it in a way that would be harmful for people on the planet.

D: *So this creates a fear so they will avoid it.*

C: Hmm, that's a good way of putting it.

D: *There is one famous skull that has the removable mandible, the removable jaw. The other ones are all made in one piece. Is there significance in that?*

C: Very definitely there is significance. When you look at the skeletal structure of the human body, the jawbone – or, in technical terms, called a mandible – is a movable part of the skull. It is the strongest bone in the human body. Think about what that bone does, the actual activity and the responsibility and the job of helping that human chew the food. The teeth are implanted in that part of the skull, so it is very, very strong. To find the crystal skull in that shape with a movable jaw makes that a more powerful one than one that does not move. Because it is so anatomically correct in its precise design, it is almost nearly perfectly designed as an exact replica of a human skull.

D: *There are many that are all in one piece.*

C: Yes. And that is for a purpose as well.

D: *So they would each contain different types of information?*

C: Exactly. And the purpose for which they were carved was different. And it is up to those who come in contact with it to discover their meaning.

D: *So different people will react in different ways around the different types of skulls.*

C: Yes. It all is about the intent and purpose of the individual who comes in contact with the skull. Whether it be one simply touching it for a healing, or one who actually owns it. And the ownership may be simply a custodianship until it goes to the next place that it is to be.

D: *Were they made by individuals or by groups using their combined mind power?*

C: There are many different skulls that are carved or sculpted or molded. Some have been done by the ancient ones with Source. Some, which could have been in your linear time, 10,000 years – even more recent than that – up to hundreds of thousands of years ago, have not been found. Then there are those that are done even *today* in your time by artists who sit at benches with modern technology and modern tools. It could be done even with lasers. So we don't say that all skulls have all knowledge of everything. Each stone, each skull is done appropriately for a specific purpose, and it is up to the individuals who come in contact with it, for that purpose to be revealed to that individual or group.

D: *I was thinking that maybe the very ancient ones used the combined mind power of several people to create them. A group of priests, or a group of people that had the knowledge of how to do it.*

C: There were several that were designed that way. Not just the skull, but a complete skeletal structure. That is, all the bones that appear in the human anatomy, have been done in quartz crystal. So there are more than just skulls that are in existence. Some are yet to be discovered.

D: *What would have been the purpose of creating an entire skeleton of crystal?*

C: To show that all structure is a hologram of itself. As a skull is done completely in a crystalline structure, so is the whole body. If the base of the human being, the human anatomy, is crystalline – which it is – then it is the whole being, not just the skull. That which you know as bone is a substance of crystalline.

D: *I wouldn't have thought of it being crystalline because it decomposes.*

C: You will find that when I say "crystalline structure," it can be as a powder. A quartz crystal can be ground into a very fine powder, such as you could blow in the wind and not see it. So that is what we speak of when we say a crystalline structure. Not as a hard gemstone. As dust, which can then decompose.

D: *Collette was wondering if she has a connection with these crystal skulls.*

C: She has a very direct connection with the crystal skull. She came from one of the planets that is of the number three, which you mentioned in the beginning. As you say, there are no accidents. There are no coincidences. So therefore the number three that you mentioned is no coincidence. The number three is a trinity. The three planets are a trinity. And she has a very *direct* connection. Her direct connection is that there – how to say this? To say it correctly through your language is difficult. (Pause) Coming from pure energy into the density of this being, it is very difficult to use words. (I encouraged it to do the best that it could.) She is from a tribe – for lack of a better word – a humanoid tribe made up of crystalline, the crystal structure. And you can explain to her, she came from a humanoid race that was *made* from crystalline.

D: *You mean these were beings that were made of a crystalline structure rather than carbon base? (Yes) But they were humanoid. (Yes) Did their bodies function as ours do in carbon base?*

C: Similar. It was as though these humanoids *knew*, and knew that they knew what they knew. It was not something that they had to go out and learn, and search and search and search to find the knowledge or remembrance. They had the remembrance. It was knowledge of time and space, not of linear time. These humanoids *were* knowledge.

D: *But they didn't function as the physical bodies we have.*

C: Yes, they did. As you look at a human now, it is flesh and blood. These were flesh and blood. As you look at the (human) bone structure as a fibrous skeletal structure, this was a crystalline structure that was *somewhat* fibrous, but much stronger. And all knowledge was held within this crystalline structure, as today the knowledge is held within the skeletal structure of the human body. It is just not as purely a crystalline structure as that humanoid race was, as that humanoid *time* was. It's a time, not a race. *It was a time.*

D: *A time. When you talk about the knowledge being in the bones of the humans, would that be the genetic structure, the DNA?*

C: Yes, yes. All knowledge is found in what you know as the DNA.

D: *But of course, that knowledge is only accessible while the spirit resides in the body and has contact with the DNA.*

C: Ahh! I beg to differ with you!

D: *I was thinking once the spirit left the body it would decompose.*

C: But when the body decomposes the DNA is still there. The DNA can be found in the bony structure. The technology has not been discovered yet that can get to the ash once one has been cremated. However, the DNA is still there. It can be found.

This sounds similar to what the people were doing in the laboratory with the strange machine that reactivated the charred bones that were wrapped and preserved, in Chapter 7, *Convoluted Universe, Book One*. Had they discovered the secret of reactivating or cloning the dormant DNA?

C: When Collette hears this she will be in awe thinking, "I've never heard of this, so why would I even believe such a thing?" So she has to look at this with openness, with honesty and remembrance, as she looks into this experience she had, of her body being a crystal hologram.

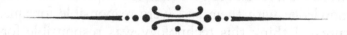

And so the debate continues about the Crystal Skulls. There have been some that were forgeries, but others that are judged to be authentic still mystify experts. One of the most famous is the Mitchell-Hedges skull discovered in a ruined city in Belize in 1924. Much controversy has surrounded this discovery, yet the experts agree that the quartz crystal could only have been created with very sophisticated technology. As confirmed by the Hewlett-Packard research laboratory, the piece was ground against its axis, and it is a miracle that the piece did not shatter into a million pieces during the manufacturing process. Tiny deviations of only millimeters would have led to parts being splintered off. US restoration expert, Dr. Frank Dorland commented: "If one flat out disregards any type of supernatural forces, then the Maya must have created the crystal skull by means of manual polishing. This is an unimaginable task, which would have taken centuries, and quite obviously superseded any political and religious conditions. It is really hard for us to imagine how such an intended, long-term goal could have been carried out from one generation to the next." Seven million working hours would presumably have been required to obtain the perfect final shape of the piece of crystal. That is equivalent to 800 years, working day and night. If one stipulated 12 hours per day, it would have taken 1600 years! (Source: Legendary Times Magazine)

I think it is obvious from this statement that the object was not created manually. I move more toward the theory of the technology that was present in Atlantis. The knowledge of how to mold stone by mental powers into the shape that was desired. In my other books this knowledge seems to have come from the ETs who lived among these highly advanced ancient societies. After these civilizations were destroyed, the survivors escaped to Egypt and probably other countries where amazing stoneworks still remain to confound the experts. They carried the knowledge with them and were responsible for amazing structures. I think this technology was responsible for the creation of the Skulls, and not manual labor.

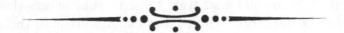

Crystals are the most abundant mineral found on Earth. It is interesting that most of the crystals sold around the world come from Arkansas and Brazil. I discovered that where I live in northern Arkansas there is a huge deposit of crystals directly under this area. There is a public crystal mine located south of here near Mount Ida where anyone can come and pick the crystals up off the ground. During a session I was told, "You only think you randomly chose to live in this part of Arkansas. You were put there for a reason. You needed the crystal energy for your work."

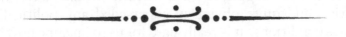

In modern times a giant crystal cave was discovered in Mexico which contains the largest crystals ever found on the planet. The Cueva de los Cristales (Cave of Crystals) was discovered in 2000 near Naica, Mexico by two miners blasting a new tunnel for a mining company. It is buried a thousand feet below Naica Mountain in the Chihuahuan Desert. The cave contains some of the largest natural crystals ever found: translucent gypsum beams measuring up to 36 feet long and weighing up to 55 tons. Geologists were stunned by the size and the beauty of the crystals when they went down into the cave to film for a BBC television series. They were unable to do much filming because of the extreme heat and humidity in the cave. Temperatures were over 136° F (58°C) and humidity at 100%, and the conditions were a potential killer. The body literally begins to cook. With special equipment they were able to stand the extreme conditions long enough (no longer than 10 minutes at a time) to film the footage for the documentary *How the Earth Made Us*, which aired on BBC in 2013. Filming was also done by 60 Minutes Australia.

So the regression was accurate that our entire planet is made of crystal, as well as our bodies.

Chapter 14

TEACHING THE KNOWLEDGE

This session was done in 2008 in my temporary office in Amber Light Motel after the flood that went through town and ruined my other office across from Granny's restaurant. I was waiting for the completion of my office in the strip mall across the street from the motel. It was not the best place for a session, (mostly because of the noise created by other guests) but it was better than nothing.

John had his own business where he worked with safe and natural animal products. His main purpose for having the session was to understand his purpose. He specifically wanted to have the veil removed to "know it all" and to understand the big picture and his place within it.

John went into a lifetime in New Mexico during the 1800s. He lived away from town and he treated people as a doctor. He had been trained in England, but he was more like a naturopath, and much of what he did was self-taught. He prepared and developed his own remedies using herbs and crystals. He grew some of the herbs and some were obtained from the Indians. They shared healing knowledge with each other. He also made salves to treat the patient topically in addition to giving herbs to help the body fight off problems. He lived a long and uneventful life and died as an old man sitting in a rocking chair on his front porch.   After he was out of the body I asked about the purpose of that life. "It was to help people. To learn. To take knowledge from several sources and combine it. And have a pure intention, pure motive." Yet he did not pass the knowledge along to anyone else, he did not train anyone. "You would think that I would have because that needs to carry on. But I don't see anybody."

Since that life was short and uneventful I had him move to another lifetime, and he saw himself in Egypt standing on the flat top of a pyramid. "I am a priest. People come to me to get

197

help, to get guidance, to get clarity, and for healing." The people would come to the pyramid when they needed help. He again was living a lonely life, with no wife. He had been doing this work for a long time, and I asked if he had been trained by anyone. His answer was a surprise.

J: I sense that I was trained, but it was not like human training. I have brothers in the stars that took me under their wing to teach me things. Psychic abilities. Healing.

D: *Tell me about it. Can you see what they look like?*

J: They're beings of light. That used crystals. Downloaded knowledge. Powers of the mind, and body energetically. Healing, counseling people.

D: *Do these beings of light live among the people?*

J: No, they don't. They're not readily accessible. I'm not even sure they're there now, after the training was done. They were there during the training, and when the training was completed, they left. They weren't living among the people. They were down there just for the training in an isolated area.

D: *They didn't want everyone to know they were there?*

J: That's exactly right.

D: *So they just wanted certain people to be trained.*

J: Yes, they did. And that's why they picked me. I was different.

D: *How were you different?*

J: I was different in my mental maturity, capacity. My intention conveyed a higher cause rather than just having an occupation. It almost appears like arrogance. But it's not arrogance. It's an inner sense of duty, a sense of calling for a higher good. And that called for some isolation.

D: *You were different from other children your age?*

J: Yes, and other people in the community.

D: *So you said they took you to an isolated place?*

J: Part of the time was spent out in the forest, in an isolated area. Part of it was when they took me up on the ship and taught me. And part of it was what to do on the flat-topped pyramid. There was astronomy taught and attention to the stars.

D: *Did they always appear to you as beings of light?*

J: They had light bodies. There were different features that would allow me to see something more human, instead of just an orb, or a ball of light. So it was like a combination of lights and form. Pure love. Pure intelligence. Compassion. Wanting to help. Wanting to teach. To benefit *me*, so I can help these people.

D: *How were you taught?*

J: Some, the old fashioned way, like a class. But more of a down-loading through crystals, through lights, through special rooms.

D: *Where were the special rooms?*

J: They were special rooms in a facility in the forest that was hidden. And a place in the pyramid. And up in the ship as well. It's like a chamber where you can see the big picture. The master plan. The gifts that I needed to have to do what I came down to do. An interesting, kind of speed-learning course. Not like you'd go to school in the 1st grade, 2nd grade, 3rd grade, and stretch it out. It was more of a quick process. I think as my body got older, I was given new segments of information. And experience of knowledge, of abilities.

D: *So they stayed with you for quite a while, teaching you?*

J: They either stayed with me, or they kept returning.

(All during these last several minutes there were sirens of ambulance, police, etc. going by the motel. Very loud, but it did not bother John. He just kept talking.)

D: *You said you were taken onboard the ship. How did they take you there?*

J: Just beam me up. It's not like I got into a little ship and they took me up. It was almost like they took me up physically right through light. And I instantly appeared on the ship. It's like I know the people. It's almost like I was one of them that agreed to come down and do this. And I got my training from them.

D: *Is that what it feels like? (Yes) That you agreed to do this, and they would help you. (Yes, yes.) That's why you were different from the rest of the people?*

J: Yes, I think so.

D: *In the mental capacity anyway. – You said the healing they taught you was mostly training with crystals?*

J: Yes, the crystals contained knowledge. And so they were downloaded into me, into my crystalline structure, so I had the knowledge in my body. And then coming down, I had an understanding of the people, of their nature, of the human body, of energy. Of the Earth: plants, food. How it should be grown. The kind of society that they had when I helped them farm so they could care for one another. Kind of like an ideal society. And I was able to energetically feel with my hands.

D: *But you didn't know all this when you first came down. You were born here.*

J: Correct.

D: Did the knowledge come later?

J: I think it did. I had to be ready physically to receive it. I had a mission and a purpose coming down. But the pieces that I was given were not all given at once. It was like you had to be ready and mature enough. And then this was learned.

D: *So things happened with the crystals before you came into a human body. Is that what you mean? (Yes) How is the knowledge stored within the crystals? Do you know?*

J: Let me ask. (Pause) It seems it was a combination of a couple of things. It was, telepathically, they did send information that was stored in the crystals. But also it had the ability of the computers on the ship to be able to send it into the crystals. So both of them. My question is intention. How does a crystal serve then as energy? How does a crystal know when to open itself to be absorbed?

D: *When to release the information.*

J: Yes. It seems it is some kind of key mechanism through intention, through telepathy.

D: *So just anyone wouldn't be able to download this information.*

J: That's correct. Only somebody who was prepared, who knew how. That had pure intentions, pure motives. And how to utilize the knowledge. Not just for the sake of obtaining knowledge, but for the sake of taking the knowledge and using it to benefit the people. So you can teach them, and they can carry on. So it's like a rippling effect. When you teach them, then they can go out and teach others. Whether it's ways of farming or anything.

D: *So you were given the knowledge, and you were using it with the people?* (Yes) *Did you teach others?*

J: Yes, I did.

D: *To pass on what you knew. Was it only crystal healing that you did?*

J: No, it was actually looking at the whole society. What dynamics make up a society? You have foods, and you had to have farming. And you have people that got hurt or got sick, so you had healing. You had trading. You had fairness. You had education. You had water storage. You had ways of settling disputes, so there was a council. But the people on the council could not have an agenda. They had to be completely objective.

D: *That's difficult, isn't it? To be completely objective. But this is the only way that the knowledge would work, isn't it?*

J: It is the only way that a civilized society could function. If you teach it in the purest form how a society could function. Where you take care of one another, you love one another. You make sure everybody has food and shelter. And take care of your older people, and make sure the children are educated. And be gentle to the Earth.

D: *Sounds like a perfect way to live.*

J: Absolutely. It is possible.

D: *It is possible because you've done it.* (Yes) *Did you use herbs also, or was it mostly crystals?*

J: Mainly crystals there. But I was intuned to plants. Everything is energetic. So we as a human are comprised of all these elements. And they all vibrate at different frequencies. And if something is out of sync, then you find something that will help the body, or that part of the body, get back into perfect vibration. It could be crystals. It could be hands-on, taking my energy. It could be a plant that has a certain energy frequency given to that person's body. It could be a detoxification program, getting rid of some things that are causing it. It could be certain herbs. It could be sunlight.

D: *So it's not the same for each person.*

J: That's correct.

D: *So that's part of what you had to do, determine what was the best method and the best way?* (Yes) *That's a lot to expect for one person to do. But you were trained for it, so it sounds like you knew when you came in. And you said they took you and trained you by yourself, after you were in the physical body.* (Yes) *Would this be the same as a Pharaoh, or is it something different?*

J: I think that's a good analogy. A Pharaoh. A leader, without the ceremonies and the pomp and the wasting time.

D: *Because it sounds like a healer, a medicine person, but there was more to take into consideration, for the whole society.*

J: Yes. A compassionate ruler that loved his people. Who was aware of all the dynamics of society, and addressed them all. And to have people who specialize in different areas, so that they could carry on the work. I was just one man, and what I did encompassed *all*. So I realized that it was important to train certain people to go to the experts in certain areas.

D: *It sounds like a very responsible job, a very difficult job to do.*

J: Very much. I enjoyed it. I was good at it. I helped people, the society flourished.

D: *All right, let's move ahead and find out what happened to the society, and what happened to you. Did it continue to flourish, or what happened? (Pause) Were you there for a long time with these people? (Pause) You can move ahead and condense time very easily.*

J: Once I felt that the job was done, and I knew the society could continue as is, and didn't need me anymore, I left.

D: *Had you passed on the knowledge to others by that time?*

J: Yes. I wanted to make sure that they could carry on. I don't think they could do everything that I could do, but from a practical standpoint it was enough.

D: *You taught them the practical things that are needed as a civilization.* (Yes) *So at that time you felt you could leave.*

J: That is correct. My job was done with them.

D: *How did you leave?*

J: (Pause) I think they just beamed me up.

D: *Were you there for many years?*

J: No, I don't sense a great many years. It seems I was around forty years old when I left. So probably ... twenty years I spent with them to help them to develop themselves.

D: *I thought maybe you lived there for many, many years and you had grown quite old.*

J: No. I was trying to see myself as an old man, and I didn't see myself. The last thing I can see is I'm very tan and fit and wise and healthy. I had a talk with the people, the leader, and let them know I was leaving. And it was time. I felt that they were capable. And so I moved on.

D: *Did they see you do this?*

J: I did that in private.

D: *Well, now that you're out of that body you can look at that life from a different perspective. What do you think was the purpose of that life?*

What were you trying to learn?

J: I had a mission and purpose. Before I incarnated I agreed to come down to learn, to grow, to mature, so for twenty years I could help the people survive. Stand on their own. Know how to treat one another. How to treat the Earth. How to eat, how to heal, how to trade, how to settle disputes.

D: *These were all very valuable things.*

J: Yes. I feel good about that life.

D: *Usually those things are accomplished by many people, and you were able to do it all. That's very good.*

I had John leave that life and called forth the SC for more information. The first thing I always want to know is why the SC chose those lives for the client to see. "You chose these two. They are similar, but the first one he was the doctor and was using herbs. Why did you choose that life for John to see?

J: So he knows that he's had experience with herbs and healing. And concocting things, combining things.

D: *That's what I was thinking because he was doing much of it without being taught. He just thought of it on his own.*

J: Yes, he did.

D: *So you wanted him to know he's done this before? (Yes) So it is natural for him, isn't it? (Yes) The second life also touched on the same theme, didn't it? Where he came down from the ship and helped people with healing. So these two lives were along the same theme? (Yes) What are you trying to tell him there?*

J: He knows this. But he needs to know that there are different dynamics to healing. With the herbs, with energy, with intention, with the guidance we're getting from our brothers from the stars. That the people out there need some guidance, some leadership, and some pure ideas that work, without being attached to profit goals. I want him to combine them all. The diets and the crystals and the herbs. And the healing, and the faith that you can heal, and not robbing people to do it. And that we do have entities that want to help us and guide us. And want us to be healthy, and not be distracted by disease. So everybody can focus on their mission and purpose. A vegetarian diet would help global warming. You wouldn't need to clear-cut all this land for cattle to graze. And it would affect the water. Teaching farmers how to farm again, and distribute their goods locally. Changing the medical community so that the healing is a more natural way, a lot less expensive way. We want him to contribute to all these things.

All of this sounded like a tremendous job for one person to attempt to do. But they said it would happen gradually. John had many ideas of working in healing and he mostly wanted to start a healing center for cancer and to teach natural healing. The SC gave him much advice, especially about buying land and getting the center started. At the center people could also learn about diet, massage and yoga. They also wanted him to go to a specific place in Mexico where he would find special herbs that he could develop into natural medications. They said he had all the information and knew what he had to do; he just had to stop procrastinating and begin. He was also told that he would eventually be traveling all over the world lecturing. "He has been given spoonful's of information. He thinks he gets it, and all of a sudden something new comes. So it's been an interesting journey that he's been on. But I think he's got it now. He's getting the knowledge now through his crystals, through his meditation, through his sleeping. And through those on other planets and planes and dimensions. But he's in a hurry. He wants to get a quicker download. However, he's getting so much guidance now. He has master teachers, guides, all around him just bombarding him with information. He has been going to sleep early the last couple of months because they wanted him to be asleep, so that they could work on him, and download all of this stuff.   So, yes, he's being guided, and will continue to be guided. He also has a special connection with our brothers from the stars. He came down here for a very definite mission and purpose that will help many, many people. And he just needs to stay open because they will communicate. He's come from the stars many times, as a way-shower, as a healer, as a teacher, as a master."

Chapter 15

LEMURIA AND PORTAL

Shirley was a psychologist who was the director at a mental health hospital.

The first thing that Shirley saw was shallow, glassy water, and she was stepping into it. There was a gold-colored reflection off the water. Shirley saw herself as a young male wearing a short, white tunic. He was carrying a staff that he referred to as a guide and healing staff that was used for ceremonies. "It directs energy. It helps me to channel energy from the Source. I have direct communication and I channel it through the staff. It comes from the Source through my body to the staff." When I asked where he did the healing, he said there was a structure nearby that he referred to as the temple. He actually lived far away, but journeyed to the temple when he was needed to work with people. I asked how he knew when he would be needed. He said, "I feel a call from the temple and I travel far to come to help the people there."

D: *Is this feeling like a voice or what?*
S: It feels like a pull or a drawing instead of a voice. I know that I need to come; that it's time.

I asked him to describe the temple.

S: It's a tall, skinny, pyramid structure that has some kind of boards that cross hatch at the top. The structure itself is made out of stone, but the opening has cloth material that is the doorway you walk through ... like a tent. You go inside and there are people there. It's big and long and it's light inside.
D: *Where does the light come from?*

S: From the stone. It lights it from the inside, a soft light. Something about the material and the stone, the structure itself lights it. And there are some families and children in there. They knew I was going to come and they are happy. I welcome the people, and I go to the center of the structure, and the staff brings the energy to the structure, to the temple itself. It changes the energy and the vibration, and all the people there can feel it. It's like a healing room.

He had been taught how to draw the energy by his father. "He gave me the staff and taught me how to use it."

D: *Is there a procedure you have to go through to draw the energy in?*

S: There's a way to focus your mind to put the energy into the staff. It's a feeling. Like pulling it out of the air and putting it into the staff and holding it there until it can be released into the temple. The energy comes from the Source, from All that is. All that is around us. It is a way of pulling it in and concentrating all your energy on the staff and taking it to the temple so it resonates in that structure and brightens the people that are there.

D: *What does the energy feel like?*

S: It feels tingling. You can feel it like music in a way, when it comes through. You can feel it fill up the space. It's like filling up a bowl with water, except it's filling it with energy and it vibrates and it feels tingly and sort of warm. The room feels that way. I go to the middle and I put the staff in the middle, and the energy is released into the room and it fills the space and raises the vibrations in the room. It heals the room. It's a beautiful feeling, wonderful and it's happy. The people are happy to be there.

D: *These are people that need healing?*

S: They don't look sick. They just seem like families, and it's happy and it's positive, like an attunement.

D: *Maybe the attunement is to keep them healthy?*

S: I don't know if they need to be kept healthy. It's a brightening. They're gathered in the room and it's a happy time. And it's a brightening to bring the energy there in that room, in that temple. It feels like a celebration and ceremony; like a special event. I do this for a while - not a day - for a time and everybody feels well.

D: *Do you know when it's time to stop the energy?*

S: I do. The room is filled, then I stop and it stays for a while. Every room helps hold it. The energy is held there with the people. There's something about the material and the shape of the building. It's designed to hold that energy longer and let us experience it, and it feels light and goldenly. Very beautiful. Once the intensity subsides, they, we, move on, move out.

D: *What do you do then; go back to your home?*

S: I do. I leave. I go back to the water, the shiny water. The shiny water feels like it's grounding. That's how I get there and that's how I leave. I go back to this shallow water that's glassy, where it's shiny and you can see the gold on the water.

D: *Is that where you live, near the water or is it further away?*

S: When we talk about where I live, I see the water and the sand and the trees.

He said he lived out in nature; he didn't need a structure, and ate the food that he found there. He had been doing this for a long time.

I decided to move him ahead to an important day and asked what was happening. "I see other people have come and it's time to go. People are getting ready and we are leaving this place. Other people are there. It's time to go because something's coming. I don't know what's coming ... not safe. Time to go and other people are there.

D: *Other people that live there?*

S: No. They don't live there. They came from somewhere else. A different place. The temple people live somewhere else.

D: *They go to the temple when they want to meet you?*

S: Yes, and I live here by myself. But other people have come here from somewhere else, many people. And it's time to go because something's coming.

D: *Do the people know?*

S: The people know. That's why the people are there. They're being run out of their homes and they've come into mine, and we have to leave because it's not safe.

D: *Why were they run out of their homes?*

S: Something came to their home. I want to say a person or an energy and they couldn't stay there, and now they're leaving. Feels like a feeling came or an energy came. Something that was not there before, and is making us leave now because it's followed them. It's not comfortable. It's like a heavy energy that is pushing us away. And they've come to me where I am, but it's not safe because it's coming there and now it's time to go. They came so we could go together.

D: *Do you know anything about what this is?*

S: It's an energy source, a negative energy source that will kill us if we stay. So we have to move away. We're going to go into the water and travel away.

D: *How are you going to do that?*

S: That's how I travel. Through the water there's a portal. That's how I go to the temple.

D: *I thought if you all were going, you'd go in a boat or something.*

S: There's something in the water. It's like a grounding pad or something. When you step on the sand into the water there's a portal that we can move through. We can do it together. I'm not the only one. The others can also do it.

D: *What is it like when you go into this portal?*

S: It's like you become the air or the light or energy. We stand in the water in the sand and then move and we go through the portal. We can go to the temple. That's one of the places it leads to. We're all going to go to the temple. We're going together.

D: *Then when you get there, you have your bodies again?*

S: That's right. They left the place. We travel to the water. When we go to the other place, it's far. It's a different place. It's a different planet.

D: *So what happens when you get to the temple? The other energy can't find them there. Are you safe there?*

S: The people are. The negative energy has affected me.

He had been saying that his leg and hand felt funny, a strange tingling sensation. I did not focus on it, but gave suggestions that he would not have any physical sensations. Now he explained that the unusual feeling was caused by this negative energy.

S: The temple is a safe place. The people got out of the water, but not me. I'm not able to go to the temple. I can't go back into my body. It has affected me.

D: *So when they come out of the water, out of the portal, they go back into their bodies?* (Yes) *Now you can't get back into your body?*

S: No. I'm staying in the water. The energy affected me.

D: *How do you feel about that?*

S: I feel good that the people will be safe in that place.

D: *What are you going to do now?*

S: I'm going to die.

D: *Because you can't get back in your body?* (Yes) *Where do you think that negative energy came from?*

S: It was sent by the people that are in control; that are ruling.

D: *This country, this land?*

S: This is a planet.

I felt that since he was no longer attached to a body, he would have access to information. "Why would they want to send negative energy to your place?"

S: To kill the people, to control the people. They don't like it because we can leave and go to another place and be brightened. They're trying to stop it.

D: *Was there a reason it affected you more than the people?*

S: It touched me and I didn't move out of the way. There are usually many people there with me. We couldn't leave quickly. There were so many people and we needed them to all be in the water so we could go, and there wasn't time.

D: *You said you're going to die? How do you do that? You can watch it as an observer if you want to. What happened?*

S: I just let go. There's no reason to stay there. I can let go now.

I told him that every life has a lesson, a purpose. I wanted to know what he learned from that lifetime. "That we're not alone; that we're in this together."

I then called forth the SC to get answers to this strange session. I asked why it had chosen that lifetime for Shirley to see.

S: For her to remember. That she's not alone; that she doesn't have to sacrifice herself.

D: *Does she feel like she's sacrificing herself?*

S: Yes, at times.

D: *In what way?*

S: To help others. She doesn't have to stand in the way and let the negativity touch her. She sacrificed herself in that lifetime, to help those people.

The SC explained that she was sacrificing herself through her job, and there was a lot of negativity there that was affecting her. This was one of the main reasons for her physical problems. In her present life she had gone through a disturbing and scary time when her eyes began acting strangely. They weren't moving correctly, but independently of each other. This naturally caused disturbance in her vision, and she had to leave work until it was straightened out. The doctors couldn't explain it, and thought she had a rare disease or probably MS, and gave her shots. "She needed time away from the job ... to see again ... to see clearly. She wouldn't have allowed herself any other time away. It definitely got her attention." They explained that there was no disease, and the shots would not affect her system. *They* have the ability to flush anything out of the system that is not needed. "It was to remind her of what she knows. To remember. She had to clear some false beliefs that she had, that caused fear. The main belief was that she was sick." I had the SC do a body scan and see if there was anything we needed to be concerned about. She had had problems with her neck. "Rigid thinking. Holding on to anger."

D: *Where does the anger come from?*
S: Perceiving other people as wrong. She will start looking at things differently now.

She was told that she would be leaving her job and going in a different direction. They couldn't tell her yet what that would be, only that she would be led. I wondered if she would be using healing, like she did in the other lifetime. "She is a healer on many levels. She heals on a bigger level than for the staff and for the client." They didn't want to elaborate further at this time, but she would be using her healing abilities.

Shirley had always felt an attraction to Lemuria. I asked about that, and they said, "Lemuria is a very special place to which she has a deep connection. She had many lifetimes there and many experiences. This lifetime we showed her was Lemuria."

D: *There was negative energy and it helped to destroy Lemuria?*

S: It did. It was a negative energy field that was sent across the land. It was intentional. The people in power sent it out.

D: *What was the purpose of it?*

S: To kill the people that could go to other places and escape. The ones that had the knowledge and access.

D: *Those were the ones they were trying to get rid of. (Yes) She also always had an attraction to crystals and pyramids. That building had the shape, roughly, of a pyramid, didn't it?*

S: Yes. But those interests are from other lifetimes. She has a long history of using these abilities. It is very natural for her to be able to do this. She just needs to remember. She's about to make big changes. She'll be making changes in herself but also the work that she does. As she remembers more and more it will help her to make those changes. The time is now.

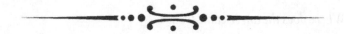

Parting message: "Remember who you are. You can do the work you came in to do."

In other cases we have been told of Lemuria. That civilization existed before Atlantis. In those days the human form was different than it became later. It was not as solid, more gaseous, so it could change shapes more easily. Later in the days of Atlantis it became more solid, and resembled more the humans that are alive today. In both civilizations they had great mental powers and excelled in the arts of healing.

There are other mentions of portals in my other books, especially Section 6 in *The Convoluted Universe - Book Two*. These are used for time travel and moving through dimensions. This is one of the main ways that extraterrestrials travel from planet to planet. Apparently in the time of Lemuria they were used more extensively by the ordinary people.

Chapter 16

PRIESTESS AT ATLANTIS

Nina worked with special education children, and also had her own healing center.

When Nina came off the cloud she found herself standing in a sandy place, almost like an oasis. But the thing that caught her attention was an opening that suddenly appeared in front of her, almost like a doorway into another dimension. It had the appearance of an elevator door. As she watched, many men and women came out and walked quickly past her. They ignored her as though she wasn't even there. They were busy talking and going about their business and paid no attention to her. Then they were out of sight, and the opening slammed shut.

Now her attention was focused on the place where she was standing. "It seems like an oasis. A place to visit, to rest. Enjoy or as we would say, 'vacation,' more than a place to live. It is warm, but not uncomfortable." She found herself dressed in short skirt-type clothes tied at the waist by something silky and flowing. More Egyptian-looking than Grecian. Bare-footed. She was a middle-aged female. Her red hair was curly and piled on top of her head with an unusual cutout decorative head piece surrounding her hair. She also had elaborate jewelry: A heavy gold scrolling bracelet that matched a similar heavy gold necklace with a red stone set into a golden round piece. The jewelry was almost masculine, heavier than what we would wear today. She also wore solid gold earrings. I have had other cases where such elaborate jewelry was used for magic or healing rituals, and had mystical powers. "Does the jewelry serve a purpose, or are they just pretty?"

N: They serve a purpose as to my status within my group. I'm more in the elite part of my group of people. It shows who you are.

217

D: *What is your status?*

N: What they call in that time: priestess, mysteries.

D: *Do you live around there?*

N: I think I might travel to that place like everyone else. It's not right there.

D: *How do you travel?*

N: By ship.

I asked for a description of the ship. Was it a normal sea-going vessel or what? "It's shiny, and more of a bubble shape." No, it did not sound like a normal vessel.

N: But the bubble is bigger in the front, and then it slims down. You could go in water, or above water. You can see through it. This is a smaller ship just for short distances, not if you're going half way round the planet. I think it's more within a confined area because I don't think it has enough fuel to go very far. It will hold five people. They bring you in, and the ship stays until you're ready to go.

In some of my *Convoluted Universe* books similar seagoing ships were mentioned as being used during the evacuation of Atlantis.

D: *But these weren't the people you saw in the beginning?*

N: Right. That was something else that those people were getting out of.

D: *When you all get back in the ship and return to where you live, what is that place like?*

N: Beautiful. It is more of an island, you could call it. It has beautiful rocks and hills, trees, and the smell of the ocean around it. And birds, and the wind blowing. It is a city, and the houses we live in are very simple. Mine is a little bigger because of being this Mystery Priestess. I have my things, I have my stones. Where I do my work, I wouldn't call it a temple, but ... I don't know the word they would call it then. The people come there, and I have my crystals, and I have waters with flowers in them. And they drink of these for things they need. And there's a place that they can lay and just relax in a tub – it's not really a tub like today – made more of stone, where they can lie in oils and herbs, flowers, and just help their bodies get well. Herbs and crystals and incantations.

D: *So they come to you if they are sick or there's something wrong?* (Yes) *Do you live in this house by yourself, or do you have a family?*

N: No, you don't marry.

D: *Do you teach others?*

N: I do the healing, but others do come to learn, more like apprentice, underneath me.

D: *Does your jewelry have anything to do with the healing?*

N: The red stone is very powerful. Protection is what I feel. And it can be used on the people if the light shines just right through it. It hooks onto the necklace. I can take the stone off and set it so the Sun goes through it until a part of a person is healed, where anything else doesn't work.

There were many people who came to her to be healed. Some of this was done through the use of crystals. There were large and small ones, and of many different colors: clear, purple, pink, green, and an orangish color. Also black, blue and deep blue, both clear and opaque. They were all used for different purposes, and the smaller ones were placed on different parts of the body, preferably the chakras. This was done after the person got out of the tub, dressed and laid on a grass mat. The larger crystals were placed around the mat. She would also use the herbs and oils. In the middle of the room was an opening made out of stone where dried plants were burned. The fumes were also considered healing, and there seemed to be incantations involved.

She explained how she came by this knowledge. "It was passed on to me by those that have come before me. I don't think it was family. You are chosen by the higher hierarchy of males if you show the ability to do this. At a younger age you're shown, and if you show as you're growing, that you have the tendencies to be this healer, then they take you and teach you. The words 'Children of Light' came into my head. If you are showing you are one of the children, or a child of light, you're mystical and you're magical, and you are chosen to go on and learn."

D: *So not everyone can do this. (No) How do you feel about that? Are you doing what you want to do?*

N: I love what I'm doing. I like helping people. It's a great responsibility, but it's very rewarding.

D: *When you went to the other place, was that on the island or somewhere else?*

N: It was another place close by. Another land not too far from our island. Our people go there for vacation.

I decided to move her forward to an important day when something was happening. "There is a gathering. It is a very important ceremony looking to the moon for guidance. There are many, many others in a circle sitting out in an open theater kind of structure. And there are those on this platform doing the ceremony. I'm up on the stage. We'll be helping, talking, performing, speaking to the great Moon, to help us for the coming of the New Year. And bringing the energies of the feminine and the love and peace. Peace." Both men and women were involved in the ceremony. "The men are there to hold the light. The women are there to carry it. Mostly the women actually do the healing, but the men need to anchor the light to come in. The men aren't really healers in the same way. They do other things. This is a very important ceremony, but it is more of a feminine thing. The moon is very close to full. At this stage it brings in this great loving feminine energy. And also it is a time when you can ask the moon for help. It can guide you with things that are important to you. Like guiding for planting, and crops, keeping the people together. This ceremony is only done twice a year."

I wanted to know if there was any type of ruler. She said there was one who was in charge, but he did not live on the island. "He comes and goes. He lives somewhere else. He comes to check." He used a different type of craft. "Bigger. Different. Almost triangular, with colored lights. And it makes no sound, very quiet. It can hover over the city. He looks somewhat different than us. His head is more elongated, he is taller. Lighter hair. He doesn't speak his voice either. He communicates through our minds."

D: Does everyone have this ability?

N: Most people can understand mind-to-mind. I can do both.

D: This sounds like a peaceful time when everyone is happy, isn't it?

N: It is. No problems right now.

I moved her ahead again to another important day.

N: I see darkness. Heaviness I feel. It's not sunny. It's dark. Like there's a gray cloud or something over this place where I am. It's heavy and kind of sad. I'm confused. I don't know where I am. It is very sad and heavy."

I decided to move her backwards to see what happened to cause this.

N: (Startled) Ohhh! ... I see people in ships. And I see stuff shooting out of the earth, the planet. Sooty stuff, and things are shaking.

D: Where are you watching this from?

N: A ship. There are many ships. There are many people on the ground. At first I thought it was the war between the

221

ships. Now I don't see that. I see something coming out of the ground.

D: *So all the people didn't get on the ships?* (No) *Why did you?*

N: I need to go so I can bring forth and preserve what I know.

D: *Was anything going on with the Earth when the ships came?*

N: It was already starting to shake. The stuff was coming out of the ground. I got into the smaller ship, and that went into the larger one. Then we were going someplace, and we were flying over, and we could see all this destruction and the darkness, and the feeling of heaviness. We didn't land. We watched. Sooty stuff. And you could feel vibrations like it was shaking underneath there. That stuff was shooting up into the air, and it forms this ... the only way I can see it is looking like a black cloud. And it's over everything.

D: *Are there others on the ship with you?*

N: There are two other women, and one man. The women are also both of knowledge. They are afraid, feeling distraught. I do not. I feel a peacefulness about it, like in awe. (This seemed like a strange reaction.) I know it will be all right.

D: *Did you know this was going to happen?*

N: I feel I did.

D: *What do you do next?*

N: At this point we are just watching it, and knowing that we will have to go somewhere else. The knowledge has to be kept. We can't let the knowledge be destroyed. It is very important for the survival of the ones who do survive.

D: *Let's move ahead. You will have to land somewhere, isn't that true?*

N: This is true. It takes a while to get there.

D: *Is it on the same planet?*

N: Yes, another place. I would say, to me, it feels like Egypt. Like that part of the world. But I don't know if it's on our Earth.

D: *Did anything happen in that part of the world?* (No) *Are there other ships or just yours?*

N: There are some that make it. And they feel some hope, and stop at another place. I feel it was Earth, or whatever planet. Whatever, it was the natural changing of things in the earth underneath it, if it is Earth. The natural things of what happens to it.

I have had many other stories of people who escaped the destruction of Atlantis by sea. Clutching desperately to their sacred scrolls and crystals they also came ashore in what appeared to be Egypt. The people at that time were more primitive and the survivors selectively chose a few that could understand enough that some of the knowledge could be passed on. Much of it was concealed within the walls of the pyramids to be discovered at a later time. Yet it could only be discovered by those who had the correct vibration and frequency to find it. Some of these people also used their mental abilities (retained from Atlantis) to build the great monuments.

I asked her to see where they eventually land.

N: Again, there's a sandy place where we come down. But I also see mountains in the background that we can travel to, to live in. We don't have to live in such a desolate place where we become our own tribe, communion. And we practice our own religions. And we have wonderful fruit trees and things that are good that we can live off of. But our knowledge still stays there. We bring that. We have to come down and share our knowledge.

D: *How do you feel about the destruction that happened on the other place?*

N: Knowing in my heart it was going to happen, I still felt sad. I couldn't change it. It was part of what needed to happen.

I decided to move her one last time to another important day. She was walking up a long flight of stairs in another temple that was made of stone with beautiful pillars. It had the appearance of Egypt. Using their knowledge they helped the people living there to build the temple. They were passing the knowledge on to a select few, one of which was a male. "Because he needs to know so he can pass it on to the other males."

We seemed to have learned as much as possible about that lifetime, so I moved her forward to the last day of her life, and instructed her that she could watch it as an observer if she wanted to.

N: I see sadness. Crying. Sadness that I know it's time to go, but I'm not quite ready to give up. The ones I have taught, there's such a bond. It's hard to let myself know that I have to leave them.

D: *Is anything wrong with the body?*

N: I don't think so. I don't feel that. I just know that it's my time to go. I am many, many, many moons older. But I felt like I was many, many moons younger. It was like I was being called home.

D: *How do you know when it's time to leave the body?*

N: I just had this feeling. The feeling just comes to me that it's calling me home.

D: *But if you're sad about it, can't you keep it from happening?*

N: I felt it was the agreement I made that I would go when I was called.

She had done much good in that life, and had passed her knowledge on to people. So I moved her to where she had left the body, and had her look back at it.

N: They put it in a resting place made of stone. It was all decorated with different colors. I was laid in the middle of this temple, and they all walked around it and said prayers.

D: Now that you are on the other side you can see the entire life. Every life has a lesson, what do you think you learned from that lifetime?

N: To go and to teach, and to help. And to know when it was time to go and that it would be all right. And how important the knowledge was that I was given for survival, for the people. And I still retain that knowledge.

I then called forth the SC and asked it why it chose that lifetime for Nina to see.

N: To show her that she can do it this lifetime. The knowledge is never lost. She must carry it forward in this life. She is working with it some, just beginning. There is much more to be brought forward. The ancient language needs to be taught. She needs to bring the ancient secrets forward. Many come from Atlantis.

D: Where was this place she was seeing?

N: A secret place.

D: Was it on Earth? (No) The original place where she was practicing these things was on the island.

N: That part was Earth. Maybe Atlantis.

D: Why couldn't they come back to where they lived before?

N: Most of where they lived was destroyed. When they got in the ships they were able to go to another planet. And she carried the knowledge, and passed it on. Now she must bring the knowledge back. For the survival of this planet, much needs to be known.

D: Is something going to happen on this planet? (Yes) Can you tell us about it?

N: There will be many parts destroyed. And there will be many who need to know the knowledge to save those who are here.

D: What's going to cause this destruction?

N: People. People that have lost the love, and people who do not believe that we are all connected. People who will not love our Earth, or each other.

D: *So people will cause this, and not a natural thing?*

N: It will be both, because it is all intertwined. Because of those who are raping our Earth, taking all the things out of the ground, and not putting it back. And poisoning everyone, and the trees and the birds and the fish, and the lakes. And they will not give up their bombs, for they think it is the power. They are so wrong.

D: *Will Nina be able to survive this, to bring this knowledge?*

N: The plan is to try and speak to as many as she can to awaken the seed, which is to help to bring the love, the compassion. And to fight – not on a warring level – but to fight on a level that people can see that we have to come together. We have to stop doing this to each other and to our mother, the Earth.

D: *This is something she must do before the disaster happens?*

N: Yes, and it's already starting. (This session was done in 2005.)

D: *Will there be time for her to spread this knowledge?*

N: There will be some time. It is starting on a very small scale. But there are others that are here to do the same from different worlds, from this world, from different cultures. There are those that are watching us. And they always say, "Do we have to pull you out of this again?"

D: *I have already met many people who are to be the healers. Many, many people are coming to me who are being told they have to help with this. And they're not aware of this consciously.*

N: No, but it's being awakened now. I think we're moving out of the minority, but the darkness is fighting so hard to keep its place.

D: *How will she be able to remember these abilities?*

N: We will guide her. There will be many she will touch. And she will know that they were together before, and the knowledge will be there.

D: *Will she instinctively know how to use this when she does her healing?*

N: No, she will learn again, to some degree.

D: *I thought maybe you could awaken the memories, so she could bring it back.*

N: I could. That would be a quicker way to do it. I could arrange that. She has a fear about using the oils and the herbs and the crystals again. There is fear because things were misused then, but not by her. – Her voice. That would be the best way for now. She is to speak of the many.

D: *What do you mean?*

N: The many in Council let her speak.

Nina told me during the interview that a strange phenomenon was occurring when she was doing her massage work with people. She had begun speaking in different languages, and she was able to understand these. She had had no training in this. Some of the languages she speaks during her healing sessions were unknown to her or the client. It would often be startling when the sounds came out. That was one of her questions, where were these voices, the different languages, coming from?

N: She has lived many times as a great healer and an alchemist. She has the secret knowledge of the mysteries.

D: *So the life we were shown was not the only time.*

N: Right. She has many, so many lives. She has an accumulation of many different types of healing knowledge. The message should be through the voice. She needs to also use her hands of healing. And yes, her flowers. Crystals too, but needs to be slowly at that, to begin with.

D: *She wanted to know why she's speaking in these other languages.*

N: They are her. And they speak when someone needs to hear them of the time in that place of her knowledge. To teach the person she's speaking to.

D: *So these are languages she knew at different times?*

N: Yes. And some come from a collective, higher power. Some are very ancient languages that are not understood by people today. But they have power, great power.

D: *She wanted to know how it works.*

N: It is the word itself, and the tone of the word. And for each that she speaks it to, it will be different. For they need to have that sound, and the way the word is said, for it to reappear within their cellular structure.

D: *Even though they don't know what the words mean?*

N: Right. Inside their cells they do.

I have had other cases where the client would suddenly begin speaking in a strange language. Sometimes it was a recognizable language, and was connected with the past life they were experiencing. But other times it did not sound like anything familiar. I have one tape recording where the client spoke for a half hour without stopping in an unknown language. I have played that tape for groups in many parts of the world (including India where there are many dialects), and no one can identify it. Mary Rodwell, a fellow investigator from Australia, has also recorded this phenomenon, and we have discovered similarities.

D: *So when she is doing the healing she is really channeling. She is connecting with her past lives. Is that what is happening?*

N: Correct. She is also to clear the waters with her voice. She is to sing a song, a song to the waters. A song to take out the negative things, the ions. All these things that people have put into the water to ruin it. She is to sing a song to it to clear it, to take out this negative energy, to send it on to be recycled.

D: *Will she know how to do this?*

N: I will say this: she goes to the water, she puts her feet in, she asks for all to come to help her. And it will flow from her mouth. There will be no problem. – Her purpose in this life is for good. Her purpose is to help save the Earth this time. Not to watch from the ship because there are many things this time that she could do to help. She is to participate instead of watching.

D: *At the beginning of the session she saw something like a doorway, and all these people came out. What was that?*

N: It was all the people she's been, many people that were her.

D: *And they didn't even notice her.*

N: No. It was more to show them to her.

D: *What was that doorway?*

N: It was the doorway to another dimension.

Almost as though these many lifetimes, representations of herself, were going past, and the SC was trying to determine which one we should focus on. The other dimension would be where they all existed, and continue to exist. It is probably one of these dimensions that we connect with when we are doing the regressions.

Chapter 17

THE STRANGE STRUCTURE

Judith is a lovely woman who works for an environmental agency. She had been having feelings of energy coming through her body and causing a jerking and movement of her head for about six years. She wanted to understand why this was happening and to have information on healing and channeling.

When Judith came off the cloud she saw an unusual and strange structure. She tried to describe it, "It's two staircases coming to a point at the top – kind of like a pyramid, kind of an 'A' shape. So you have one on the right that's going to the top, and one on the left, and they join in the middle. And it seems to be the outside of some sort of long building. It's kind of a tan color, or a light clay color. It doesn't seem like adobe. It's hard to tell. I've never seen anything like this. I'm right at the base of it, in the middle between where the two staircases meet. I have no idea where I'm at. I have no idea what this is." The unusual structure sat in what appeared to be a clearing in a jungle setting. "The forest seems to be thicker around. The trees are like a canopy. I get the sense that this might be a hot place, but because of the canopy of the forest, it's cooler. This is the only building, the only structure I'm seeing from my vantage point. I don't understand the purpose of having stairs that just go up and meet at the top like that. It doesn't make any sense, there's no platform or anything. That's weird. The stairs just go up to a point, and that's it! You can just go back down the other side!" She continued to walk around the building, looking for an entrance. "There are no openings on this side. Let me look on the other side. I don't see any way to get into this thing! It's like there's no door! That's very weird."

I then wanted to get a description of this person. She was wearing a very primitive type of sandals that appeared to be made out of some type of fiber. "They're man's feet! They're not my feet!" she exclaimed. She was wearing a thin gauzy cotton type of robe that started above her knees and wrapped around her body. "It's like one, long piece of material that wraps and comes up from the back, and across one shoulder, and is kind of tucked in, tied." It was definitely a young male body, very healthy and thinly muscular. She had light tan colored skin, and dark, dark hair. She was clean shaven with very little hair on her body. She was wearing a shiny gold hat with a portion that came down over her ears. "It's *very* shiny. – It's not pointy, it's rounded, but it's not completely form fitting to my head either. – The hat has a purpose, something to do with energy. Something to do with honing an energy." She then gave a surprised gasp. "It's like it's gathering energy and it comes to that shiny hat. And then I can use it for something. I don't know how. But it's like a transducer, or a gatherer of energies. There's something about the metal, there's something about the shape of it."

D: *Where does the energy come from?*

J: I think it must come from other dimensions. That's the sense I get. It comes from other dimensions. It's like a universal energy – gathering point or something. It comes into the hat, but it comes in contact with my head, with my brain in a sense. What am I doing with this? It affects my brain in some way, my brainwaves or something. It's a way of gathering it to the self, in a sense. It's a way of pulling it in. It's almost like the energy is everywhere, but this focuses it. I can definitely feel the energy running through my system. It feels really good. Is it healing modalities? It has something to do with that structure. (Long pause) I went to the wall, and inside.

D: *How did you get through the wall?*

J: I just walked through it! There's no door because, I guess I don't need one! It definitely has something to do with the energy. It does something to the molecules in my body.

D: *Oh! So you were able to just pass through the wall?*

J: Yes. It's kind of dark, but there's kind of a glow inside. It's like there's no source of light at all, but there's a glow that comes from nowhere. Kind of a goldish glow, with some magenta type of color in that space. – On the outside this building is long, but inside it's almost like there's no space in a sense. I don't get the feeling that there's length like there was on the outside.

D: *What do you mean, there's no space?*

J: Well, you know when you look at a building from the outside, and you think, 'Oh, you'd have to walk from one end to the other, and it would take you this long because it would take you this long to do it on the outside. But when you're inside, the space has changed. It's different. – It's like there's no space inside. (Laugh) I don't know how to explain that. There's no space inside, but there *is* space inside. It's like you're in a different building altogether.

I have come across this idea of the distortion of space in my work on UFO abduction cases.   There have been times when the person entered what they thought was a small craft, only to find that it was as much as five times larger on the inside.

D: *Is there anything inside of it?*

J: There's this glow around, but it doesn't illuminate the walls. It's just there. Where is it coming from? There's definitely energy inside here. It's like I'm humming with the energy inside this place.

D: *So that's different from the energy coming from the hat? It's two different kinds of energy?*

J: There's the energy from the hat, and then there's this. It's not the glow that's creating the energy. It's like I'm now in a space *of* this energy. It's like the energy is here in the space, and I'm utilizing the hat to get me into a kind of – maybe frequency? Where I can get into that space inside that building.

D: *Because the hat was necessary to go through the wall, wasn't it?*

J: Yes. But it's getting me into a frequency where I'm compatible. Inside the structure it's like I'm more in the source of the energy. And the hat gets me in touch with the source so I can get to it. And it gets me in touch with the energy so that I can get to the source.

D: *Is there anything else inside there that you can see?*

J: No. It's almost like there's another dimension. There is no furniture, objects. There's no space. But there *is* space. It's very spacious. I feel like if I was walking, I could walk forever around, and there would be no boundaries. But at the same time there's no space.

D: *But this energy is a good energy?*

J: Yes. Definitely. It's like a higher vibrational energy.

D: *What do you do with this energy?*

J: I'm gathering it inside there. It's being infused in me, and I'll take the energy source out with me once I leave. And I do something with it when I leave. I know when I don't need to be there anymore, and I'll just leave.

D: *How do you leave the building?*

J: Just walk out. I form in my mind that I now want to leave, and I just walk out. And the next thing I'm outside of the wall, but I didn't see the wall inside. It's like by forming my intention I walk through the wall. And now I'm outside again. I form the intention of going back outside of the source of the energy, and then I'm outside of the wall. I'm outside of the structure. It's like a portal into this certain dimension where this energy is.

D: *You didn't need to go any further into that dimension? You just went there to gather the energy.*

J: Yes, because when you get there there's nowhere to go because it's all there in that place, in that moment in that place. It's all there. And it's like you lose your body, in a sense because it changes your molecular structure. So if you were able to walk, there's nowhere to walk because you're just in that energy. And that energy is everywhere in that place. I don't know how else to explain that.

Rather like the aborigine in *Convoluted Universe, Book Two*, when he went into the side of the mountain and disappeared into another dimension.

Now that he was outside the structure again he walked away following a path through the forest. "It's a village. There are other people there. I'm the only one wearing this hat. I'm trying to figure this out. Do I make these hats? I'm coming back and there are these pieces of metal. And I do something with this metal. It's like I fire this metal? I shape this metal?   This energy is infused into this metal. And so I go there and I gather up this energy and then I come back and I work with this metal. And I'm able to take this energy and somehow put it into the metal. – I'm trying to watch what I'm doing here. I'm making different shapes out of the metal. Some of them are rods, and some of them are more like ball structures. More like balls, or elongated rods of metal. When you start out with this metal it's really dingy and dark. But I do something with it and it turns into this really shiny, shiny metal. In a completely different structure than I started out with."

D: Hmm, I wonder if that energy has anything to do with that.

J: I think it does!

D: You make these different shapes, and then what do you do with them?

J: I'm watching myself do this, and I'm feeling the feelings of this person. – It's nothing special to him what he's doing. He works with the energy; it's like a no big deal situation. It's something that he just does. I get the feeling he wishes he could be doing something else, but this is his job – his lot in life, basically. Not that he's unhappy, but it's just no big deal. You know when you're so good at something and it's so easy for you, you kind of get bored a little bit? That kind of feeling.   He puts these objects on this tray that has an edge around it. The tray is made out of a different type

235

of metal. And it's spinning around, his fingers spinning around in this thing. You know when you're making a vase from clay or something, that thing spins around? And you're forming the clay? It's like that. These pieces of metal, he puts them all onto this tray, and now it's spinning around really fast. I don't know what it's doing. I have to get a different vantage point and see what's going on. And they kind of stick to it. They don't flail all around, they stay. So maybe that's kind of a magnetic thing that holds the metal in place? And it's spinning it around, spinning it around.

I asked her to move ahead and see what he did with it eventually when it was finished.

J: The thing has stopped now, nothing looks any different. But there's something that happened with those things, energy wise, when you're doing that. And he's picking each one up and he's testing it. With his mind he's feeling it and seeing if it's right. And then he's putting them into a box. You know when you go to get a bunch of wine, and they have a box. And there is a slot for each individual wine, like a cardboard in between? It's kind of like that. This is made of metal too, and he's putting each one in different little slots to keep them separated from each other. And he takes these, and he's going to sell these to people. I think they're healing rods or something. He shows people how to use them. He doesn't make a lot of money because if the energy does dissipate from them it takes a long time. (Laugh)

D: So they can use it for a long time.

J: Yes. I think they use it on other people, too! So he's not making lots of money.

D: But they're used for healing? (Yes) What do you see them doing with them?

J: He likes these oval ones, these long, oval ones. They hold them in both their hands. (She held her hands in a cupped position.) And close their eyes. And the energies run through them. And they concentrate on what they want to heal. For instance, if they have some sort of injury, or they have some sort of illness, malady – they concentrate on that disk, or rod, or whatever. Different rods do different things, and it just heals it.

She explained that they would cup their hands and hold the disk shaped ones, and then put both their hands around the long rod types.

J: I can feel the energy running through it. (Pause) I think the long, thin rods have more to do with the physical. Physical things like an injury, maybe a sprained ankle or something like that. And the oval ones get you more in touch with spiritual things. The shape definitely changes the function.

D: *Is he the only one that can get the energy and make these things?*

J: Yes, he's the only one in that area.

D: *So he makes these and sells them to the people.*

J: Yes. It's not about money. There's no money there. But it's trades or something like that. I don't get the sense that the people worry about money. Or they don't worry about, "Do I have enough," or something like this. People can barter or that sort of thing. There are not many material things, but that's not what these people are about anyway.

I then had her leave that scene and move forward to an important day.

J: I'm looking at a huge diamond in the sky. It has many facets. It almost looks like two pyramids put base to base. It's beautiful! It shimmers like the sun on water, and it's just up in the sky. And I'm looking at it. – I can't say it's turning on its axis, but it's doing something. It never loses its shape,

237

but it changes slightly, constantly. It makes it look like it's moving back and forth a little bit.

D: *What is this thing?*

J: (Pause) It's a messenger. (That was a strange response.) It's a messenger. It's telling me something. I'm all by myself. I'm in a clearing again. It's a different kind of clearing. I didn't know that it was going to be there.

D: *Maybe that's why it's appearing to you, because they didn't want the others to see it?*

J: Yes. I don't know if the others *could* see it, anyway.

D: *You said it's a messenger, and it's telling you something. How is it telling you?*

J: I don't know. Through energy. I'm getting these waves and waves and waves of energy. But it's not like you can see this energy coming from it to me. I can just feel it. It's far away, but I can feel the waves hitting me.

D: *But you are used to working in energy.*

J: Yes, but that energy was just there. And this energy is full of information. It's telling me things that are going to happen, in a sense, and the way that I need to deal with it. And the way that I need to instruct others to deal with it. You know, these people don't really care about this stuff. I am one of them, but I am not one of them, in a sense. They like the fact that these rods can heal, but they don't have any appreciation for it. They've lost their appreciation for the changes in the seasons, and the changes in things that happen in life.

D: *Kind of like they take everything for granted, you mean?* (Yes) *What did you mean that you were not one of them?*

J: I have a lot of understandings about energy and how it works. There's just no one who cares! There's no one who wants to learn about it. They don't understand that if I'm gone, no one makes these rods anymore. Nobody is going to be able to be healed after that. It's like they take it for granted and they don't understand the consequences. *I* understand the consequences. The consequences are that they could move forward to the point where they don't need these things anymore. And the rods are a tool to help them understand that they could move forward with this. But because they have the tool that takes away their aches and pains and this and that and the other things, that's enough for them. They don't want to move forward. And so once these tools are gone, they're going to revert back. They're not going to move forward, they going to revert.

D: *They wouldn't even try to make any because they wouldn't know how.*

J: They have no idea.

D: *Did you say that you are not from there?*

J: Yes. I mean I stand way apart. And I think maybe I'm not from there originally either. I'm so different. But because they don't care, I don't care about what I'm doing anymore either.

D: *If you're not from there, where did you come from?*

J: I came from the place where that diamond is.

D: *The messenger?* (Yes) *Is this why you can relate to it?* (Yes) *But it sounds like you've been there a long time.*

J: Yes, I have. I've been here way too long. Way too long. And the society hasn't moved forwards. They're going to end up moving backwards. It's taken the excitement out of the whole thing for me because I'm making these things, and they're using these things, and I'm going to be gone at some point. And then they're not going to have them anymore. And it makes me sad that they don't even care. No one is thinking, "Wow, we really need to learn more about this."

D: *Were you born there? Or how did you get there?*

J: I was found by someone as a baby in the forest. I was just found there. I was left there by these beings.

D: *The beings from the diamond craft?*

J: I think so, yes.

D: *What do these beings look like?*

239

J: They're very tall and thin and white. Tall.

D: *Do you look like them?*

J: No, I'm more like a human. They're not human. How did they get me?

D: *You can find out if you want to. (Pause) Can you see where you came from originally?*

J: I was born on a ship. I was born in that diamond thing. There are a few people on this planet who live there. It's as if they've transcended or something.

D: *Do they look human?*

J: Oh, yes, they're just like the people on the planet. I don't know if it was genetic engineering or something. There was something that took place when I was conceived.

D: *That made you different from the others?*

J: Yes. So I could go down and help.

D: *That was the idea anyway.*

J: Yes. But it didn't work.

D: *Well, let's move back to where you were standing outside looking at the diamond shape, and you said it was a messenger giving you information. You said it had something to do with something that was going to happen?*

J: Yes. It's not direct information like saying, "Okay, this is going to happen, and this is going to happen, this going to happen, this is when it's going to happen." It's not like that. It's like an organic knowing about things. So I can feel when things are going to happen, or when bad things are going to happen. And basically, I'm going to leave this place soon.

D: *You said you were getting bored anyway.*

J: Yes. But am I going to die, or am I going back on the ship? I don't know.

D: *We can find out. We can condense time and move ahead to when it happens. How do you leave the planet?*

J: (Pause) I'm back on the ship with them.

D: *How did you get on the ship?*

J: It was like when I kept going to that building. It was the same kind of thing. It's like I was transported there.   It could have been from the building. I went into the building and then they were able to – I was just there on the ship. I was there. – But I'm really sad.

D: *Why are you sad?*

J: Because I feel I let them down.

D: *You did the best you could. The rest was up to them, wasn't it?*

J: Yes, it was. But these tall beings had hopes for this. They were trying. I was their hope that this could move forward.

D: *But they didn't take advantage of it. It's not your fault.*

J: No, but I always think, "What could I have done?" Because now I'm at a different vantage point.   Now I think of things: well, maybe I could have talked to them more, or maybe I could have ... I had some sort of disdain for them. And so I didn't try as hard as I could have. There are two beings that are talking to me. (Pause) I'm telling them that I feel I failed. (Pause) They're just imparting a feeling to me of non-judgment, and it's okay. It's not that they talk. It's an imparting of information through the energy. The situation didn't work out the way it was hoped to have worked out. But I did the best that I could, and they understand that I was run down emotionally about the whole thing.

D: *You can only do the best that you can do.*

J: (Softly, wistfully.) Yes.

I then removed Judith from the scene. There did not seem to be any purpose in taking her to the day of her death because that could have occurred many years from then. I thought we had covered the main points of the story anyway. I then called the SC forth to explain the session. "Why did you pick that for Judith to see?"

J: Because we wanted Judith to know that this is what she does. She knows she feels energy. That is connected to that lifetime, and all of her experiences, all of her lifetimes.

D: *Do you mean that all the lives she's ever lived she's worked with energy? (Yes) On the planet Earth or somewhere else?*

J: On many planets. The lifetime she was just looking at was not Earth. In most of her lives she's dealt with energy. Other lives were learning lives so that she would be able to deal with certain facets of the existence, so that she would be able to then utilize the energy better.

D: *But in this life she hasn't used it yet, has she?*

J: She's using it; she's not using it consciously.

D: *She said she feels this energy moving through her, and it can be quite strong at times.*

J: Yes. She's still learning how to work with it physically.

D: *Where is that energy coming from that she experiences?*

J: It's coming from other facets of herself. It's filtering down into this dimensional plane where this part of her exists. She understands what's happening in a certain sense. This is who she is, she's had a problem accepting it. There are certain things that she needs to come to terms with before she can work with this energy effectively in this plane. First of all, she needs to accept this as part of her existence. Secondly, she needs to deal with the more human emotions, dealing with unworthiness, fear of being different, things of that nature. She has to do some work on herself first. Then she'll be able to do the healings that she wants to do. She'll be able to channel this energy in different ways. There are many, many ways to channel this energy. She only thinks of what she knows. Healing is one. The transference of information is another. But the way she thinks about it is just verbally. There are many ways to channel information, not just verbal. She knows this on other realms, but she doesn't understand it here.

D: *Because as humans we work mostly verbally.   That's the way we operate.*

J: Yes.   She can use this in any way that she wants. Healing is something she is interested in because she's interested in helping people. The energy was withdrawn for a short time so that she could adjust to certain things. But now the energy is coming back again, and she'll learn how to deal with more energy more effectively. She does control it, but she doesn't understand the way she controls it.   It's not the conscious part of her mind that she thinks she should be able to control it with. So as she stretches into other dimensional planes she will automatically gain more control over these abilities, and the energy that she is. She will come to a certain state of knowing, an organic knowing. The knowing, the information, will just be there. As she comes to accept who and what she is, the knowledge will come with that. This energy is an energy of knowledge and healing.

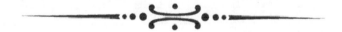

D: *Why is the age of three so important to Judith? She always keeps going back to thinking about the age three.*

J: It was at this age that she fully came into the body. It was at this age that she still had knowledge of who she was on other levels. It was at this age when she decided to stay and explore.

D: *Do you mean before the age of three she was not totally in the body?*

J: No, her consciousness was not totally in the body. This is actually a normal occurrence with children at that age. Until they're at a certain age they're popping in and out all the time.

I had been told that we do this up to the age of two, but I suppose it can actually be longer.

D: *Then this was important because she decided to stay and fully enter into the body?*

J: Yes, and she was also still aware of herself on other levels, and made a very strong decision to utilize that knowledge in ways that she could be of assistance here. This is a very ripe time when she was still not completely conditioned into the ways of this realm.

Chapter 18

ATLANTIS

Mitchell was a difficult case and I really had to work to get to the point where we could get information. This sometimes happens when the client is a "control freak," or is in an occupation that causes them to focus more on their left brain. The left side of the brain is the part dealing with control, analysis and numbers. When I get a client who is an engineer, a CEO of a big corporation, an accountant or a math professor (Ugh! The absolute worst!), I know I will have to work doubly hard to move them out of that side of the brain, and over into the right side where the pictures and memories are located.

In Mitchell's case he was able to visualize, but they were all scenes from this life. I moved him backward through this life until he was a baby. Then I tried to move him beyond so he would end up in another lifetime or on the spirit side planning his present life. Yet nothing seemed to work. I am very patient, and after over 45 years of doing this I have a large bag of tricks. When working with this type of personality I have to work harder and pull out many of these tricks, but it can be done. The longer the person is under the deeper they are going into trance, even though they may be trying to fight it. I can eventually break down that resistance and get to the point where the information will come through. Most hypnotists don't have that kind of patience to keep trying, so they wake the client up too soon. I know if we keep at it, it will happen. It just takes more work.

In Mitchell's case I tried several different methods and although he was visualizing, he was not getting past life scenes or any useful information. He had already been under for an hour, so I knew he was deep enough that I could try to call forth the SC. At first he even tried to control that and keep it from coming through. That old stupid conscious mind can be powerful sometimes, even though that is not the part I want. That part knows absolutely nothing useful, yet it does not want to give up control. Finally I saw the signs that the SC was winning the battle and I would be able to communicate with it. Even so, I had to be alert when the conscious mind tried to slip back in. When I knew it was there, my first question was, "Why didn't Mitchell see any past lives?"

M: His fear of failure gets in the way.

D: *Why is he afraid of failure?*

M: Because he's been told for a long time that he has potential.

D: *He has wonderful potential, doesn't he?*

M: Yes, he does. And he has fulfilled some of it.

D: *But he still fears failure?*

M: He feels the fear of failure. He's also suffered. He has a hard time surrendering, because sometimes when he was not able to be in control, he suffered.

D: *You mean in other lifetimes?*

M: In other lifetimes and this lifetime.

D: *That's why he doesn't want to see those other lifetimes?*

M: He does want to see them, but he's holding himself back. Fear of being out of control and suffering the consequences.

I then had a conversation with the SC about the helpfulness of seeing some of these things. If Mitchell knew the cause he would be better able to understand its effects on his present life. I suggested that the SC just tell him about some of the significant lives. Mitchell didn't have to see them if they thought that might disturb him. The SC could just tell him about them. That would be a safe way. "Was it in a certain time period?"

M: This was from many different time periods. It has happened several times.

D: *That's why it's hard to just pick one?*

M: Yes. He's aware of failing in Atlantis.

D: *How did he fail?*

M: He wasn't strong enough. He didn't have the emotional mastery to stay in the place he needed to in order to work the energies in the way they needed to be worked. To work the energies through the crystals requires being very centered.

D: *Were there others doing the same thing?* (Yes) *How did they direct the energy into the crystals?*

M: With their minds. They had control of their intention and their attentions, which you can't do if you're in an emotionally fearful place. Emotions interfere when out of balance. When in balance they can empower intentions.

D: *Was something happening that created fear?*

M: He doubted he had the ability to match the power of those with other agendas. The ones directly in his presence were working together. Others in Atlantis had other agendas. The egos got in the way of these technologies, and their egos got in the way of higher agendas.

D: *There were two different groups?*

M: Yes, although the other group had factions, they weren't exactly united in their agendas, although they were all egoistic. They were trying to harness Mother Earth's energies. Their intentions were control, in today's terms, of military uses. Definitely not for the higher good of humanity or of nature. They were succeeding in harnessing the energies, but not in control of it. They didn't know what they were doing. Their egoistic beliefs in their own abilities were not in line with reality. They weren't as powerful as they thought they were.

D: *Playing around with something they weren't supposed to?*

M: Correct. His group was trying to support Mother Earth in maintaining balance.

D: *They were doing this by projecting energy into the crystals?*

M: Yes. A more harmonious, loving energy, you might say, when their own emotions were out of balance. That was difficult.

D: *That was hard for humans to do, to overcome their own emotions?* (Yes) *But in those days they had no control over their emotions?*

M: They did at one time, not at the end. Not enough.

D: *So in the end when they were doing this, he doubted his own abilities?*

M: Yes. At the end in his heart he knew they were not going to be successful.

D: *There were two powerful energies working, weren't there?*

M: Yes, which is usually the case in these realms of duality. His intentions were good. He did the best he could.

D: *So he didn't really fail. It was just too difficult, too big of a job. What happened at the end? They weren't able to maintain the positive energy?*

M: Correct. It was like an incoming wave meeting an outgoing wave at the shoreline, and then they come together. There was a rapidly moving, energetic response, which was large enough to rearrange the Earth.

D: *That would be a terrific power, wouldn't it?* (Yes) *One was canceling the other out?*

M: No. One was larger than the other. The negative one.

D: *You said it ended up rearranging the Earth? What do you mean by that?*

M: Atlantis was torn asunder, although not completely all at one time, but the process was begun.

D: *So it was a gradual process?*

M: There was an immediate loss of souls. Atlantis and the remainder over time followed. It is a protective device.

D: *What do you mean?*

M: When powers assembled by the mind go beyond the growth of consciousness, rather than allowing destruction of all, those minds will be removed to start again. That's the protective device. Shut down the consciousness that's going awry. The technology is removed from control of that consciousness. The slate is wiped clean to some extent to allow the consciousness time to catch up, even if that requires time to start over.

D: *But this can take a long time to start all over again.*

M: It can appear that way, but time is really not a significant issue in the overall scheme of things.

D: *So this is why Atlantis had to be wiped out?* (Yes) *There were also many good people there, weren't there?*

M: Yes, that's true. Keeping in mind that all that is wiped out is a physical aspect.

D: *What happened to Mitchell in that life? You said he wasn't able to fulfill all that he was doing?*

M: True. His physical body died.

D: *You said some of Atlantis was destroyed gradually. How was it destroyed?*

M: The physical aspect of what was called Atlantis was eventually covered by the seas for the most part. It is an efficient way to wipe the slate clean and to remove the offensive technologies.

D: So he died in the water when it came in? (Yes)

Refer to the chapter in *The Three Waves of Volunteers*, Chapter 31 (Keepers of the Grid), for a more detailed explanation of the incredible power that was unleashed and almost destroyed the Earth. Everything had to be destroyed to keep that from happening.

D: *So he has carried this sense of failure, but he was fighting insurmountable odds.*

M: Yes, he was.

D: *So he shouldn't feel personally responsible for something he couldn't control.*

249

M: That's true. The residue was in his emotional body. The emotional residue carries forward into other lives.

D: *So he had other lives where he felt he had failed?*

M: Yes, yes. For Mitchell the emotional dynamic of what he carries has often become a self-fulfilling prophecy. It is a good time to let go.

D: *Because we don't want him to continue carrying it any further. The karma should be paid by now, shouldn't it?*

M: There are no "shoulds." It either is or it isn't. It would be a good time to let it go.

Then the SC agreed to remove the residue from the emotional body. But first it had to have Mitchell's permission because of free will. Mitchell readily agreed. I asked it to tell me how it was going to remove the residue. "It can be wiped clean. It's a matter of calming the waters." Even during the work Mitchell's conscious mind was trying to interfere. The SC said he was trying to come back in. I knew that would only hinder what was being done, so I had Mitchell stand over to the side and watch and listen, but not interfere. He agreed to do that. He was breathing heavily while the SC worked on the emotional body. While it was doing this I continued with Mitchell's questions. Of course, there was always the main one, the eternal question, "What is his purpose?"

M: He's been around for a long time. He was involved in anchoring the energies in different areas of the Earth. He had the foundation energies for the different indigenous cultures and the wisdoms that they hold. It was part of the creative process.

D: *What do you mean?*

M: Earth is a school. It has different classrooms. Different classrooms carry different frequencies to support different expressions of culture knowing creativity. Each culture had its own music, its own language, and its own frequencies.

D: *How do you want him to do this now?*

M: It is what he has done without realizing it at the time. Traveling throughout the world always meeting shamans, different teachers in different cultures. His being there acknowledged their presence and the validity of their cultural gifts, and served to reawaken those wisdoms that are emerging. And in Mitchell's case, he was carrying pieces of those original energies ... from the original anchoring of those energies. His presence is like a key in the lock to open a door to the full emergence or re-emergence of those frequencies. – He was there before the cultures emerged, but planted the energies.

D: *He probably didn't have a physical body at that time, did he?*

M: No. It's a place like Machu Picchu. The reason that Machu Picchu was there was because the energy was already there.

D: *And the people who built these places felt that energy?* (Yes)

Question about any karma to repay: "Karma is a personal thing. He's done a good job of balancing old karma – *old* being a tricky term since there's only *now* – while not creating new karma.

D: *So at least we accomplished what we'd set out to do in this session, even though we had to go over and under and around to get there. But that was his belief system that was blocking the whole thing, wasn't it?*

M: Yes, his fears.

D: *But you know me, I don't give up.*

M: Thank you. (We both laughed.) We will be supporting him.

Parting message: We appreciate his heart, his heartfelt intentions and his integrity, and appreciate all he's doing to bring humanity to their full potential. God bless you, Mitchell. Thank you, Dolores, and bless you.

I have other cases that are similar to Mitchell's. One such case involves Cathy from Nevada who went to a crystal city where they used energy very similar to Atlantis. But it was on another planet. The SC said other planets went through similar problems because that civilization met the same fate through the misuse of crystals. She is to bring back her knowledge of the use of the crystal energy and use it for healing.

Another case is Christy from Memphis. She used a frequency machine for healing that utilized light to regulate frequencies to bring the body into harmony. It relied on the person's mind power. It could be operated by one person and produced pure energy. It was real, it was effective, but it sat unused. The other healers preferred to use crystal machines. They were powerful, yet they distorted the energy. They were crystals in boxes with some type of fluid. Light shining through the boxes generated the power from many people in the room. It was used for the wrong purposes (especially sexual) and distorted the effects.

And yet another case is Denise from Memphis. As the Atlanteans learned more about the use of energies and their knowledge expanded, they were fascinated by the manipulation of energy. They discovered new ways to experiment with it and direct it. They lost sight of using it for positive purposes in their life, such as healing and balancing. When the energy (multiplied by many people concentrating and giving it increased power) was used for negative reasons it became misdirected and distorted and turned destructive. It became so powerful it turned in on itself. This was one of the reasons for the destruction of Atlantis.

Chapter 19

THE HIDDEN RECORDS OF ATLANTIS

Julie was a young college student who did not seem to have any serious problems. She mostly wanted to have the session because she was concerned about which career to pursue.

She came down on a desert with yellow sand as far as the eye could see. She was standing next to what at first appeared to be a wall, but was, on closer examination, found to be a very large pyramid. It was a solid structure that was smooth and very shiny. "It's shiny and it's warm... very powerful. You can feel the heat coming off of it. I think the heat is just the power of the many. It's a comforting feeling. As I walk around it, there's something on top of it, like an antenna or something."

I asked her to become aware of her body. "Rope sandals. I can feel the heat from the sand. White cloth around my waist going just to my knees. A top of some kind, but nothing I've really seen before. Sleeveless, kind of like a vest. - Reddish skin. Very dark brown hair tied in the back by something." She was a young man, maybe in his late twenties. He was wearing gold bracelets decorated with swirls. Also wearing a large pendant (about the size of a fist) around his neck, that had a carving on it that he did not describe.

J: I'm looking for the door.

D: *Do you want to go inside of some reason?*

J: Yes. I'm trying to find something.

D: *Do you know what you're looking for?*

J: The library, I think. Books. There's a brick I have to press in the side of the wall. Then part of the wall moves away.

There's a stairway down. I go down the stairs. I have a torch. The stairs lead to a passage. I turn right. Thick walls on either side and at the top. The passage is barely bigger than I am.

He kept walking and turning corners and down more stairs until he came to a wooden door. "For this one I need a key."

D: *Do you have a key?*

J: Yes, that's what my necklace is. The pendant. I press it to the door and turn it. There's an indentation on the door that matches my pendant. There's a dial with the pendant on it, and you spin it on the door. You hear the locks creak and then it opens.

D: *So not just anyone can go in there. You have to have this special key.*

This seems very similar to Deb in the *Crystal Skulls* chapter, except they sound like they are in different parts of the world.

J: It's a very, very large room, high ceilings, lots of books. And everything seems to glitter. Like treasures hidden away ... a lot of knowledge. I'm looking around the room making sure nothing's gone. I am the guardian of this room. I don't think people know I'm the guardian. I think it's a secret. I do something else, but I do this as well.

D: *What is the other job that you do?*

J: I write.

D: *Do you do it in this place, or in another place?*

J: Both. I'm writing on stone.

D: *Is it hard to write on stone?*

J: I don't use my hands. I think the words and they appear.

D: *That's like magic.* (Yes) *What are you writing about?*

J: History of a civilization no longer there.

D: *Can you tell me some of the things you are writing?*

J: The symbols don't make sense. I don't understand them *now*. They're not words. They're an alphabet that I don't know.

D: *What do you do with the stone whenever you finish the writing?*

J: They're stacked against the wall. They become part of this library.

D: *But nobody else can see this but you?*

J: They're not ready to see it.

D: *These are things that just you know and nobody else?*

J: Now, yes.

D: *What do you mean by "now"?*

J: Those people are no longer there. That civilization is gone.

D: *The ones who built this pyramid?*

J: No, not this one.

D: *A civilization in another place?*

J: Yes ... lots of water.

D: *How do you know about that civilization?*

J: I believe I was sent away so others would know when they needed to.

D: *And you were supposed to preserve the writing of the history of it? (Yes) And you came to this place. And here you are trying to write the history so people will know?*

J: Yes. It's very important.

The other place where he wrote was in a village that was near the pyramid. The people were unaware of his work in the pyramid. In the village he scribed letters for very important people. There were not many people who could write. He was essentially living two lives. In the village he had a normal life with a family. "I live in a very nice house, nicer than the other ones." He also wrote books. "They would call them fiction, but they are stories of a time that has passed."

D: Do you write those also with your mind?

J: No, I write those by hand. I sell them. They're very popular. They are based on times of the past.

I moved him forward to an important day, and he said he had gotten very old. "It's time for me to leave the town and I hand my pendant down to another man."

D: You're passing on the knowledge?

J: Yes, but not the knowledge - The guardianship.

D: So it will not be lost?

J: So it will not be found yet. It will be found eventually.

D: Did you show the other man how to do the writing with the mind?

J: No, that's finished.

D: You have all the history of the place you came from? (Yes) So this man doesn't have to know that? (No) He's just supposed to watch it. He doesn't have to know all the magic that you knew. Maybe some of those things can't be passed on. Is that what you mean? (Yes) Can you tell me some of the history you wrote about of the place you came from? It will remain secret. I won't tell anyone. (Oops!! Only a few thousand readers!)

J: They lost respect. They no longer respected one another. There was too much competition, not enough brotherhood. They no longer loved one another. They wanted to prove themselves better than one another. They disrespected nature as well, and nature didn't like that. There were earthquakes and much water, too much water.

D: Were you there when it happened?

J: No, but I could feel it. I think I was connected to those who were there.

D: Do you think eventually someone will locate the records?

J: Yes, when they're ready.

He said he was already very old, so I had him go to the last day of his life to find out what happened to him. "I'm already gone. They've loaded me onto a boat with many candles and they are pushing me out into the water."

D: What was wrong with the body? Were you ill?

J: No, I think just old. I was never sick.

D: Is that the way they do it when someone dies?

J: That's the way I wanted. I wanted to go back to be with my brothers and sisters.

D: What do you mean by "going back"?

J: To the water ... back where I came from. I think I was just tired. I had done what I had to do and it was time to go.

D: What do you mean, "You came from the water"?

J: I think that's where I traveled from to get to where I was.

D: Whenever the other civilization went down? (Yes) So you wanted to return and they respected that by putting you on the boat and sending it out.

J: Yes. I'm gone. I saw the boat being pushed, so I left. Now I'm floating back up.

D: Do you know where you're going to go?

J: No. Just float.

D: Are you glad to be out of the body? (Yes)

I asked him to look back at the entire lifetime and see what the purpose of it was. "To bring the knowledge, but to keep it safe as well, so those in this era don't repeat the mistakes."

D: Where you are now, can you see if that knowledge is still preserved at that place? (Yes) No one has found it yet? (No) That's good. It's still safe and protected from anybody changing anything.

I then called forth the SC to get more information. I asked it why it chose that life to show Julie. "To write is to be able to find the knowledge. It's important to spread the knowledge to the people. Writing is a good path."

Of course, this was one of her main questions: What was her purpose? What was she supposed to be doing? She had many talents and many paths she could take. She had already traveled much of the world. The SC said that was one of the paths she could take, and it was an important one. "She's getting an impression of the world, of it being a globe. Her travels, those experiences will influence the writing. She's learning not to judge. Much travel. By teaching people to learn to live with one another and not to judge a book by its cover. The photography. The image will be very important as well." There was much more information given about her career, and her personal life. Some things she could not know yet, "Suspense is the spice of life."

D: *The civilization she was talking about, was that Atlantis or another civilization? The one that was destroyed?*

J: Some have called it that.

D: *She said she wasn't there, and didn't die when it went down.*

J: No. She was sent away to save the knowledge because she was still connected to the people there. She felt them when they no longer existed on this plane.

D: *That way she could retain the memories to write about it?* (Yes) *How did she travel?*

J: By boat, before the last disaster.

D: *The last disaster? People have said there were a series of things that happened?* (Yes) *Does that pyramid still exist?*

J: In a different form. It is changed, but it is still there.

D: *In those days, she described it as smooth and bright. How has it changed?*

J: Another was put on top, a different shape.

D: *Something was built over it?* (Yes) *What happened to the original?*

J: It was destroyed somehow.

D: *But the knowledge was underground, wasn't it? (Yes) So that wasn't destroyed, was it?*

J: No. Those who needed to know built a new form and a new tunnel.

D: *What does the new form look like that was built over it?*

J: Much like a cat. Very big, but not quite as big as the forms that surround him.

D: *What do those forms look like?*

J: Much like the ones that were destroyed.

D: *So they built another entrance. You said it's like a cat. Is the entire structure like a cat?*

J: No, it was supposed to be, but it was changed at the last minute, and the face is someone that ruled that land. An ego changed it.

It was obvious she was referring to the Sphinx. This also sounded very similar to the story in *The Convoluted Universe – Book Two*, Chapter 3 about the Cat People. In that story the original Sphinx had the face of a woman and the body of a cat. And it was changed when men came into power.

D: *I think I know what you are talking about, and they say the face is too small for the body. (Yes) Was it originally the face of a cat?*

J: It was originally meant to be. It was changed before it was finished.

D: *Do you think in time this knowledge will be uncovered?*

J: Yes. It is not long, but people won't know immediately. It will stay secret when they find it.

D: *Why will it still stay secret?*

J: Too much power. There's power in knowledge, and of keeping knowledge from others.

D: *So they won't want people to know.* (No) *But eventually it will come out.* (Yes)

It has been said by many (including Edgar Cayce) that the Sphinx sits on a Hall of Records. I have spoken to people who have explored underneath the Sphinx, and they said there are tunnels down there. One of the reasons they have not been fully explored is because they are normally full of water.

In some of my other books it is said that the entrances to the rooms where the records are located are protected by something similar to electrical fields. So you would have to be of the correct vibration and frequency to even come near them. The ancients incorporated many very clever protective devices.

Chapter 20

ATLANTIS EXPERIMENTATION

Amber had worked as a nurse for many years, but quit after she experienced "burn-out." She wanted to try a different career and was now working in an office.

This session began as a normal, typical past life regression, but it took a strange twist before it was over. I always expect the unexpected.

Amber saw herself as a forty-year old man sitting in the crow's nest of a large ship with big white sails. She saw that they had stopped near an island. All she could see was lots of jungle and a rocky beach. There were no docks, so the sailors were lowering boats and rowing toward the land. The man did not go with them, but stayed on the ship and watched from the crow's nest. He saw the sailors pull their boats up on the land and get out and go into the jungle. He knew they had landed there to look for food, or anything of value. They had been at sea for about thirty days and their supplies were running low. Only a skeleton crew remained on the ship. "It's tedious, it's patience, but it's boring. It would be more exciting to go with them."

This could have taken some time, so I moved time forward to see if anything happened. "I'm on the railing watching them. They were attacked. There were savages. They're fighting. They're trying to get away from them and are coming back to the ship."

D: *Were they able to get any food, or do you know?*

A: No. It was an ambush. Not many make it back. Many of them were killed. It was like a slaughter. They were caught unaware and were surprised. Some of them got on the boats. They're hurt. They're bleeding. They make it back on the ship, but they don't live. They were hit by something

261

like poison darts, from spear tips or something. They are puffing up and turning colors: blues and blacks. We're afraid we're going to get that. We're pushing them overboard. And I'm trying to raise anchor and get out. There are not too many of us left. We're a skeleton crew and we're trying to get away.

D: *What about the captain?*

A: I want to say he's a sissy, not much help. He's weak and not a good commander.

D: *So he didn't go ashore with the others?*

A: He did, but he made it back. He let our men die. He was chicken. He was a coward.

D: *So there aren't many of you left to take care of the ship?* (No) *Are you able to do it?*

A: We do it, and are heading out to sea. We know enough to do that, but I don't know if we will survive. I don't think we have enough food.

D: *They didn't have enough time to find any, did they?*

A: No, and we're down to the bare minimum. We have to try something. We have to try. Either that or die at the hands of the savages. We have to get away from them. We're raising the sails now. We just want to get out to sea.

D: *How do you feel about the situation?*

A: We're in a "damned if you do and damned if you don't." If we stay we die, if we take the risk. The only choice is to go and try to survive at sea.

D: *Have you been sailing long?*

A: My whole life ... I started out as a cabin boy.

D: *Then you're away from home for long periods of time, aren't you?*

A: I don't have a home. I don't have a family. I just jump from ship to ship. – I'm thinking I should have never signed on with this ship, with this captain.

D: *Did you have feelings that he didn't know what he was doing?*

A: I didn't know it at the time. I don't think I realized he was such a coward.

I was going to have him move forward to see what happened, but before I had a chance to do that he announced, "We don't survive at sea. We don't have enough water. There's no wind. We're dead in the water. We're all fading, fading, fading. We ran out of food a long time ago. Now the water is gone. We've lost men. There's no wind. We're all dying slowly. I'm one of the few remaining." I moved him forward to see what happened. "It's quiet. The ship is rocking. Everyone's dead."

D: *Are you one of the last ones?*

A: Yes ... I'm leaving too, though. I know it's coming to an end soon. There's no wind.

I moved him to where it was all over and he was on the other side, and asked if he could see his body. "Yes. We're just kind of lying there. There's no life." I then asked what he thought he learned from a life like that. "Patience. I want to say 'patience,' even patience in dying. I wasn't one of the first. I was one of the last to go. Patience in death, even in death you need patience. I learned patience, and I have to rely on myself. I can take care of myself."

D: *Yes, your entire life was always taking care of yourself.* (Yes)

Because the lifetime had been short I knew we had enough time to explore another past life. So I had her leave that scene and move to another appropriate time where there was something else she needed to know. When she arrived there she found herself in the courtyard of a big stone building like a church with a bell tower. She called it an "abbey." She saw that she was a young nun dressed in a white habit, and she knew she hadn't been in this place very long. She was all alone in the courtyard because the other nuns were tending the gardens.

Then she noticed something that surprised her. "My knees hurt really badly. It seems like I can't move. I'm in a chair ... an old wheelchair. I can move my upper body, but my legs are straight out. My knees hurt. I don't know if there are braces or.... I use my arms and I wheel. I can't go everywhere. I think I just sit out there." During all this conversation she was repeatedly yawning and trying to talk over it. I wanted to know what happened to her, and she said she had been thrown from a horse. "Not even that long ago, so my family brought me here because I'm damaged goods. No one would marry me. I wouldn't be able to be a wife and mother. I didn't want to come here, but they didn't know what to do with me. Maybe they thought I needed quiet. They didn't know how to take care of me, and what would they do with me?"

D: *Do the nuns take care of you?*

A: They do.

D: *Do you like the church, that kind of life?*

A: No, it wasn't what I wanted to do. I'm bored, but I can't leave.

She kept yawning, "I'm tired. I think I drank something to make me tired. I think they gave me something. A tea."

D: *What did they give you the tea for?*

A: I think for pain. It doesn't hurt as much now.

I moved her forward to an important day. She announced, "Somebody's coming to the abbey. They're all bustling about ... bustling, bustling and preparing. I'm not able to help."

D: *Is there anything you can do from a wheelchair in this place?*

A: I read, but their books are all uninteresting. ... They're all bustling about preparing. Somebody's coming. There's a carriage coming up. I'm not allowed out. I'm hidden. They put me in bed again. Something I was drinking. I think it is this tea, and it makes me tired." (She was still yawning repeatedly.)

D: *It sounds like they are giving you something that makes you sleepy. Why are they hiding you?*

A: They wanted me to sleep. They gave me a tea. I'm so tired. I can't figure out what's happening.

D: *That sounds like medicine. They help you get into bed?*

A: Yes, I need help to get in and out.

D: *Were you able to see who was coming?*

A: Looked like someone important giving money or donations or something. I sleep through the whole thing.

D: *Are they nice to you?*

A: Yes, they're okay. I'm a burden to them. Another mouth to feed ... and no help. And I don't want to be here either.

D: *Where do you eat?*

A: We go into a big brown room and we have meals. It's on the ground floor, so I can get in there with the wheelchair. I sleep through most meals, too. The tea. I just sleep all the time.

D: *That's not good, is it? Can you refuse to take the tea?*

A: I think I can, but I don't know what it's doing to me. I don't associate it.

I moved her again to another important day. "They're poisoning me with the tea. Poisoning me! That's how the other nuns are going to get rid of me. They're making it stronger and stronger so eventually I won't wake up. That's why they're always out in the garden tending to their brews. Tending to what they grow that they know how to make."

D: *(This was a surprise.) How did you find out they were doing this?*

A: (Still yawning repeatedly.) I heard them talking, "She's younger. She'll need more."

D: *It takes too long to die otherwise?*

A: I think so.

D: *Is it because you're a burden?*

A: It's because of the money that came with me. My father was wealthy and gave them large gold pieces to take care of me. And they have to make it like I'm comfortable, and then he sees I am still alive and he keeps giving them money. (She was yawning so furiously it was difficult to understand and transcribe.)

D: *But if you die then the money will stop, won't it?*

A: They have to fake it. Tell him a lie and fake it.

D: *So they won't tell him that you died? Then they won't have to take care of you, but will still get the money? (Yes) So now that you know what they're doing, can't you do anything about it?*

A: I'm too drugged. I have too much of it onboard to fight them. They force it down me. Not all the sisters know this thing, just the senior Mother Superior and one other. The other ones think they're just caring for me.

D: *So it was the Mother Superior's idea to use the herb?*

A: Yes. They force it down me. The other sisters think it's helping. They think it's medicine. They don't know. They don't know the mixture.

D: *Don't they think it's strange that you sleep all the time?*

A: They think that I'm just sad and depressed. She has them all duped. She will continue to collect the money, because I am young and my father thinks I can stay there for a long time. And I can't do anything about it.

I moved her again to another important day. She announced emphatically, "I'm dying!"

D: *Was this from the medication?*

A: Yes. I'm in my bed. I'm in the cell. Some of the nuns are around the bed. Not all of them. Some of them are praying.

Mother Superior is here. She wanted to make sure that I died.

I moved her ahead until it was over with, and she could look back on it. "I see my funeral, the procession."

D: *Did they notify your family?*

A: No. I think my father died. I think that's why they killed me because when my father died there would be no more money. They didn't want to continue to take care of me. So it was safe to kill me.

I knew that from that out-of-the-body position she could see the entire lifetime from a different perspective, so I asked her what she thought the purpose was of that lifetime.

A: Not to be dependent. I can't be dependent on other people. They were interested in *their* best interests. Your best interest isn't their best interest. They won't have your best interest at heart.

D: *Oh, so it's better to just depend on yourself?* (Yes) *So that's an important lesson.*

I then called forth the SC to get some answers as to why it chose these two lifetimes for Amber to see. "The first one was the man on the ship who died. Why did you pick that one to show her? What were you trying to tell her?"

A: To trust herself. She knew not to take that assignment and she did it anyway. She didn't trust what she knew, her intuitions.

D: *How does that relate to her life now?*

A: The same. She doesn't trust people. She doubts herself. She knows, but she doesn't trust. In that life if she had listened to her intuition she wouldn't have died on that ship.

D: *Does the way she died of starvation have anything do with her life now?*

A: Yes. She's always worried that there will not be enough food, won't be able to ever get it or find it. Or she won't be able to come by it easily.

D: *In that situation it was impossible to get it.*

A: Right. But in this day and age there is plenty, around every corner.

D: *She doesn't have to be afraid of finding food.* (Right.) *Is this part of what is causing her problem with eating?* (Yes) *She says she is always hungry.*

A: Yes, because she was always hungry and there wasn't any food. On the ship once it was gone it was gone. (She was still yawning.)

D: *Why is she yawning so much? Why is the body doing this?*

A: She's releasing it.

D: *Good. That's what we want; release all of that junk from those two lives.*

Amber had an overweight problem. She was eating constantly because she always felt hungry, no matter how much she ate. It was obvious that it came from the lifetime where she died of starvation on the ship at sea. I did a lot of work, with the help of the SC, to release all of that because it had no place in her present life. We could leave it with the other man. She didn't have to worry about starving. She could get rid of the hunger. There was plenty of food now. Once this was realized then the extra weight could come off.

D: *That was very clever that you showed her that life, but then you also showed her the life of the young nun who died very tragically. Why did you show her that life of the nun that was poisoned?*

A: She gave up in that life.

D: *She didn't have a lot of choice though, did she?*

A: She could have, but she gave up. She lost all fight.

D: *But they were forcing the drink on her.*

A: There was a part of her that knew what it was, and she accepted it anyway as her fate.

D: *She didn't try to fight it then?*

A: No, and in some regards she welcomed it.

I wanted to know if there was anyone in that life that Amber knew now in her present life. They said there wasn't. I was surprised because I would have thought the Mother Superior had certainly incurred karma. "Yes, she has been taken care of." So she didn't get out of repaying karma. Her debt no longer involved Amber.

Amber had injured her left knee in high school. It was still painful, and had spread to involve both knees. Stairs, in particular, were a challenge. She had difficulty going up stairs. The doctors suggested surgery as the only solution. I wondered whether Amber's physical problems were connected with the nun's damaged legs. The SC said they were not, "She gave up. It was easier to give up."

D: *But she must have designed those circumstances before she went into that life, as we all do.*

A: Yes and no. It was just an accident. It's very complicated. Everything with an action has a reaction, so it changes minute by minute.

D: *It didn't start out to be that way? (No) What was the original plan?*

A: The original would have been that she live a healthy, normal life.

D: *Then after the accident, her parents didn't want her anymore. They didn't want to take care of her.*

269

A: No, it's not that they didn't want her. It's that they didn't know how and didn't know what to do. They thought they were doing the best for her.

D: *So those parts were not part of the plan: being put in the convent and the nuns taking care of her?*

A: Right. Her family was convinced ... talked into it. She knew otherwise, but she didn't fight it.

D: *Does the way she died of the poison have any significance in her life now as Amber?*

A: All things have significance. Be careful who you trust.

D: *So the first life was telling her to trust her instincts, and the second one was telling her to be careful?*

A: Of whom you trust. You have to know the balance. Trust yourself ... when to know ... who to know ... who to trust.

D: *Sometimes it can be a delicate balance.*

A: Very delicate.

By now the reader is probably wondering what these two stories have to do with lost knowledge. Although they are interesting, they do not seem to fit the theme of this book. But I have learned never to underestimate "them". They are full of surprises. So the session took a fascinating twist.

We moved on to discuss her physical problems. I thought that her knee problem was related to the nun's life, but it wasn't. This symptom usually means the person is not going in the right direction. That they are holding back. But the SC said it was different in Amber's case. "Sometimes you have to slow down. She's impatient. It's stubbornness about almost everything." They wanted her to learn how to heal it herself, instead of having surgery. I kept trying to get them to heal the knees and they kept refusing. This was a first, and I wanted an explanation. They said the problem came from another lifetime, but not the two that we had covered.

D: *What happened in that lifetime?*

A: They weren't put together correctly. They weren't built correctly.

This was confusing. I asked for an explanation.

A: They took her legs off and they put different legs on. She was part of the Atlantis experiment. They took her legs and they gave her animal legs, something with hooves. They cut the knee.

D: *I always thought in Atlantis they were experimenting with the genes. I didn't know they were experimenting with actual animals and humans.*

A: No, this was before they learned to work with the genes. She was a female. They took her legs off and put the animal ones on.

D: *You said it was not done correctly?*

A: That's what caused the pain.

D: *Was she able to live like that?*

A: She did, but it was painful. It was a painful surgery.

D: *They were just doing that out of curiosity?*

A: Yes and no. Some curiosity, some thought they had really found something to help. They thought there would be a way. First in using animal to human transplant, then in using the animal. That it would save other humans. They thought they had discovered the connection.

D: *But they didn't, did they?*

A: Not at that point, no.

D: *Did they realize they were going to cause pain to the person they were working on?*

A: Well, it was an interesting situation: pain as you are, or pain you might have.

D: *You mean there was something wrong with the person's legs?*

A: Yes. They thought they were helping.

D: *So that gives it a little more justification.*

A: Right, and some had good intentions, not all. And then they evolved from there. For the most part most of them had good intentions. With anything you have good and bad, and when they realized they couldn't do that, some pursued and some tried to stop. And then some tried to advance further, and then again there was a question of right and wrong at the time - disagreement, not right or wrong - disagreements.

D: *So they thought by transferring the animal legs this would at least give her something? This was their intention, and later they went to experimenting with the genes?*

A: Yes. They evolved later. And again it started out with good intention, but sometimes those who know can't stop it. They try to fight it. They try and it's about perseverance. And they try to overcome.

D: *When they exchanged body parts, did they work?*

A: Sometimes, sometimes not. It was pre-artificial; it was the very first artificial limb. In her case it was painful. She was able to move and walk around, but there was still pain.

D: *I have always thought that with the connection of an animal to a human, the body would always reject it.*

A: Yes, to some degree, but they were able to figure out how to maintain it.

D: *So in Amber's case, her body is remembering now? (Yes)*

This would certainly explain the pain in her knees now. So we had to set about releasing the memory and returning it to the past where it belonged. "So something happened in that lifetime to cause her legs to be damaged. Then she had the damage to her legs in her life as a nun. There's a pattern there, isn't there?"

A: Yes, it's time for the pattern to be removed. It's time to stop the cycle.

D: *So you're stopping that pattern?*

A: Yes, it's like weaving, like unraveling a thread. Now I'm removing the pattern. It'll take some time. To disintegrate, be removed and to stabilize. There's a layering at the knee, that's why it will take time. There are layers and layers caused by multiple things. So it's layers, big onion layers, layers, layers. Layers, layers and layers.

Amber wanted to know how to connect to the SC directly and be able to ask her own questions. "How can she communicate with you?"

A: She does already. There is no AHA!

D: *That's what many people think it should be. So it's just a voice they know instantly. It's not an AHA moment.*

A: No, it's very soft. We're very subtle. We don't like to influence because you have free will.

D: *But many people don't recognize those small subtle things.*

A: No, you don't.

D: *Another question she wanted to ask: She said she has always felt unworthy and not valued. Where does that come from?*

A: Many lives. Yes, those lives of Mother Superior wanting to eliminate her, the captain not listening, are also a pattern. We have to unravel that too.

Parting message: She is loved. It's that simple.

D: *Her present life sounds like it's a lot easier than those other lives anyway.* (Laugh)

A: Yes. Sometimes you need a break.

D: *Yes, I call them "resting lives."*

Chapter 21

THE ORIGINAL STONEHENGE

Original temples dating back to Babylon were designed with pillars evenly spaced all around the outside. Some had the roof open to the sky. These were intended as an observatory. The priest would sit at a designated spot in the center of the building and observe and record the movement of the stars and planets as they passed between the open spaces of the pillars. These records would have been kept and observed for hundreds of years. Thus a record of the movements could be accurately measured. These records would become part of the sacred knowledge, and only those of the secret mystery schools would have access and be able to interpret the meanings. This would have been the birth or the beginning of astrology and astronomy. Of course, the original teachings (and what stars to observe) would have come from the ETs. Much of the knowledge originally given would have meant observing planetary bodies that were invisible to the naked eye. Thus they used highly advanced instruments such as telescopes. (Probably similar to the "far-seeing devices" in my book *Jesus and the Essenes*, that were used at Qumran.) Much of this information was essential to the ETs because it related to their home planet or constellation. They wanted to keep track of the movements so they would know the best times to journey there or communicate. So some of the astrological information would have importance for Earth to plot the passing of time and the seasons, and some was important for the ETs themselves.

It was very important to be able to calculate time, especially the passing of the seasons, so the developing species would know when to plant and when to harvest. Thus the importance of erecting the structures, to keep track of the seasons and to train certain people to be able to interpret the information and to give it to the people. So the original ones were built by the ETs, not the primitive humans who were living there at the time.

The knowledge of the use of the mind to create and levitate etc. was perfected in some highly advanced civilizations. And carried to Egypt and other places by survivors after the destruction of Atlantis. The ETs were still living among men and sharing advanced knowledge during the time of Atlantis. Because of the abuse and misuse the abilities were taken away. It was similar to blowing a fuse, and the knowledge could not be allowed to be given back to mankind. However, now that we are entering the New Earth these abilities are returning. Our psychic abilities are reawakening as the Veil is thinning.

It began with the basic tracking of the seasons, then later developed into the more sophisticated system of astronomy. Maybe also so the ETs could keep track of their own home planet and its position. The structures could also be seen from space and served as markers for spaceships orbiting the planet, so they could know where their brothers were located and working.

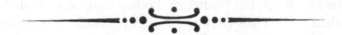

This pattern also continued with the building of stone circles and monoliths such as Stonehenge, New Grange and many others throughout the world. It was a marker for the passing of the seasons and the positions of certain important stars and planets. Their courses were plotted in relation to the lintels and stones.

This was a highly advanced science by the time of Atlantis. The knowledge was carried by the survivors to Egypt and other parts of the world. This is explored in my *Convoluted Universe* books.

Why was the building of the temples and stone circles, and the marking of the passing of the seasons so important? The monuments and the knowledge date back so far in time that man was just beginning to master agriculture, planting, harvesting and the caring of livestock. The traditional explanation is that these basic humans built these masterpieces. How is that possible when they were just beginning to move from savagery to the rudiments of civilization? We know that during these early times ETs lived among the developing people and gave them information and gifts to help in their steps of evolution. They knew how to harness the abilities of the mind, especially the ability to levitate and mold stone. Remember that everything is energy, and it is possible to manipulate energy. So why is it so impossible to think that ancients knew how to use the power of their mind to manipulate the cellular structure of rocks and other matter? These secrets were passed on by the ETs to special humans so they could use this knowledge and teach a select few.

Every culture in the world has their legends of the Culture-bringers. These were special beings that came and dwelt among the people and taught them the basic rudimentary skills to begin to develop a civilization. For example, the Corn Woman in the American Indian legends; she taught them about planting and agriculture. There were others who taught about hunting and gathering, about the development of fire, how to use natural materials to build shelters, etc. Because these beings could live as long as they wanted, they were treated as gods by the people.

The more complicated secrets and mysteries were not given until later in mankind's development.

In *Convoluted Universe, Book One* there is the story of the beginning of civilization as told by Bartholomew. In that story the ETs built complicated machines and devices that were used to harness the energy of the Sun, Moon and Stars. When they left Earth the knowledge of how to use these devices were given to certain priests and was supposed to be passed down in Secret Mystery Schools. However, the ETs could not foresee the greed of humans for power (a common flaw that has caused much trouble throughout history). There were certain people who wanted the control of the devices for their own use. They killed the priests, and because they did not understand how to utilize the devices they would not function. The devices themselves ended up being destroyed.

In my sessions I have always asked why couldn't the ETs come back and tell the people they were not using the knowledge correctly. But we must remember the laws that were set down in the beginning of the development of life on this planet. "Let us give this beautiful planet a creature with intelligence and free will. And see what he does with it." This information was given in *Keepers of the Garden*. We are the only planet in the universe that has been given free will. That is why we are called the "Grand Experiment." Then there is the prime directive of non-interference. "Once a civilization has been established, you cannot interfere with the development of that civilization." The information and devices etc. are given to the people as a gift, and then they stand back and watch and see how it will be used. It is the people's free will what they do with it, and many times we didn't use it for the purpose intended. But to return and try to explain it to the people, that would be interference.

My client, Sharon worked in Hollywood in the movies as a double and also behind the scenes on the set. She was attending my class in Burbank, CA, and wanted to be the demonstration. I agreed and the session began.

When Sharon came off the cloud she found herself at Stonehenge in England. However, it did not look the way it appears today. If anyone has ever traveled there they know that the structure is no longer complete. Most of the upright stones are still in place, but some of the top ones (lintels) that connected the upright pieces are missing or fallen. It is still magnificent, but only a shadow of what it must have been originally. She was seeing it as it appeared in its original state many, many years ago. "It's really, really green and all the pieces of the rocks are still there. They are complete all the way around, complete in a circle. All of them are new, and they are complete."

D: *What do you think as you look at it?*

S: Pride and power. Like my people, my friends there, we are really proud of this place and the work that we do with nature.

D: *What kind of work do you do with nature?*

S: We have rituals with nature. We do something to honor nature, but it aligns us with the Earth itself so we stay one with Earth. We stay peaceful and loving rather than some of the hordes of people at the other places. They aren't as civilized as we are. They tend to become aggressive, and they stray away from this place where a portal resides and connects to another earth.

D: *Do you feel there's a portal there?*

S: It is a portal. Opposed to a feeling that I would have, it is. It's not how I feel about it. It is. Whether I believe it or not, it is there.

D: *So your people believe it is there?*

S: It's not a belief. It is the truth whether we believe it or not. Whether you turn your back from this place or not, the place exists and has power and peace. And you can find love on the deepest level. It is more profound than anything that a physical life yields.

D: *Can you see this portal?*

S: For me, as I sit on this horse observing on the outside, I see that the green center opens and it's whole. So it looks like it's green and land, but in truth when the stars and the Sun and the planets are in particular places, this is sort of like a ... it's a mechanism that when these pieces are in alignment with the planet or the energy of the stars, then it's an opening. And the person or persons standing in the center ... their physical body seems to stand on the grass, but in truth a dark hole opens and their spiritual body goes down to the center of the Earth. And realigns to remember from whence their bodies came. I'm looking at it because tonight there's going to be a gathering ... a participating. I'm kind of an officiate. I help the people that live in the village. I have a purple cloak and somehow the cloak defines my position as some kind of helper or go-between. I can hear the stars when they twinkle.

Sharon saw that she was male in the "prime of life." I asked some more about the significance of the purple cloak. "The cloak itself was a gift that I received from my elders when I achieved a state of – how would you say? – It's enlightenment, but there are levels. Enlightenment means 'in the light,' so we're all in the light. The entire little village, too, the butcher and the baker. My life is dedicated solely to communicating and helping the people to stay in alignment with this portal."

D: *With nature or the portal?*
S: The portal is even more than nature. Nature is like a portal, too, so if the people had to go away from our place, they are to remember by being in nature. And if they are among the trees and the grass, then we're at peace and they can remember how it is where we live. Right now I'm not with anyone. I'm just on my horse and I'm here observing today, because in a fortnight – I don't know what that means – a fortnight ... pretty soon at night I'm going to officiate. It is important. They are giving me this opportunity. My elders have given me an opportunity to – officiate is not the right word, but – (He had difficulty finding the correct words.) facilitate, I guess, and I am going to be in the spotlight at the ritual at night on the north. I will be on the north -- in the north -- I want to say "a pillar," but they're not pillars. I'll be under that one and all the congregation of the people will look toward the north. It has to do with the time of the year, but nature has a spring, a fall, a winter and a summer. And so I stand at the north, so all the congregation of people will face north on this night.

Whereas on other nights, they face one of my other brothers. Not a brother by birth of mother, but by the elder grouping with which I am a younger member. The people are regular people, the butcher, the baker, and those who come from the village.

D: *I think this is a great honor that you are going to be able to participate in this.*

S: It is. I am humbled and empowered by the idea of this.

D: *Did your people build these stones? Did they have anything to do with that?*

S: No, not the people, no. The elders know of these. I don't know if they're people, but they're not the village people. They're not, but my elders are really old. There is an ancient one among us and he knows those answers.

D: *Do they know where this structure came from?*

S: Only the ancient one, our eldest elder, could give you that detail.

D: *But it's been there all of your life?*

S: Yes. And if I live this life ... I'm not sure I aspire to be that person, the ancient one, but all of us could evolve to become him. And as we work our way into the ranks of higher knowledge, those things could be revealed to me as well, because I am of that ... it's not caste because we are not above people. But we just have dedicated our lives to staying connected, rather than being a village, a butcher, a baker. I was chosen from my family because the elders came and told my parents. My mother was proud. My father wasn't happy because he wanted me to work with him in the fields. (She began to cry very hard, and found it difficult to get words out between sobs.) Even though I was called to be with elders, I feel bad that I didn't live the life to help my father in the fields. (Still crying.)

D: *Do you think you would have been happy living the other life with your father?*

S: I am a being who seems to be always happy, so it was not of consequence to me where I was. I was just so happy to be here and see the green grass, and to experience the Earth from this point of view of being a person with feet and a body. I can tell where I came from. I did not care if I was a son of a farmer or with the elders. It was with the elders that the elders recognized my light and they came to take me, but as far as me as this man, I did not really care. I just wanted to experience the treasure of this planet from the point of view of being part of, as opposed to looking down at it. (Crying again.) I had been working for the Source in another capacity, and always I would pass by the Earth any chance I could, to look down upon the paradise of God's work manifest. And it was this giant treasure of earth, air, water, and I wanted to experience it from a human aspect. The most important thing is just to be on the Earth and appreciate the beauty of the blade of grass, the beauty of it being green. The beauty of the trunk of a tree and that it's brown.

D: *But you're going to participate in this ritual, these ceremonies, on that night.*

S: I'll stand at the north.

I moved him forward to an important day and Sharon immediately began talking about the chaotic scene she was watching. "The town is being invaded by hordes. Hordes are coming and the people in the village are running around in fear and worry, and the ancient one has gone. My elders have taken him to a safe place, a cave or something. I am on the hill (Stonehenge) and I am trying to be calm." Which would be very difficult to do with all the turmoil surrounding him.

S: I am calm, but I am trying to tap into the Wisdom of the Pillars so I can channel calm to the villagers. It feels like the other brothers have gone, but I will stay behind because I feel for my family and my neighbors, and the neighbors of my neighbors. I feel that my presence will help. I would rather try to bring peace, as best I can, for them.

D: *Do you know who the people are who are invading?*

S: They are blonde people of Norse. They have these sticks with sharp balls on the end, and they live for the violence. They live in the forestry area edge of the other water. And they are very large and very simple. They carouse or they are – what do you say here? – I guess I would say, a Norseman. They are the most excellent warriors that man right now would know.

D: *And your people are not violent. This is why everybody is frightened.*

S: They are peaceful and so would have gladly brought out welcomes and garlands and that, and partied with the maypole. But when the first one went to welcome, they were murdered. These people really revel in the fact that they can kill, and they pride themselves on being able to kill swiftly. They aspire to kill quickly, as if it's a failure or you are less than a good warrior if it takes more than one blow to kill. They are almost as if a machine.

D: *So you are watching this?*

S: I cannot actually see it with my own eyes, as I stand with my palm against the south pillars, left side of this. But I can see it in my mind and my heart, and I can hear it. And I am aware of the people as they pass (their spirits), and I can even tell who they are. And so I am trying to tell them, "There's the light," so they can get to where they need to go. (Began crying loudly.) I am only one, so I am limited in my ability to do much, but to help them to pass over in this way so horribly. (Sobbing.) I will do my best until they find me. The end will be later this day where they will slay me in the center of the circle. (She was crying so loudly it was difficult to understand her.)

D: *You're doing the best you can. You are only one person.*

S: I didn't set this in motion. They set in motion a mantle of this warrior way that will now reverberate from our time for many eons. I am confident that all my friends and neighbors and my mother and father, and even myself will reabsorb into the (Still crying loudly and difficult to understand) ... center, because of the power of which I held. It would send a power of killing. It reverberates when you throw a pebble into the center of water, and it reverberates out. By them doing this thing for fun, of killing me in the center in the ritualistic way, it is different because they know that I am important to the people below in the village. They didn't just whack me. They all will have their own darker ritual, dark being a killing light. It will do this in the center, and because the portal is for the amplification of humanity, they will send a vibration of this killing way through time through their future, all of the future of Earth. And it upsets me because it will lead to the destruction of Earth. And the life we could have had for this planet to evolve will now not go as the ancient one had said it was supposed to, when the people would come.

D: *So it doesn't matter what type of energy. This place is so important that it amplifies energy. So in this case it is amplifying negative energy.*

S: The Norse way will then permeate the Earth through eons of time. There will be more wars, and my people will take on the mantle of the north and become great warriors on the sea.

D: *Tell me what happens.*

S: They kill my corporal body and they took my horse.

D: *Did that happen at the place of the pillars?*

S: They killed me at the center of the center. It was bad for them and all the future generations. Now I will reabsorb to the Source and because I was killed in that way, I will now have to play a game on Earth for some time.

D: *Do you have to go and rest?*

S: The rest will not be required for long because I was purely Sourced when I was in body, and so now I will begin the game of the wheel. The game of what you would call "karma." This has now entrenched me to the game of Earth, and that way it is going to take me from my original duty to

Source when I flew around the universe as a sort of messenger. I carried messages for Source throughout the universe, but now I will lose my chance to do this job. Because I merely wished to look upon the Earth, but in so doing, I have now entrenched myself into the wheel.

I then had her leave the man there and moved her forward so I could call forth the SC. The rest of the session revolved around Sharon's questions and the SC gave her many suggestions.

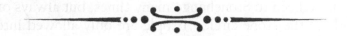

After awakening, Sharon said she was still receiving information about the incident at Stonehenge. The negative energy was so strong that centered around the execution that it contaminated the place, and spoiled the powerful positive energy that it had before. This was part of the reason the stones were disturbed and some of them toppled. It was to destroy the focus of the energy, and this would, in effect, close the portal there. The ancients realized the power of the stone circle. If some energy remains (and it is felt by some sensitive people), it is not even a portion of what it was at the time it was being used. Even though Stonehenge still sits at a vortex and a juncture of ley lines, I do not believe the portal is functional any more. The same way the energy has been weakened at the Great Pyramid. History says that this was also what happened at the stone circle at Avebury. The Romans knew there was great power there and deliberately destroyed parts of the earthen circle that surrounds the town, to break up the power. There originally was a mile of stones (called the Avenue) leading to Avebury. Many of these were broken up and used by the locals, thus destroying the focus of the energy.

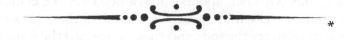

*

After this chapter was written I went to Ireland and England in August 2011 where I was featured in a Sacred Sites tour. People accompanied me to New Grange near Dublin, Ireland; Glastonbury, Stonehenge and Avebury in England. At each stop I was to talk about what I have discovered in my work relating to these ancient places. At each stop we were accompanied by a local historian, and of course, my version did not agree with their version of history. They were quoting what had been passed down, and I was talking about what I discovered during my regression work.

I have been to Stonehenge many times, but always on the outside of the stone circle. People are only allowed into the center of the stones by special permission. On this trip we were allowed to enter the circle, but it was very early in the morning just as the sun was rising. Except for the security guards we were the only ones there. There was a gentle rain falling and it seemed to let up for a brief time while we were in the circle. I was surprised that the center is actually smaller than it looks from the outside. There are two circles, one within the other, and the outer one is the one visible from the outside. When we entered I noticed there were two lintel stones on the ground on my right. I said, "Those stones should not be there." Maria Wheatley, who knew the local history and is an expert dowser, said they were originally on top of the upright stones and had been toppled. They were so huge that I wondered who would have been able to knock them down. If the purpose was to close the portal they could have been brought down by ETs, but that is only my speculation.

I told the story of this regression, and Maria pointed out where the north pillars were. We were able to get a visual of where the brothers would have stood during the ceremony before the villagers. (Maria said there was evidence that a village had existed nearby.) I wanted to know where the exact center of the circle was, and Maria pointed it out. She had dowsing rods with her, and as she walked over the center the rod began to swirl wildly in a circle. Some of the others in the group wanted to try the rods and they performed the same way.

I think that was evidence of where the ancient portal would have been located. Of course, the energy was not near what it would have been when it was active, but some still remained. The group formed a circle around the portal and Maria led us in a meditation. We blessed the man's spirit who died there, and focused on removing any leftover negativity of the violence that had occurred there. There was a feeling of peace as we left the circle. On the way out we passed another group of people who had been granted access. And I said, "I don't think they are going to have the same experience that we just had!"

Later Maria showed us a photograph she took as we were walking toward Stonehenge just before sunrise. She just put her camera on a fencepost and took the picture, and it showed a huge orb directly over the center where the portal would have been located.

I found this picture on the Internet of Stonehenge in 1877 before the restoration project that started in the early 1900s.

This is an aerial view of how it looks now.

Chapter 22

MOUNT VESUVIUS AND THE DESTRUCTION OF POMPEII

Barbara came into a place that made her very happy: A large city with cobblestone streets and beautiful buildings. "Everything is so clean and bright and beautiful here! There are many buildings and they are all white. All the buildings have paintings on the outside, and also on the inside. It's a very clean place. The buildings are not huge, maybe a couple of floors, but most of them are one floor. They're so pretty inside. They're just incredible, beautiful things. There's something special about this place to me. It's unbelievably beautiful, so much attention to art, to detail." When I asked her to focus on her body, she saw that she was a young girl about eleven or twelve, standing barefoot on the street wearing a short white tunic. "It's so pretty. It's just pretty, pretty, pretty." The city was full of people all going about their business. They were all dressed very similar to her. "More people than I know. People are just having lives and doing things ... buying and selling things, but I am just hanging out, I guess, playing. There are some wagons but they're not around right now. There are animals."

She lived in the city with her parents. "My dad's got money. I see all these silver coins around, money. I'm not exactly sure how it comes to us, but he does something. Money is nice. Money makes things not an issue, but wow! It's so pretty." She described the inside of the house and there were paintings on the walls. "It's colorful and beautiful, and it's really a skill to be able to make those things. They are paintings of people, scenes, scenes in life, scenes of people. Sometimes you can pay someone and they'll make you a picture that way or with little stones. It's such a skill to make things that are beautiful. This is part of our life. The outside of our house doesn't have much on it. It's white and red, but inside there are these stone pictures of my mother.

And there are pictures of birds. Nobody in my house does that. They pay people to do that, and give them money." She slept on a mat, and said she didn't have to worry about food or cooking. There were people who cooked for the family. "That is done a little bit away, and there are women and sometimes men too that take care of this. And you tell them what to do and they do it. They bake it and then it comes to you. They are servants, but you do have to tell them. If you don't tell them, they don't know what to do. But the mother does that. Mom does that. Father is not in the house so much, but comes and goes and brings in the money and everything is done." She did not go to school, but her mother was teaching her. "My mother tells me how the house is run, and you learn what to do. I like to look at things, see things, and experience beautiful things. I wish I could make these beautiful things."

I decided to move her ahead to an important day and she said she was only a little older, about thirteen or fourteen. But it was a scene of chaos. "It's like the world is turned upside down." She became upset. "You can't breathe. The air is full of dirt and it's hot and … you can't breathe." I gave her suggestions for well-being so she wouldn't experience any physical discomfort. "Oh, my goodness! I don't know what to do. It's so scary! Everybody I see is so afraid and nobody knows what to do.'

D: *What happened?*

B: The mountain blew up! Earthquakes, earthquakes, earthquakes and Boom! And there's all this dirt, dirt, dirt. Dirt in the air and everywhere, and it's so horrible. And I don't know where to go. (She was crying.) Nowhere to go! I don't know where to go!! The dirt is in the air, and EVERYWHERE! It's hot and the air is so *bad*. It's really bad! It's horrible! – I'm going in the house and I'm going to hide and maybe I'll be okay … maybe.

D: *Were you outside when it was happening?*

B: It was happening, and it's gotten so much worse, and no one knows what to do.

D: *Has it been going on for a while?*

B: Not long, but long enough. It's so overwhelming! It's just ... all this is just ... it's gone! It's not clean. It's dirty.

D: *And you think the safest thing is to go and hide in the house?*

B: I don't know if anywhere is safe. It's bad! (Crying)

D: *I guess you can't run away?*

B: Where??? – I'm going to hide in the corner where I have been sleeping. It's as good as anywhere. It's all gone! (She then began to moan loudly.)

D: *What?*

B: The body ... I'm above it.

D: *You're not in the body anymore?*

B: Not in the body.

D: *What happened?*

B: The body stopped working. It couldn't breathe. It was hot. It was this poison stuff. It was awful! – Now it's okay. I'm above the body. Way above the body looking down, looking out.

D: *What do you see as you look out over the city?*

B: It's just all covered. There was nothing that could be done. No hiding.

The amazing thing about this was that it sounded like the eruption of Mount Vesuvius that destroyed Pompeii, and she described the city as beautiful and clean. The site has been excavated and this was not the impression that the scientists got from the ruins. Of course, it was all covered with volcanic ash, so it would probably appear different. Many paintings made from little stones still remain on the walls and floors.

D: *It was such a beautiful, clean place, but now you're above it. What are you going to do now? You can't go back. – You're smiling. What's happening?*

B: There's a light in front of me. It's a soft light. Wow! There's a lady forming in the light. Ah!! (A deep breath.) It's much better. (A sigh of relief.) Just surrounding... surrounding... surrounding me... so nice. I think she's taking me somewhere. And there's no bad taste or that smell and all the dirt. It's just wonderful. I'm going somewhere and I'm going to learn things. She takes me and drops me off. There are lots of books... well, I think that's what they are. We didn't have these in the other place, but lots of things, all kinds of things, information. It's things to learn, things to know.

D: *What does this place look like?*

B: Big, big, big, big, big. There are books, books, books, books everywhere and some table-like things. And you're supposed to figure out, to learn things.

D: *You said there's lots of information there?*

B: Oh, my goodness! Everywhere. Everything you can possibly imagine and wow! – I don't think I'm going to be making beautiful things now. I think I'm going to be looking at books.

D: *What are you supposed to do there?*

B: Absorb information, learn things.

D: *Is there anybody there to tell you what you're supposed to do?*

B: There's an old guy with a long, long beard. He's getting books for me. (Sarcastic) There's so many! Later I can pick. Now I have to learn *this* stuff. It's about how things work. – There are so many books, but you have to start somewhere.

D: *Are you going to open the books and see what's in them?*

B: I can do that. (She laughed.)

D: *What's funny?*

B: It's a book about leaves. (Still laughing.) Tree leaves.

D: *Tree leaves? He wants you to look at that?*

B: Yes, because there are so many different, different kinds of trees. And part of how you tell the differences between them is by the leaf. I didn't know that before!

D: *Why does he want you to have that information?*

B: It's important. That's what he says. It's important and I need to know.

D: *Can you ask him why it's important?*

B: For something else, for a job later? It's important for later, for me to know the differences. This didn't happen before, but needs to happen in this place.

D: *What are the other books?*

B: Oh, about different plants. – There are books about everything you can imagine and then some, but I get the ones about plants. He picked them just for me.

D: *Why does he want you to know about the plants?*

B: To help things grow. How do you know how things grow, how it works, if you don't know the differences in the plants? I will need this information sometime. He tells me I need to know this. This is important. Some of the plants are sick, and I need to know about the difference in plants so I can help them. At some point I need to go, I need to work with plants and help things grow. This is a place you come and study and learn things.

D: *Is that the only place you go, just to read the books, or do you go somewhere else?*

B: This is all I'm seeing is this place with books, and this old guy, and he picks my books. And he says, learn this and I read and read and read some more. I didn't know I could read actually (Baffled) and learn. And there you are and this is important for later; not for now.

D: *Okay, let's move ahead and see if there's somewhere else you have to go.*

B: I keep hearing that I don't get to leave until I've learned everything in those books.

It was obvious that she was in the Library on the spirit side, which contains all the knowledge that ever has been or ever will be. This could take a long time to do the learning, so I condensed time to where she had learned all the knowledge that was required. "You've learned and absorbed a lot of information about plants. What do you have to do next?"

B: Leave.

D: *Where do you go?*

B: Into a baby.

D: *Does anyone tell you what you're supposed to do?*

B: More old guys. They are very strong and very powerful. They're together. I mean, not connected together, but they come together and they tell you. "Okay, now you've learned that. Now you need to learn some other things," and you get to pick a little bit, but they tell you.

D: *They make a lot of the decisions?*

B: They do. I need to go and apparently I need to work with people, and work with plants because things aren't growing right.

D: *But do you make some decisions about where you go or what you do?*

B: You can decide *when* sometimes. They let me decide when, and to whom, but I have to do this job. It's a job.

D: *Because the plants are not growing correctly?*

B: So that the plants *will* grow correctly. They're not now. It's like the plants are sick somehow. There's something wrong with them. And maybe they don't need to be in this place, but somewhere else with other things, but the people there don't know. So they need someone new to come there and tell them and help them because otherwise, there would be no food. (Concerned.) Food would go away.

D: *Why aren't the plants growing correctly?*

B: Things have changed outside and old people do the same old things. So they need new people to come in to do something different. Knowing something else so then there's still food. Otherwise, everyone dies.

D: *The plants are that important?*

B: What do people eat?

D: *So everything is not progressing. It sounds like things were going backwards.*

B: Just sick. Things got sick. Things change and people didn't change like they needed. They need change.

D: *So they think you'll be able to help?*

B: One of the helpers. There are others.

D: *And your job will be to work with the plants?*

B: Work with the plants and make some changes, little changes that will wind up being big changes.

D: *Does it have to be big changes?*

B: Ultimately, but little changes can be handled easier than the big, big changes.

D: *So how are you going to do this when you go into the baby?*

B: The baby doesn't do much. The baby has to grow up, but the knowing will still be there.

D: *Did they tell you how you are going to be able to make these changes?*

B: Go to a family where they are already growing things.

This made sense, because in her present lifetime Barbara was born to a poor family of farmers that lived in the country. Thus Barbara was raised close to nature.

D: *And you said you're allowed to pick the ones to go to?*

B: Yes. They grow things.

D: *Is that the only job you'll be doing when you come back to Earth?*

B: Working with the plants is supreme. Getting along with hard people is also important. Difficult people.

D: *Why is that important?*

B: To learn flexibility. It makes more things possible.

I asked about the purpose of seeing the past life we had just gone through. "I know what that was about. Mount Vesuvius blew up. I knew the place when I saw it. It was Pompeii. I could see it. Barbara has been there in this life, but it looked very different. She has seen it."

When she saw Pompeii in this life it was an emotional experience with a foreboding of disaster that still hung over the place. The members of the family in that lifetime were in her life now, playing different roles. I asked what she learned from living there and dying in such a way. "Letting go, letting go, letting go. It was a short life. She loved it there, but there was fear that came through after the mountain blew up, there was fear. She was left with not being able to trust. The perfect and the beautiful, you can't trust. It was incredible! Something so beautiful could turn into something so terrible. The feeling that nothing was safe. There's still some of that left in her present life."

D: *What was the purpose of dying like that? To live a short life?*

B: That was payback for something from another time. She's had times when she has been very cruel, very cruel. On some level she knows already. This is why there are big abusive powers -- not just power -- *powers*.

D: *Many different powers?*

B: Oh, yes, big energy.

D: *Was it on Earth?*

B: Sort of, but not this Earth. Almost like a different incarnation of Earth.

D: *So the Earth has many incarnations, too?*

B: That's what's coming. It's like a new incarnation is coming anyway. It's coming.

D: *This was an old incarnation of Earth?*

B: Before the present incarnation of Earth. She's very powerful. She has been afraid of her own power. It's the fear of her power because there was so much misery created. Not just for her in other times and spaces, but misery was created because of her love of her powers. The fascination, the charge, the power of, "I can make this happen." That was what she was thinking. (An evil voice.) "I can make this happen." Her power was unbelievable.

D: *In that life were there humans on that incarnation of Earth?*

B: Beings, like humans, but there were dinosaurs, animals.

D: *Did everyone have access to this power at that time?*

B: Many people did, yes.

D: *So she was playing around with it more than the others?*

B: She was really bad, more than most. It was almost like wanting to be the king of the world -- the queen of the world -- the power.

D: *Did she harm other beings?*

B: Yes, yes. Not alone though.

D: *What happened in that life?*

B: Destroyed. More earthquakes and water. Water, not ash, water.

D: *So did she bring this on?*

B: Oh, yes, she was part of that. Misusing the power. Wanting to see what would happen. No thought of consequences.

D: *So she was harming others even before the big thing happened?*

B: That wasn't the reason. That wasn't the intention. It was not about wanting to harm others as much as, "I want to be powerful," or "I want to be important." That's what she was thinking and so were the others there. And thinking that what they were doing would make things better somehow, and they would be important. It wasn't, "Oh, we're going to end this all." It wasn't that thought, but that's what happened. That was the consequence. It was destroyed by water, water, water, water, water, so the payback in this other time, happy, happy, happy, happy. Earthquakes, ash, ash, ash, ash, ash, or dust, dust, dust, dust.

D: *Only this time she had to be on the other side of it.*

B: Yes. That karma is gone now.

D: *That's big karma.*

B: Yes, but the fear is still there. She has that fear that the powers, powers, powers can eventually harm other people.

D: *Is that one of the reasons she hasn't used it in this life?*

B: Yes, totally. She had many abilities as a child, and she still does.

D: *She kind of buried them, but now they're coming back, aren't they?*

B: And scaring people as they do. She knows she has to use these abilities now. She knows to not go crazy with it, not so much ego. That was an ego life for all of those people. Everyone was living in the ego, thinking they were with the gods. That it was all fine and whatever they did there would have no lasting consequences. It simply didn't matter. They could push, push, push, push. It would all be fine.

D: *So that memory is still in the back of Barbara's mind.*

B: Completely from memory, the fear of stepping into the powers. It's about being comfortable with them, finding comfort, finding ability. The little abilities are coming back. But the fear is huge for her. She has to learn trust. And it's very hard to trust again when actions destroy everything. And there's still that self-importance. Just letting all that go. It's almost like some decalcification groove. Something in there that is like a rock. That rock of fear that can't go away.

D: *Well, it serves a purpose because we don't want her to go in that direction. – When she was in the library she was studying about plants. Do you want her to use that knowledge?*

B: She has lots of plant knowledge. It's easy for her. She needs to be doing what she's doing. She studies. She learns. She helps people. That's what she needs to do.

Barbara was then given much personal advice, especially about her marriage being over and that it was time to move on. All that karma had been repaid. Her present husband had been a part of the destruction with her when they abused their power, so they had to come back together in different roles. Her dependent mother had been her servant in another life and Barbara had not treated her well. So now she was in a position of having to take care of her.

Parting message: She'll be fine and she needs to know that what's happening in her life is the highest good. This is freedom for her. And that her life hasn't really, in some ways, started. It's just now beginning.

D: *She was worried about getting old. I told her she has many years left, yet.*

B: She needs to look in the mirror. And that's the culture. The culture is messed up.

D: *You told me one time that age is not what it used to be anyway. Age is not the same.*

B: You have one hundred year olds running around driving cars. Age is not what is used to be!

Chapter 23

GOING TO HELL

When Catherine came to my hotel room in Sydney, Australia in 2007 for the session, she was walking with a cane and so bent over that she resembled more an old woman than her real age of late 40s. Her lower back caused her tremendous insistent pain. This was the main reason for the session, to find some relief. She was also going to attend my class there in a few days.

She was born into a family where she was ignored, abused and mistreated. She was considered an "accident" and her mother never wanted her. Her whole life as a child was being told she was not good enough, and whatever happened was her fault, so she received no sympathy. Her father ignored her totally because he did not think she was his child. Her parents had to marry because the mother was pregnant with her older brother. He was treated better. But the father did not want any more children. Catherine said she could only remember five or six sentences he ever spoke to her. He totally ignored her. She left home and went to college, specializing in psychology. When she married it was more verbal abuse and suffering. Her sex life was no good, mostly because she didn't want it. She had two children and the son went with the father upon divorce. Her second marriage wasn't any better. (Was it any surprise that all of this had affected her back?)

She got a job trying to help women who had experienced child abuse, and the children who were in the middle of it. It would seem to be the ideal solution because she could identify with it. Instead it created a great deal of stress. Working with their stories and problems brought all of her old memories back. All of the old garbage she had never dealt with. She finally couldn't handle it anymore and transferred to doing the paperwork, the office work, instead of dealing directly with the victims.

Her father had died in his 50s. He had also been a victim of the mother's constant rage and anger. Her mother (now in her 80s) is still terribly angry at everything. She had always blamed Catherine for the failure of her marriage, and her unhappiness. Even now when she called her, it is only yelling and accusations. No sympathy or understanding.

She did not like her job and a few months before this session she had a heart attack and quit. (That is one way to escape an undesirable situation.) She had explored past lives with other hypnotists in the hope of finding some answers. Many came up where she was involved with nunneries or monasteries, most often as a nun. In one that she explored the most, she was dropped off at a convent as a child of five. Unwanted, she stayed there and was totally ingrained with the dogma of harshness, strictness and obedience. She lived there all her life, eventually training the new initiates in the same way, passing on the bitterness and the need to suffer. She had explored these past lives and used meditation, and thought she had cleared most of it. But it became obvious from our session that she had only touched on the cause. The need to suffer in order to go to Heaven was deeply ingrained, and came into this present life strongly.

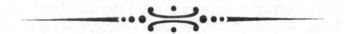

Catherine came off the cloud to find herself as a young adult male dressed in a short toga type garment. He was standing on a rocky shore looking out at the ocean and the waves pounding against the rocks. He immediately became emotional, "I'm afraid of going back to the city. I'm afraid of what I'm going to see." He began to cry and sob, "The mountain exploded. There's so much fear because of the mountain."

D: *Were you in the city when it happened?* (No) *Is it still exploding or is it over with?*

C: It's happening and people run away and they don't know where to run. I hear them and I see them running and screaming. They are just having a lot of pain and fear and panic. – The smoke. And the ash is covering people up in the street and they're suffocating. The wise men said it's because the people are so bad. That people were lascivious and worshiping gods and devils. They weren't being honest proper people anymore, and they were going to have to pay for their sins. The wise men wanted them to stop the drinking and the carousing and the prostitutes and …. Some of the people had great fear and believed them, and some of the people laughed. They are being paid back.

D: *So the whole city had become corrupted?* (Yes) *Did you believe the wise men?*

C: I don't know who to believe considering the leaders and the people don't want to listen to the wise men. And the leaders want us to follow them into the drinking and debauchery, but the soothsayer of the wise men says, "Don't do those things. It's wrong and it hurts humanity." And because they had too much wine, they get into hurting people. They are saying we're going to be paid back. The people weren't listening to them.

D: *Were you doing these things?*

C: I'm only about eighteen and getting into manhood, but not knowing the right road. And I don't want to be doing the wrong thing and be punished. There's no way to know the truth. There's no way to know if the leaders should be followed, or the people who drink every night and carouse. Or to be a prude and not follow them, or follow the priest.

This was not his home. He had come from Rome to visit cousins living in the city. "The terrible city. I'm visiting these cousins and they're taking me places to gamble and drink, and I'm not used to it. Who is right? (Very forlorn.) Who is true? How do we know the truth? Why can't we hear the gods directing us? Why do we only hear the gods through people lying and trying to control us? It's so hard. I want to hear the truth. But I want to be like the priest."

So it had come to the point where the mountain was blowing up now. "I'm on the beach watching, hearing the screams and the people running. And they are saying, 'See, I told you if you didn't change, this would happen.' And others are saying, 'Oh, this is stupid and not from that.' It's terrible, terrible things and terrible times.

D: *Do you have any idea what you're going to do now?*

C: Stay at the water. Stay at the water. Don't go near the cloud of smoke. (She was breathing heavily.)

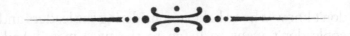

I had another regression that may have been at the same time or another place where a volcano was erupting. In that story the woman ran into the ocean to escape the lava and ash, thinking it would be safe there. However, no place was safe. The water became so hot that the people were cooked alive. So it seemed as though in a situation like this there would be no safe place, no matter what the decision. Also the young girl in the previous chapter tried to hide in her house to escape the ash, but she was suffocated there.

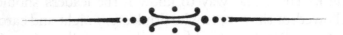

I condensed time to see what he decided to do. "My god, I can't decide! I can't decide whether to stay at the sea, or go up to higher ground, but in a different direction from the spewing mountain. (Panic was setting in.) I can't make a decision. (Crying) I can't make a decision. I'm alone and I don't know how to decide. (Calming down somewhat.) All right, don't be afraid right now. Don't be paralyzed by your fear. Make a decision. (Asking himself.) What if I make a wrong decision? ... Well, so what!"

D: *It'll still be your decision. What do you want to do?*

C: Stay here for now. Take no action because it's safer. I don't see any lava, just the smoke and the ash, and the people burning up from the ash. – Now I'm running through the streets. People have fallen and some of them are covered with hot ash.

D: *Why did you go into the city?*

C: To see what's happening because I don't know what I'm doing. I don't know what to do. I better run away. – So many have died a terrible death. I hear the screams.

D: *Let's move time ahead and see what happens to you.*

C: It's all quiet now. The terrible fear about making a decision is gone because it's been made now. The decision has been made over the terrible, terrible fear. The fear of not being able to make a decision is over. He's dead.

D: *How did you die?*

C: By the ash, the hot ash.

D: *But you didn't have to go back into the city, did you?*

C: But I didn't know what to do.

D: *You were safe by the water.*

C: But the ash came. I had to run. It even came to the shore. (Crying) I had to run. I had to run right into it. – Now it's quiet. I'm just floating and the others are confused and lost. They don't know what happened. They don't know. It's a terrible shock, terrible, so many in fear.

D: *So many dying at one time?*

C: Yes. Terrible. – I'm just lost right now. I'm still feeling the pain ... the searing pain.

I took away any remaining physical sensations, so he would be able to talk without that residue distracting him.

C: The searing pain, the guilt and not making a decision has never left me. (He started crying again.) I'm stuck there. People are moving away, but I'm stuck there in the body, not living, not dying.

D: *Why are you stuck there?*

C: Because I need the body. I will be tanned and punished by God.

D: *Is that what you're afraid will happen?*

C: Yes. It's all of God.

D: *But you don't need the body anymore. The body doesn't function anymore. You can't make it move, can you?*

C: So when it's safe to move away, will I find worse in hell, and burn in hell forever?

D: *That is what you're afraid of? (Yes) Is that what they told you?*

C: Yes, they did, they did. Old hags and the old vicious people pointed their boney fingers and said, "You will go to hell!"

D: *But you weren't doing anything bad. You didn't do what the others were doing, did you?*

C: No. No, I didn't, but I wanted to try it.

D: *Yes, that's normal, but you didn't do it. I don't think you have to worry about being punished for something you didn't do.*

C: But I went somewhere to a hellish place after death. They said that, "You will burn in hell forever." And I went there because I believed it. Because I had so much fear. But they were wrong. They need to learn that they were wrong. What they said was based on their fears and false knowledge. And they had no true religion. They were fake and they taught me fake things that I believed. And so I couldn't make a decision. They were wrong. They taught with fear and with falsehoods. And maybe there was harm in those who drank and gambled and were in debauchery. Maybe there was some harm, but it wasn't all harm. I believed and was afraid, and I didn't really even have a chance to try life. I didn't have a chance to do anything because I was pulled into too many directions, and there was no truth to believe in.

D: *Do you think that was part of it because you couldn't make a decision about the problem?*

C: Yes, I couldn't make a decision. – But I don't have to be in that hellish place. They made me believe I had to be there. Now I know, and it's such a relief. I don't have to be in the hellish place. I believed them all.

D: *Where do you go now that you realize that wasn't real?*

C: It seems I can go to the light. They said I was unworthy.

D: *But you know you don't have to believe them.*

C: No, I don't. I can go to the light. I see people floating away to some nice place. They're all flying and following each other up and up and up, and I didn't go there. I was down.

D: *That was because you believed them. Now you can go somewhere else. (Yes) What is that like?*

C: It's this long … like a beam of light. And all the souls who left their body and died, they're all floating. And they are two and three abreast, and they're all in a big line one after another. And they're heading toward these clouds of light. It is golden, and music is coming from there, and it looks so nice. And I didn't think I could go. I didn't think I was worthy. There are beings who are pointing the way, helping the stragglers get in the line and go forward, go up.

D: *The ones that were stuck.*

C: Yes, like me. And people came to pull us out of the mental hell we went through. But it seemed so real. We can be free.

D: *What is it like when you get there?*

C: We're enfolded in the comforting light, and all the fears have gone away, and all the sin – the perceived sin – can fall away. The searing pain caused by being burned by hot ash can fall away. You don't have to keep it forever. (In awe.) You don't have to keep it forever! (Crying) I'm so relieved to know that it doesn't have to be forever. They said I went to hell forever.

D: *(Laugh) But they were wrong!*

C: I'm so relieved to know. I should never have believed them. I should never have believed them.

D: *It was the circumstances.* (Yes) *You were there to learn and to make a decision.*

C: I think it was to move away from the gambling and the drinking. They took us to a false place with false teachings. I can let them go, and I can let the pain go, and I can let the fear of becoming a carouser go. Let it all go. I want to let in the truth. There is truth to this place that we're going to.

D: *Let's move ahead until we're there. What is it like?*

C: Breathe... I couldn't breathe on the ground. That stayed with me forever. Now I can breathe. It's very beautiful, full of beams of light bouncing and shining everywhere. And I can breathe and I can be acceptable again. (Whispers) I can be acceptable.

D: *Is there anyone there that talks to you?*

C: Not anybody that I know, but many people are around and they are friendly and beckon to come closer. But I just can't believe it's okay for me to be here.

D: *(Laugh) Of course, it is.*

C: And to not be in pain anymore, and to not be in guilt and eternal damnation.

D: *It's perfectly all right for you to be there.*

C: (Angry) Those people taught me the wrong things. Now those of us that were stuck and lost are being taken into a sort of temple of shining light where we can be allowed to recover from what we went through. I see some of the others. They didn't have the stuck period. They just went straight to the nice place and started to recover right away. But those of us who got stuck, we need help.

D: *What is this temple like?*

C: On the outside it's all columns and beautiful. Inside it's like... now I'm in a pool. They said this pool will heal me from these terrible wounds, and that terrible pain. A pool that will heal all of the stuck pain, and the terror and the horror and the pain. It's golden water that shimmers, and you wave your arms around the golden shimmering light while you're standing up to your armpits.

D: *It just washes everything away?*

C: It does. And my eternal soul is still alive. They told me it was going to die in hell. I didn't know I could still live. (Amazed) They tell you your soul is going to die and you believe it. You don't know you can live!

D: *You can't kill a soul. It's not true, is it?*

C: No. They just could hide it because we believed. I don't need to follow them anymore. – Now I'm sitting with other people in the beautiful place and garden, and people are eating grapes. And I'm allowed to join them now. I've been away a long, long time. And I'm allowed to be here and to be saved, and to have life that I didn't have for a long, long time.

D: *Are you going to stay there for a while?*

C: I need to have teaching, new teaching. The real truth about God and life, and the kind teachers are going to teach us all the things to counteract the false things we had with the old stuff. And I can be peaceful here. And we can grow because our learning was stopped. They said we don't have to return to Earth until we learn many more things.

D: *They want you to be more prepared?*

C: To do it better next time. We weren't prepared, and we didn't do it right, and we believed false beliefs and we didn't become ourselves. So now we have a chance to be given teaching, so that when we go again we become ourselves, our real selves. To be able to think for ourselves, and be individuals. To be ourselves, to be real and live our destiny; fulfill our potential. It was taken away from us and now it is being restored.

D: *It's time to come back and do it the right way.*

C: Yes, with proper knowledge and with proper encouragement.

D: *Are you going to be able to remember it when you come back to a physical body?*

C: I don't know about that, but I know the people now encourage us and will let us be our real selves and want us to be our real selves, instead of being squashed and hidden like before. They want us to be who we really are and that's much more than I ever believed.

D: *Let's move ahead to when you have learned everything they want you to learn, and you are getting ready to come back to a physical body. Does someone help you or tell you when it's time?*

C: Yes, we're in a class that teaches how to go back. These are the ready ones now getting instructions about going back.

D: *What are the instructions?*

C: That you can have your true knowledge with you even though it may not emerge immediately. It is always there and you can call on it and you can connect and you never need to lose your connection. And go to the Earth in a body and stay connected.

D: *Do you get to choose what kind of a life or physical body to come into?*

C: No, I don't think I've done that yet.

D: *Let's move ahead to where you have the instructions. Do they allow you to choose where you go?*

C: Yes, and they're helping me choose a good one this time. It builds my soul and restores my spirit.

D: *They don't make the decision for you?*

C: No, they are showing me the different ones and they help me choose a good one. You don't have to have bad lessons like that all the time, and the pain all the time. You can choose a good one. You can develop music and become a pianist, and you can choose things that build and enhance you instead of tear you to pieces and destroy you.

D: *Which one are you going to choose?*

C: I like nature and science and there can be science. I can study the universe.

D: *Do you pick the family?*

C: We seem to be going together in a group to a planet where we can study physics and the universe, and all the secrets of the physical life and how to help people do it better. It's a place where we're going to be working together and have wonderful teachers and we won't have the problems of Earth. You won't get torn to pieces and half buried. You'll be able to do it in the light.

D: *They thought this would be a better choice than coming back to Earth?*

C: Yes, a better choice to help humanity. Otherwise, we'd be stuck in those little hell holes forever. – We get to build something different. Of peace, and learn what you can do without being broken.

D: *What kind of body do you have in that lifetime?*

C: It's not like Earth. It doesn't get hurt as easily. It's tough and leathery, sort of a reptilian looking thing.

D: *It sounds like you're very intelligent though.*

C: Yes, but any place we can be intelligent because we were so stupid on Earth.

D: *So you stay there for a while on that planet? (Yes) Do you become a scientist?*

C: Yes. It feeds my soul and fills my soul with knowledge and information in helping many other planets and races in their time in a physical body. This is to help them. It's to ease the suffering because the suffering causes too much damage.

D: *Do you do all of your work on that planet?*

C: Oh, no. We go in ships. We have the whole universe to study. How the stars explode and how the planets will develop in their body. And it's so vast and beautiful and we can be part of it. It's very strange because we can go out and see stars and galaxies one minute and now we can go and see something else the next minute. I don't know how that works. Back and forth between different dimensions. We want to learn and to teach. Because there's so much to heal from the Earth experience, and they've given me this chance to heal now.

D: *Do you ever go near Earth again while you're exploring the universe?*

C: I haven't been there yet.

He seemed to have finally found happiness after the terrible ordeal he had been through. So I decided to take him to the last day of his life in that lifetime and see what happened.

C: The shining, golden light that started in my heart and expanded throughout my body and the energy body and ensouled in the spirit, has permeated my being and the others who are also leaving.

D: *What happened to the body you are leaving?*

C: It just dissolved into dust.

D: *There wasn't anything wrong with it?*

C: No. When the golden light came we knew that we were healed and we knew it was time to go and bring the knowledge that we learned to other species and planets. So now we are a floating, golden ball of beingness. We go to the council with knowledge, and we communicate with other beings that have had other knowledge. And wear silvery balls and glimmering, shimmering colors of balls of light. And together we give the information to the pool of knowledge for all to use, so that the broken planets can draw this knowledge for their healing.

D: *Is it like a huge pool that collects everything?*

C: Not exactly a pool, it's these bubbles. Each being is like a shimmering bubble and all their knowledge together forms like electrical currents that flow to the universes. To all the places that need it. And so a planet in trouble like Earth was, can call on that electricity to come to them. It comes like a golden current and it brings the healing. And it becomes available for the whole planet.

D: *How can the whole planet receive it?*

C: Well, it can't, but as they become ready they open up and receive it. And it gradually heals the planet and the people and the brokenness that was there, the damage.

D: *Do the people on the planet have to desire this?*

C: Yes. Somebody has to call on it. Otherwise, it flows right over the planet and they miss it completely.

D: *So they have to want help?*

C: Yes. And so the many, many bubbles of light ... each one of the beings, continuously gather at the central place and bring the knowledge and the information and the helpfulness to share with all. And they come and go, so we brought our bucket of knowledge and dumped it in. And they can choose to go somewhere else and get another bunch of knowledge to bring back. – We don't have to stay broken forever. Now we're fixed.

D: *Now I'd like you to move ahead to when you decide to come back to Earth and into the physical body of Catherine, the one that you are speaking through at this time.*

C: Oh, her! She was broken, but she doesn't have to be. Now she's got me. She was in that broken place in many lives on Earth, but now I have come to her. A lost part of her, and now the golden, shining light can be in her, too, starting now. She will be pleased. She was faithfully hanging onto all the misery, but now she doesn't have to.

D: *Can you explain to her why she chose such a dramatic life with her parents?*

C: She had to continue being broken. She had been hanging on to every bit of brokenness from every experience, and she had to continue hanging onto it. She thought she was being faithful to God by hanging on to the brokenness.

D: *She thought she had some other lives where she was religious.*

C: Yes, so with all of that she kept building the brokenness each time. Making it worse, and hanging onto it. She thought she was doing the right thing. It was her way of being faithful. It was just misplaced.

D: *So when she came into this life she thought she was going to have to continue having the trauma and bad experiences?*

C: That's right. Just continue being broken and dysfunctional and suffering, all because they told her -- somewhere they told her -- God loves it when people suffer in His name, and she believed it. Now because she saw Vesuvius she knows it was false teachings.

D: *What about her parents? Why did they all choose to come back together and experience this?*

C: They were gentle souls and still had so much learning to do, and they shared some of the same false beliefs, and so it all unrolled. They all shared distant and primitive lives full of superstition and fear. And so they had that connection of believing superstition and fear. It was almost unconsciously continuing the suffering. – I see the mother now. She so believes that inflicting suffering is good for souls, so she does it and does it and does it, and has never realized how wrong it is.

D: *But Catherine doesn't need to be caught up in that anymore, does she?*

C: No, no. She doesn't want to be caught in it. She didn't know how to get out.

D: *But now you can help her, can't you?*

C: Yes because new information has entered and penetrated the place that was locked up with the pain. Now her whole life will change. Because the change in that distant planet, where the healing and the science took place can be with her now ... starting now in this life.

I switched to asking about Catherine's physical condition. They said if she had continued on the path she was headed that she would have died. She was following the wrong path.

C: The heart was shriveling because of the brokenness, but now she's learned that if a relationship ends, you don't have to shrivel up and die because you are self-sufficient and a strong individual. And so now the shriveled heart can be healed. It's done shriveling!

They then focused on Catherine's back, the major source of pain and crippling effects that were holding her back. The pain went from her neck all the way down her back. The doctors were talking about surgery as the only option.

C: Extreme tension and rigidity and hanging on for dear life to the old ways. Let it go! The bones can now be restored. I can do it now. Let the electrical energy surround the whole spine; restore the whole energy that restores the bones. The electricity just wasn't working. The bones will all be fixed once the electricity and the energy moves through in the next few days. The pattern for healing is now there. She didn't think she could be inter-dimensional, but the spine was in the inter-dimensional hellish place. It was still being held there. It was inter-dimensional, just not a place she wanted to be. But now it's inter-dimensional in a healthy pattern. The channel of light has been opened. She thought she had no power, but holding that spine in that dimensional hell took so much power to do. She had *lots* of power. – Her whole body is tingling with the energy.

Message: She'll be so glad to join in my work of bringing light to planets and waking people up and helping them live and so, so glad and her happiness and desire of her heart to do this work.

D: *You said "my." Am I communicating with the subconscious?*
C: I'm the one that was on the science planet.
D: *So you mean you've been assigned now to work with her?*

C: Yes. It's the part of her that she was cut off from and felt so lost. And the work is galactic. She wanted to be part of the galactic work.

Parting message: Just listen more. Listen more because the truth is there. Don't give up.

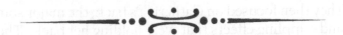

In our session she died as a man during a volcanic eruption. A glob of molten rock hit him in the stomach causing severe burning pain. The man died confused in Pompeii and then incarnated into religious lives in order to find his answers. This was probably part of the hellish place he spoke of. It didn't work. He was taught the answer was suffering and that followed through into Catherine's life.

The other part that emerged during our session was another splinter or aspect that found the correct way. That part could now merge with her and take away the false belief in the need to suffer. Enough is enough.

Also there was the suffering at the convent by the denying of food, living on very little. Eating as much as they could because you didn't know how much you'd get at the next meal (or if there would be another meal). (Notice that the man in Pompeii died of stomach injuries.)

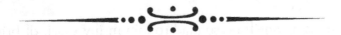

After the session Catherine was surprised to find that she no longer had any back pain. Also she looked softer and younger. She had volunteered to help with my lecture the next night, and was also attending the class. When she arrived at the lecture she was smiling and talked about how good she felt. At the class, before we started she said she wanted to tell (and show) the students what had happened. She walked and ran in circles all around the room, laughing excitedly. She said the day before she had spent four hours walking all over Sydney with no discomfort whatsoever.

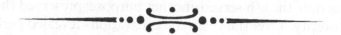

Sadly this type of fear still exists in our world today, and it is caused by the Church. My daughter, Julia, was a nurse in Intensive Care for many years. She said the saddest cases were those people who were dying in fear. They had lived a perfectly good life with all its challenges, and have harmed no one. Yet the Church had told them that unless they were perfect they were going to Hell. Since no one is perfect, they were terrified. They knew they were dying and the Church had convinced them that they were going to go to Hell. I think this is a great disservice for any religious organization to make a person afraid of dying. They should tell them about the beauty and wonder they will find when they cross over. That they will not be alone and that they will be reunited with their loved ones. That the other side is a place of unconditional love where no one is judged, no matter what the circumstances of their life have been. When they leave their earthly body they are simply going "home," and it is not a place to be feared, but welcomed.

There is much more information about what death is like and all the wonderful places you can go on the spirit side in my book *Between Death and Life*.

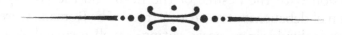

For those who do not know the history of what occurred at Pompeii I will give a condensed version. I have been there when we traveled by bus from Rome through Naples to reach the ruins. Mount Vesuvius stands majestically hovering over the entire landscape. There was smoke coming from the top, showing that it is still active. Scientists say it is only a matter of time when the volcano will erupt again, and I felt an uneasy feeling being in the vicinity. It did erupt in AD 79 and buried Pompeii in ash (just as was described in the sessions). Besides destruction, the ash served another purpose; preserved the city for posterity. Over the years the excavations revealed perfectly preserved buildings and artifacts. From the ruins it can be seen that it was a large city. It is now considered one of the richest sources of knowledge of the Hellenistic and Roman world because of the remarkable preservation.

Thus we have two different versions from people who died during the eruption of Vesuvius, and they are both essentially correct. They are just reported from different viewpoints. The first one was from the viewpoint of a child living in Pompeii during that time, and she saw it as a beautiful clean city. During the excavations they found perfectly preserved buildings, and they had remains of paintings (stuccos) on the walls, beautiful murals. And also pictures made from small stones or mosaics. These were not only found in the public buildings, but even in the family houses, beautiful wall paintings (just as was described in the session). There was also a great deal of industry, agriculture and commerce, so the girl's father could very easily have been a wealthy man. Seeing it through a child's eyes, she only saw the beauty. She did not see the dark side of Pompeii.

The man's version of Pompeii was also correct. Among the paintings in the buildings were found explicit scenes of sex, and also statues with exaggerated sex organs, as though they had an obsession with the desires of the flesh. So the young man's version of debauchery was also correct. The Romans were well known to divulge in excesses, eating as well as sexual pleasures. In some ancient ruins they found what they called a "vomitorium." They would eat to excess, go and vomit, and then return to eating again. This type of world must have been very confusing to a young man coming into it from a life in the countryside. So it is easy to see how he was riddled with guilt when he died so violently.

Here are the ruins of Pompeii with Mt. Vesuvius towering in the background.

Here is a mosaic found in one of the homes.

Research shows that the concept of hell originated in the second and third century after the New Testament was written. The concept of hell has been used by over-zealous Christian preachers for centuries as a way to frighten their flocks into obedience, but it has no basis in scripture.

Chapter 24

HIDING JESUS' TEACHINGS

This session was done as a demonstration during a class in Ojai, California. I would pick a student in the class to perform the demonstration on. I never knew in advance who it would be, and I was always apprehensive about doing a demo in front of a large group of people. I never knew what would happen, and it is not the best setting for the subject either. I call it a "gold-fish bowl" setting because there is no privacy, and they are also nervous. It is done in front of the class and anything can happen. Normally it amazingly has always worked, although I never know what information will come out. On a few occasions the person I picked has been difficult and I really had to work to get them into a past life. It is normally a "left-brainer," or in other words, a "control freak." I want to show the class how to do the technic and how simple it is to use. In these cases the students said they liked seeing how I would handle a difficult case. They think they learned more from that than an easy one.

This was what happened when I asked Betsy to be the demo. When she came off the cloud all she saw was dark and then confusing images. Her left brain was very active trying to understand why she couldn't find something. This is always my explanation for skeptics who say the client is inventing a story to please the hypnotist. If she was going to make up something, why didn't she? After a while she began to see disjointed images and then scenes from her early years in her present life. It was interesting that these referred to arguing she heard between her parents while she was alone in her crib. I don't give up. I persist until I finally break down their resistance. After about a half hour of this confusion I asked her to move forward to something that was important and appropriate for her to see. Then we broke through the left brain barrier and were in a past life.

321

B: I am like a nun. I live with a group of women and we are studying books. We study teachings. We're in France and we're studying the teachings that we brought with us. We don't go out very much. We are afraid to go out.

D: *You said you're like a nun?*

B: Yes. I'm in an order of very bright women who are studying agnostic teachings of Jesus of Nazareth.

D: *But you said these were teachings you brought with you?*

B: Yes. We came away from that place ... the place where he was crucified.

D: *So you were there at that time?*

B: I was there. I was there with the others and we saw what happened. We were all there and we knew it was going to happen. He'd been our teacher and we loved him very much.

D: *So the whole group of women was studying with him?*

B: Yes, we were very special students of his.

D: *Did you see what happened to him?*

B: Yes, he was crucified, of course, and I saw the whole thing. I tried not to look very much, but afterwards we had to leave. And we had to take our teachings and go somewhere else. He told us we would have to and so we obeyed. Otherwise, the teachings would have been lost. And they were looking for us, too because they knew about us. That we were special disciples of his, and so we had to get out quickly. After his body was taken care of we left very quickly and went to France.

D: *Otherwise, you would have been in danger?*

B: Definitely. I would have and some of the others. By association it would have been me as well, but mostly our leader.

D: *How did you travel to France?*

B: We walked. Well, part of the way we walked. It was a long travel. It was a long trip. A good deal of it we walked.

D: *You all stayed together?*

B: We all stayed together.

D: *How did you find the place you're living now?*

B: It had been arranged and so we just followed the woman who knew ... our leader. She knew and there was a man who was leading the way. He knew. It had all been prepared. We knew this would happen so we took the teachings and we left.

D: *Did you remember them?*

B: They were written down. Many of them were written. We wrote more later on. It was written and we had to protect them. It was very hard. That's what they really wanted were the teachings and we had to protect them from being torn and lost. He told us different things than he told the others. We learned more than the others. These were secret teachings as far as the others were concerned.

D: *These were different than the men disciples were taught?*

B: Different than the men disciples and they were very jealous that he taught us those things, and they didn't want us to have them. They thought that if we had them, since we were women that they should have them. Of course, that's how they are, you know.

D: *Yes, I understand. That's why they were jealous of your group?*

B: Very much so, especially of our leader. She was the one they really despised. They pretended to love her, but they deep down didn't love her at all.

D: *Did the men go in a different direction, or do you know?*

B: I do know that some men came with us, but not the ones we were afraid of. They stayed back and went their way. They had a different dispensation. Their job was to take the teachings that were verbal teachings and to spread them verbally. But those that were written were precious and they were given to us. And we went and we studied more, and He came after He was back again. He came and visited us in that place in France.

D: *Who came after you were in that place?*

B: Jesus came. They called him Yeshua. He came.

D: *After he had been crucified? (Yes) Was he in spirit or body?*

B: He was in spirit and in body.

D: *Both together?*

B: Together, yes. He came with his physical body just briefly. Just for a time to do the teaching and then he left. He left but I knew him and he knew me -- very casually -- not in much depth, but he was my teacher.

D: *Did he go somewhere else after he left your group?*

B: Yes. He went back to his Father. But he came several times.

D: *To make sure you were doing what you were supposed to be doing?*

B: Yes, to question us and to leave more teachings. And we wrote these down. And no one knows about this, I don't think. I don't think anyone knows.

D: *Then it's very secret. It's very precious for you to protect all of this.*

B: Yes, that's true. We are honored and we lived all alone for many years. We never went out. We stayed inside. Even our leader stayed. We were away from everyone for years. We wanted to be like him. We thought we could be like him. We knew we could be like him because he told us we could. And he wanted us to be teachers as well, but we couldn't be with the men. You know they wouldn't allow it, so we came here.

D: *That was a very good decision.*

B: Yes, we think so.

I decided to move her ahead to an important day in that life. That would be one way to get more information because otherwise she just stayed in the place where they lived.

B: It was a day when we tried to go out and found out they were still ... we heard that they were still looking for us.

324

We thought that we could find women ... bring other women into our group. We were becoming very small and we needed and wanted to spread the teachings in our own way.

D: *Your group was dying off?*

B: Yes, they were dying off. We had maybe five or six left so it was important to not let it be the only way we had. Some others had to know. So we went out, and we found out things had not changed very much at all, and still many did not know what we knew.

D: *So what did you decide to do?*

B: We decided we had to take these teachings and put them somewhere. Not just where we would have them alone because certainly we all could die and there wouldn't be anyone to have these teachings but us. So we arranged to take them out and to bury them, and we did that. We had the help of some male disciples to do that. We wanted to protect them, and we trusted these men. They were our friends. Not all were the same, you know. We had some friends who thought differently of us. There were many men that wanted to study with us, but of course, (Laugh) not in those times.

D: *Where do you bury them?*

B: We took them out and buried them in several places, not just in France. There were some that were buried close to where we lived. But then there were those that were taken back to where he was crucified, and we buried them on the seashore very close to that place.

D: *This place where you went out and buried everything ... where you had your group. Was it near a city or a town?*

B: Yes, it was ... Le Deuce ... Le Blanc? Something like that or close to that name.

D: *That was the name of the place where you had the group?*

B: Yes, close to the city. We were living in a temple actually, an old church. There were other knights around that protected us in that place.

D: *So when you buried the teachings, was it near that city?*

B: Some of them, yes, and then some of the knights took off to other places and buried.

D: *I think that was very good that you wanted to protect these things. It's good to protect knowledge, isn't it?*

B: That is extremely important, the precious, ageless, teachings of all times. Those that teach the way, the way to God. That is what I have always wanted and it was my privilege to know him. And it was an honor to be able to be in his light and to radiate that light and to do the teachings.

D: *You did a good job.*

B: I think so.

D: *And you did try to protect the teachings.*

B: Yes. There weren't very many people to listen however, not where we were, but I think they would have been good. I wanted to teach large groups, but that was not my destiny in that life. But we did something very important in that life and I like doing things that are important, very important. You know some people can't see things that are important, but I can. I can see important things. I know them immediately and that is what I do.

I thought we had learned as much as we were going to be able to from a woman living a cloistered and isolated existence. So I moved her ahead to the last day of her life and asked her what was happening.

B: I am in the bed and my sisters are with me. They are very old now. We are all old. (Laugh) We lived a long time, and I'm sad because I lost so many others, my sisters. And I am among the last and I'm thinking now of my life. I'm thinking of him. I'm thinking of the future. I'm thinking of the greatness of those teachings. If only others could know.

They're not what they seem. They're not what they're being taught now. The beauty of the teachings has been lost.

D: *You were able to teach people, weren't you?*

B: No, not enough ... not enough. Not of the *True* teachings. Only the superficial teachings, only those that could be understood. There was no one to understand the depth of the teachings. That was the problem. We had to protect them from those that were not able to see and understand them.

D: *You weren't able to spread them like you wanted to.*

B: No. We had to bury them. But someday someone will discover them and they will be taught and that was my job.

D: *So they were not lost.*

B: No, they were not lost, and I die happily that way knowing this. My life has been fulfilled. I did a very good job. I'm very pleased. I would not have it any different although I was very alone. I would have liked to have *known* more people. I'm so alone in it all, alone with the teachings.

D: *I think you did a good job with it. You tried.*

B: Thank you. I did indeed.

I moved her to the other side where she was out of her body and asked if she could see her body. "I can see it far away. I'm just drifting away, drifting away."

D: *As you look at that lifetime, every life has a lesson. What do you think you learned from that life?*

B: I learned the love of the teachings and I learned that they must be preserved and hidden. And that God is within. Despite what the Christians teach today, I know the truth and it is not what they say. It is not what they have done with it. I can see that now.

D: *You think you learned that in that life?*

B: I knew that I had the teachings all the time. I learned about the oneness of God. I learned about the way it was taught, and what happened to the teaching *after* it left our hands. Yes, I learned that.

D: *What do you think you are going to do with that lesson? It's an important lesson. Now that you're out of that body, what do you think?*

B: I'm going to protect the truth and I am going to make sure that the truth is preserved. And that others unfold in spirit as I was able to because I knew the truth, the truth about who we are.

I then had her drift away from that lifetime and called forth the SC. The first question I always ask is why the SC chose that particular lifetime to show the client.

B: Because she doubts herself. She doubts she is who she is. She doubts and she is afraid.

D: *What is she afraid of?*

B: She is afraid of being different than others. She is angry because her family never saw her difference and if they did, they didn't support it. Her mother tried ineffectually, not very well. But she pretended to be letting Betsy dabble here and there, but not as far as seeing that little difference, then nurturing it and education. She needed more education, and she's angry, very angry that she's not cultivated it earlier so she could have done something for the world. More than she's been able to do in this life. It's so hard ... so hard for her. It didn't need to be so hard.

D: *Did she make it that hard?*

B: Well, I think she purposely came into this life and was given circumstances to work out karma. She knew from the beginning who she was. She could not escape the karma that she had to pay so she would try to jerk out and she would try to do this and do that. And nothing, of course, would work because it was not *our* will. It was not what she was to do. She never liked the contract idea. You know she didn't want to have to do that. She wanted to get on with it.

D: *What was her contract?*

B: The contract was to help these various men in her life find themselves and to learn something about themselves, sometimes to see their own weaknesses and to then go on. She had to learn that she didn't belong there and to go on. They just had to finish off their karma together and it was a lot of suffering for her. She felt angry at these men because she couldn't get on with it again. She knew where she had to go, but she had to do this first. That first one was a thing she had to fulfill. Poor dear, she suffered. Oh, my, he was quite a guy. He crawled up from under a rock in Norway. That's what we used to say about that one. (We laughed.) He was quite a character. She had to live with him and he really frightened her. For a long time he was beating her and she was coming back for more because of the Christian guilt to not leave this marriage and to stick it out. She felt guilt and she stayed and he did his thing over and over and she didn't "get" it. She stayed much too long. He almost could have killed her, but she was wise to see that finally and got away. He eventually got on with it so she only has herself to blame for that, if you want to feel blame, but she could have broken it earlier. I know she wonders about the karma of that one. She does not want to come back with that one, and I don't blame her. I think we can say that it's finished. It's finished. She got out of that one and it was smart. She had to go through him. She also had to go through the *other* one, the second one, Dennis. There's no karma there with that one. They simply had to meet. Dennis had to grow up and go on, and Betsy had to see that these were weak men who were holding her back.

D: *Were these people she was involved with in other lifetimes?* (Yes, yes.) *So they had karma.*

B: Yes, they had to get it over. And then, of course, there was the music teacher, one of the loves of her life. Of course, they were never married but that was another lesson. You know, attachments, attachments. She couldn't really see who she was because of a previous life where she was in music. And all of a sudden she thought she was to be an opera singer, and we couldn't convince her that was not where she should be. She stayed too long. Oh, my goodness! She finally had to lose her voice. We had to take away her voice entirely to get her out of that one, and he loved her. And then, of course, there was the other one, the last one. We won't even talk about him. Finally she has found a partner. This is one who needs a partner and so she found the right one.

The SC then discussed the major problems Betsy had had with her mother all her life. These were still continuing and it was time to let them go.

D: *You know that Betsy is so interested in metaphysical teachings. Does that come from that lifetime you showed her?*

B: Yes, she has been a part of this pattern for many lifetimes. Other religions as well, but always in the thick of it, surrounding some great teacher of some sort. Which she was in the life of the Buddha. She was a friend of his wife, and she received the teaching at that time. She has been in the life of Mohammed, but a follower, not so much a part of his inner circle.

D: *It seems like her destiny has been to study ancient teachings and to pass them along.*

The SC discussed her fascination with ancient teachings now, and how she has been going from teacher to teacher to absorb as much knowledge as possible. "We have so much more for her. There's more she is capable of. It's time to move on. The teachings are very important, and she has gotten herself in with people who love these age old wisdoms and teachings, but not many people will take the time to go through them. There's only two or three of those books that anyone can understand." I remarked that it was similar to the lifetime she was shown where they didn't have very many to pass the knowledge on to. – I decided it was time to ask about the healing of her body. Betsy had many physical problems and symptoms.   She was in constant pain that had been escalating over the past forty years and she was on heavy pain medications. The pain was over most of her body as she had problems with her back (scoliosis and degenerating disks), her pelvis (rotated and damaged floor), hips, knees, ankles, wrists and shoulder blades. She had severe allergies and had been having breathing difficulties since childhood.   In addition to these issues, Betsy also had high blood pressure and problems with her eyes and she was on numerous medications. I thought it best to have the SC do a body scan since there were so many health issues.

B: She needs this body to be healed. She has wanted it for so long. She didn't know how to come to me. I think that she couldn't make the contact to the fuddled brain through the drugs. We tried. We tried to reach her when she was begging and asking, but she couldn't make the connection. There was nothing we could do. The drugs were definitely in the way of the light we wanted to send, which could have saved her, could have healed her right on the spot.

D: *But now in this state you can help her, can't you?*

B: She can be helped and we want to do this. We have wanted it for a long time, so let's get on with it.

D: *She won't be able to resist you.*

B: Oh, yes, we have her right where we want her. We are going to do a big scan from top to bottom and see what's there.

D: *I call it a body scan.*

B: Oh, of course. And we'll just let the light go from the top to the bottom and then we'll find out where we missed. We have a technique we want to bring in. The technique of light that will be the new way of healing in the New Age. The Space Brothers have it, you know.

D: *I didn't know that.*

B: Everything is of light. Everything is light. We just have to learn how to focus it. – We are going to start with the top of the head. We're going to stop for a considerable time and work on the brain. We're going to take the light and pull the light through every molecule in her brain and get all that toxicity out. That stuff makes her brain unclear.

With other clients the SC has many times said they were rewiring the brain. This could be how they do it. I always ask them to explain how they are doing the healing because I am curious, and it is good for the client to hear the process on the recording.

B: I don't have to concentrate. I have this instrument at this time, an instrument that opens this light energy. And it's capable of breaking through the frequencies necessary to balance them with light. It's quite difficult to explain to you, but here it is.

They then moved on to her chest cavity and they were appalled by what her allergies and the drugs had done. "You wouldn't believe. This Las Vegas (where Betsy lived) is not good for her. She needs to leave as soon as her mother makes transition. We've got to have her out of there. Her body is sensitive, mostly because she spent so much time on another planet. There are two ways we can do this. We can make her body not react to the allergies, which is *my* preferred way, so she can go anywhere. Or we can make her not allergic to the allergies she experiences in a certain place if she wants to just stay there."

D: *You do it the way you prefer to do it.*

B: Well, I'd like to just get rid of ALL of it. You know, it took us so long to get her here, let's do it right! (Laugh)

D: *You do it the way you want to do it. You're the boss. (Laugh)*

They also mentioned that the nasal spray drug she was taking was creating a problem with a rebound reaction. They repaired the damage, but she would have to be patient as the nose learned to breathe without it. They then moved on to her liver/kidney where they saw congestion and they proceeded to do a detox. They then moved to the pelvis area.

B: She's had two surgeries and we have to tear out all that. This part is not easy. The doctors messed the surgeries up. And she would be moving toward a life of misery and perhaps incontinence. Surgery is so archaic and primitive. My goodness!

D: *They want to operate again.*

B: No, absolutely nonsense. This is so easy.

They then worked on all the joints and repaired them. "There is a tingling sensation now. I'm sure she can feel it." A problem with her pineal gland had caused trouble sleeping, and she was taking medication for that also. The SC definitely wanted her to get off all of the drugs. She had also been taking drugs for depression, but they also fixed that without being asked to do so. "We handled that. She's all right now. It came from all those lives of being held back as a woman. You know women have a terrible time with karma, the collective whole. They have accumulated so much. You're bound to get depressed after a while. She absolutely carried that into this life, and then no love from the father compounded it. So there, we've done that and balanced that. Now we have to do the back." Betsy's back was the main problem she wanted to address, but they felt they had to fix everything else first. Now we could go to her back and help that. Betsy had been born with a curvature of the spine.

B: It started out when she was a woman in Africa carrying around those baskets. Being born in a time when women did carry heavy things. It began there and so it was continued on in various lives. There were accidents and wars where she was broken. She broke her back in a war and they didn't have ways of patching that in those days, so she carried that forward as a memory.

D: *She doesn't need it now.*

B: No, she doesn't need it. She's going to be shocked when she can stand up straight. She'll love it. She is wondering if she will feel any of this. She's feeling something happening. It is the alignment. We will continue. This back thing is not an easy thing. We're trying to get her off this medication, so we don't want it to take very long. Maybe we just want to heal it right now. She wouldn't have the pain without this straightening of the back right away. Yes, the pain is going to be gone. We would prefer to do the straightening over several months only because it is hard for *us*. It is a lot of work.

D: *I know what you can do.*

B: Yes, I know you do. (Both laughed.) Well, let me see.

D: *Whatever you think is most appropriate.*

B: Well, I think it would be very good for Betsy if she could really see a miracle. (Pause)

D: *So what are you doing?*

B: I'm gazing at a triangle and fixing her back at the same time. The pelvis is rotated so it takes it awhile to rebalance. To readapt the balance of the neck, the shoulders, the whole works. I think we've accomplished miracles today. She'll be surprised and she won't need the meds as much, if any at all. She really needs to see her doctor though to go off them slowly. It won't be difficult, though. That is the main thing. There won't be any more pain and all the withdrawal symptoms that you usually experience. The body will just get used to not having that drug in it. I'm trying to say there won't be any pain, sick to the stomach maybe. I think it's enough. We will continue on. It will continue on even though I am not here, so if you wish the rest you may finish.

D: *Well, you know we have a class, don't you?*

B: Oh, yes, that's right.

D: *And this is very important for them to learn this, isn't it?*

B: I hope we have been instructive. I hope they have learned a thing or two.

D: *We want to teach them. They can do it themselves.*

B: Yes, we would be so happy to work with them as healers. Yes, the world needs more, so let it be.

D: *Get away from surgery.*

B: Oh, my! Don't even mention the word. (Both laughed.) We have removed all the discomfort from the back. That is so! I've done a great deal today but during sleep we'll even assist more. There will be more of a release of the discs as she sleeps. We do a lot of the work on the back in sleep time because it is so sensitive. The whole system, the whole spinal fluid, cerebral spinal situation is in the back.

D: *Then you have the conscious mind out of the way so you can work without interference.*

B: Yes, it's so good.

D: *You said it would take several months to complete the straightening?*

B: I don't think it's going to take that long now because I worked on her. Thank you for allowing me more time. I think she'll be surprised. She'll notice a difference.

D: *Wonderful! Then she'll believe it!*

B: That's what we want. Belief is very important, and she has a particular problem with all of this, you know, the esoteric approach. Believe only what you yourself really believe, not because someone told you. It has to be something that you know. She will be a new person.

D: *She was ready to leave, and it's not time, is it?*

B: No, it's just beginning.

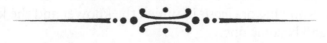

Parting message: She's worried so much that she hasn't done a good job. She's so worried and has to do this and do that, and she's worried about the "other" side that we're going to be disappointed in her. No, she's doing a fine job. Everything is just fine. She needs to quit the guilt and know that we love her. I will unconditionally. She can do no wrong and we should have more like her. She is doing her part in the great plan. She is listening to her higher self and fulfilling her purpose in life.

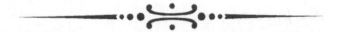

When Betsy awakened and got off the bed, she was amazed that she had no pain. She also noticed immediately that she was standing straighter. Later she was sitting on the floor doing yoga positions, as the students watched. She laughed as she said she had not been able to do those in many years.

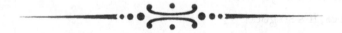

According to Stuart Wilson and Joanna Prentis in *The Power of the Magdalene – The Hidden Story of the Women Disciples*, Mary Magdalene left Israel after the crucifixion on board one of Joseph of Arimathea's ships and her party landed in southern France, which was then known as Gaul. It is stated that there would be a balance of the male and female disciples, there were six circles of twelve, making 72 male disciples, and six circles of twelve making 72 female disciples – a total of 144 disciples in all. Mary Magdalene was part of the first of twelve female disciples. Could this be the same group Betsy mentioned being a part of? Also within this text Stuart defines the Gnostics as a loosely-knit movement which was active during the very earliest years of Christianity. They believed in a mystical state of Deep Knowing or *Gnosis* in which the knower and the known merge and become one.

There is still great debate of their motives and ethics by the Church.

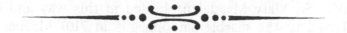

The Relics of Saint Marie-Magdalene at La Sainte Baume Diocese of Frejus-Toulon, Southern France

Provided Courtesy of: Eternal World Television Network

Translated from the French by: Deacon E. Scott Borgman

The region of Provence was evangelized in the first century by Christians from the East. Tradition has called them the "Friends of Bethany" or as we know them to be Lazarus, Martha and Mary Magdalene who, it is told, came to the south of France in the following way:

In the year following the execution of St James in Jerusalem, the persecutions were amplified. Lazarus and Martha were thrown into prison and Mary Magdalene, having wanted to visit them, was made prisoner as well along with other members Christian community of Bethany: St Maximin, St Marcelle, St Susan and St. Sidonius.

The Jews, being afraid of the crowd if they were to execute the prisoners, placed them in a boat without sail or rudder, and a great ship towed them offshore and abandoned them in the open sea. Singing and praying they found themselves landing on the shores of Gaul at the place called Saintes Maries de la Mer. The trip had been made at a miraculous speed.

They traveled by land to Massilia (Marseille) where they were given a good welcome. They preached the Gospel and Lazarus, in his capacity as bishop, baptized many people. Mary Magdalene retired to a cave in the mountains which was difficult to access; there she lived in severe penance. Martha went to Avignon and Tarascon.

St. Mary Magdalene died near Tégulata (St. Maximin). On the site where the sarcophagus of St. Mary Magdalene was found, during excavations under the Basilica of St. Maximin, tombs from the 1st century made of bricks and tiles were also discovered.

Was St. Mary Magdalene buried in this way and then transferred to the marble sarcophagus in 710? Maybe. The essential thing is the Tradition affirming this and the constant pilgrimages to the Ste Baume, a place venerated by Christianity from the early centuries, before the monks carried some of the relics to Vézelay in Burgundy during the ravages of Provence by the Saracens.

The presence of Lazarus, Martha and Mary Magdalene in Provence was recognized as true and belongs to the Sacred History of France. It was also acknowledged by all of Christendom in the East as well as in the West. People came from all of the countries of Europe on pilgrimage to the graves of "Holy Friends of Jesus".

Chapter 25

CONCLUSION

As I stated in the Introduction, this is not new knowledge. This is new, *old* knowledge. It has been here for millennia, but was reserved for the select few who devoted their lives to understanding and teaching it. Because knowledge was power, usually people in authority felt threatened by anyone or anything they couldn't understand, so they tried to get it by any means they could. Many were tortured and killed for this knowledge. Many of those souls are back now to help mankind and the planet in the movement forward. Their mission is to ensure the mistakes from before are not made again. Much of the skills, abilities and knowledge are returning to those who are open to them to be used in a manner to assist one and all. That is why there are so many people drawn to do healing work as "lightworkers" or are in the helping professions. Most of the people who come to see me, fall into one of these categories.

This is an exciting time we live in right now as our home, our planet, moves into another dimension. It's all a matter of frequencies and vibrations. And people are waking up at an alarming rate. It can be confusing at times, but we all signed on to be here at this time. We must never forget that we chose to be here and we are here for a reason. These sessions are just a few examples of how we are coming back to remind ourselves who we are and what we can and *should* do. It is no longer knowledge for a select few, but for all of us. As we all awaken and raise our frequencies, we are helping each other and our Earth to accomplish her mission of raising frequencies to be fully in another dimension.

I am continually being given more and more information about our heritage and why we are here and will continue to do my part in helping to uncover this hidden, sacred knowledge for all of us to learn.

Author Page

Dolores Cannon, a regressive hypnotherapist and psychic researcher who records "Lost" knowledge, was born in 1931 in St. Louis, Missouri. She was educated and lived in St. Louis until her marriage in 1951 to a career Navy man. She spent the next 20 years traveling all over the world as a typical Navy wife, and raising her family. In 1970 her husband was discharged as a disabled veteran, and they retired to the hills of Arkansas. She then started her writing career and began selling her articles to various magazines and newspapers. She has been involved with hypnosis since 1968, and exclusively with past-life therapy and regression work since 1979. She has studied the various hypnosis methods and thus developed her own unique technique which enabled her to gain the most efficient release of information from her clients. Dolores is now teaching her unique technique of hypnosis all over the world.

In 1986 she expanded her investigations into the UFO field. She has done on-site studies of suspected UFO landings, and has investigated the Crop Circles in England. The majority of her work in this field has been the accumulation of evidence from suspected abductees through hypnosis.

Dolores is an international speaker who has lectured on all the continents of the world. Her seventeen books are translated into twenty languages. She has spoken to radio and television audiences worldwide. And articles about/by Dolores have appeared in several U.S. and international magazines and newspapers. Dolores was the first American and the first foreigner to receive the "Orpheus Award" in Bulgaria, for the highest advancement in the research of psychic phenomenon. She has received Outstanding Contribution and Lifetime Achievement awards from several hypnosis organizations.

Dolores has a very large family who keep her solidly balanced between the "real" world of her family and the "unseen" world of her work.

If you wish to correspond with Ozark Mountain Publishing about Dolores' work or her training classes, please submit to the following address. (Please enclose a self addressed stamped envelope for her reply.) Dolores Cannon, P.O. Box 754, Huntsville, AR, 72740, USA
Or email the office at decannon@msn.com or through our Website: www.ozarkmt.com

Dolores Cannon, who transitioned from this world on October 18, 2014, left behind incredible accomplishments in the fields of alternative healing, hypnosis, metaphysics and past life regression, but most impressive of all was her innate understanding that the most important thing she could do was to share information. To reveal hidden or undiscovered knowledge vital to the enlightenment of humanity and our lessons here on Earth. Sharing information and knowledge is what mattered most to Dolores. That is why her books, lectures and unique QHHT® method of hypnosis continue to amaze, guide and inform so many people around the world. Dolores explored all these possibilities and more while taking us along for the ride of our lives. She wanted fellow travelers to share her journeys into the unknown.

Other Books by Ozark Mountain Publishing, Inc.

Dolores Cannon
A Soul Remembers Hiroshima
Between Death and Life
Conversations with Nostradamus,
    Volume I, II, III
The Convoluted Universe -Book One,
    Two, Three, Four, Five
The Custodians
Five Lives Remembered
Horns of the Goddess
Jesus and the Essenes
Keepers of the Garden
Legacy from the Stars
The Legend of Starcrash
The Search for Hidden Sacred
    Knowledge
They Walked with Jesus
The Three Waves of Volunteers and the
    New Earth
A Very Special Friend
Aron Abrahamsen
Holiday in Heaven
James Ream Adams
Little Steps
Justine Alessi & M. E. McMillan
Rebirth of the Oracle
Kathryn Andries
Time: The Second Secret
Will Alexander
Call Me Jonah
Cat Baldwin
Divine Gifts of Healing
The Forgiveness Workshop
Penny Barron
The Oracle of UR
P.E. Berg & Amanda Hemmingsen
The Birthmark Scar
Dan Bird
Finding Your Way in the Spiritual Age
Waking Up in the Spiritual Age
Julia Cannon
Soul Speak – The Language of Your
    Body
Jack Cauley
Journey for Life
Ronald Chapman
Seeing True
Jack Churchward
Lifting the Veil on the Lost
    Continent of Mu

The Stone Tablets of Mu
Carolyn Greer Daly
Opening to Fullness of Spirit
Patrick De Haan
The Alien Handbook
Paulinne Delcour-Min
Divine Fire
Holly Ice
Spiritual Gold
Anthony DeNino
The Power of Giving and Gratitude
Joanne DiMaggio
Edgar Cayce and the Unfulfilled
    Destiny of Thomas Jefferson
    Reborn
Paul Fisher
Like a River to the Sea
Anita Holmes
Twidders
Aaron Hoopes
Reconnecting to the Earth
Edin Huskovic
God is a Woman
Patricia Irvine
In Light and In Shade
Kevin Killen
Ghosts and Me
Susan Linville
Blessings from Agnes
Donna Lynn
From Fear to Love
Curt Melliger
Heaven Here on Earth
Where the Weeds Grow
Henry Michaelson
And Jesus Said – A Conversation
Andy Myers
Not Your Average Angel Book
Holly Nadler
The Hobo Diaries
Guy Needler
The Anne Dialogues
Avoiding Karma
Beyond the Source – Book 1, Book 2
The Curators
The History of God
The OM
The Origin Speaks

For more information about any of the above titles, soon to be released titles,
or other items in our catalog, write, phone or visit our website:
PO Box 754, Huntsville, AR 72740|479-738-2348/800-935-0045|www.ozarkmt.com

Other Books by Ozark Mountain Publishing, Inc.

Psycho Spiritual Healing
James Nussbaumer
And Then I Knew My Abundance
Each of You
Living Your Dram, Not Someone Else's
The Master of Everything
Mastering Your Own Spiritual Freedom
Sherry O'Brian
Peaks and Valley's
Gabrielle Orr
Akashic Records: One True Love
Let Miracles Happen
Nikki Pattillo
Children of the Stars
A Golden Compass
Victoria Pendragon
Being In A Body
Sleep Magic
The Sleeping Phoenix
Alexander Quinn
Starseeds What's It All About
Debra Rayburn
Let's Get Natural with Herbs
Charmian Redwood
A New Earth Rising
Coming Home to Lemuria
Richard Rowe
Exploring the Divine Library
Imagining the Unimaginable
Garnet Schulhauser
Dance of Eternal Rapture
Dance of Heavenly Bliss
Dancing Forever with Spirit
Dancing on a Stamp
Dancing with Angels in Heaven
Annie Stillwater Gray
The Dawn Book
Education of a Guardian Angel
Joys of a Guardian Angel
Work of a Guardian Angel
Manuella Stoerzer
Headless Chicken

Blair Styra
Don't Change the Channel
Who Catharted
Natalie Sudman
Application of Impossible Things
L.R. Sumpter
Judy's Story
The Old is New
We Are the Creators
Artur Tradevosyan
Croton
Croton II
Jim Thomas
Tales from the Trance
Jolene and Jason Tierney
A Quest of Transcendence
Paul Travers
Dancing with the Mountains
Nicholas Vesey
Living the Life-Force
Dennis Wheatley/ Maria Wheatley
The Essential Dowsing Guide
Maria Wheatley
Druidic Soul Star Astrology
Sherry Wilde
The Forgotten Promise
Lyn Willmott
A Small Book of Comfort
Beyond all Boundaries Book 1
Beyond all Boundaries Book 2
Beyond all Boundaries Book 3
D. Arthur Wilson
You Selfish Bastard
Stuart Wilson & Joanna Prentis
Atlantis and the New Consciousness
Beyond Limitations
The Essenes -Children of the Light
The Magdalene Version
Power of the Magdalene
Sally Wolf
Life of a Military Psychologist

For more information about any of the above titles, soon to be released titles,
or other items in our catalog, write, phone or visit our website:
PO Box 754, Huntsville, AR 72740|479-738-2348/800-935-0045|www.ozarkmt.com